Cognitive Psychoanalysis

Cognitive
Psychoanalysis

Irving Bieber, M.D.

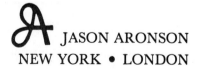

JASON ARONSON
NEW YORK • LONDON

to Toby

Contents

Part II
Clinical Perspectives

Part III
Critiques

Preface

Psychoanalysis is a phenomenon of this century. Although its beginnings and intellectual roots are embedded in nineteenth century philosophy and science, it has revolutionized psychiatry and profoundly influenced the intellectual life of the twentieth century. In 1900 the publication of *The Interpretation of Dreams,* in which Freud first described the oedipus complex, was both revelatory and shocking, but it laid to rest for all time the naive idea that children are asexual. Psychoanalysis continued to develop apace, especially in the United States, where it achieved its greatest recognition. But even a brief account of the development of psychoanalysis must include Breuer's seminal contribution that behavior could be unconsciously motivated.

Joseph Breuer was a noted medical internist. During the course of treating a patient who became well-known as Anna O (Breuer and Freud 1893–1895), he discovered that her neurotic symptoms were linked to antecedent psychological trauma. He observed that when the memory of the traumata was recovered, that is, made conscious, and the events were reevaluated and restructured to accord with reality, the patient's symptoms disappeared. Complications arose when Anna became sexually attracted to Breuer and she developed the delusion that she was pregnant and he was the father of her unborn child. Greatly discomforted by this unexpected reaction, Breuer abruptly brought to an end his relationship with Anna and he abandoned his interest in psychology. He did, however, share his observations with Freud, who was greatly interested in his colleague's information. Undaunted by transference reactions, or by the hostility of patients and colleagues alike, Freud proceeded with his investigations of human motivation and behavior. His discoveries require no documentation here.

He also became absorbed in theory building and he constructed a model of mental functioning that he termed the metapsychology. His theory of neurosis was based upon the primacy of instincts. Initially, he proposed that libido was the only instinct, that it was activated through excitatory processes in erotogenic organs and that these processes created psychic tension and became the source of psychic energy. He viewed psychopathology as the outcome of disordered sexual development and functioning, as he broadly defined sexuality.

In 1920, Freud added the death instinct to his theoretical schema; it became the aggressive instinct. Libido built; aggression destroyed. Each instinct was thought to be part of the affective, not the cognitive, system. In the structural part of the metapsychology, the id was conceived as the reservoir of the instincts and was said to be totally unconscious and noncognitive, while the ego, the reality aspect of the mind, was predominantly conscious and cognitive. The superego contained the distillates of parental and cultural indoctrination and values, and it, too, was predominantly cognitive. The other two major elements of the metapsychology were the energic and genetic components. The former was concerned with the distribution of psychic energy; the latter, with the development of the instincts—oral, anal, phallic and genital.

By the 1930s, the metapsychology had become progressively inadequate as a conceptual system encompassing and explicating the wealth of new data accumulated by the increasing number of psychoanalysts. The group of dissenters who had already discarded the metapsychology began a revisionist movement—Karen Horney (1937), Abram Kardiner (1939), Sandor Rado (1956), Harry Stack Sullivan (1956), and Clara Thompson (1959). During this period a classical analyst, Heinz Hartmann (1951), also began to formulate new theoretical views which emphasized and enlarged ego psychology. Freud's instinctual theory had postulated two sources of psychic energy, libido and aggression. Hartmann postulated a third source, an independent ego energy which supposedly energized such functions as learning and curiosity. By postulating a cognitive type of energy, he fundamentally altered the libido theory, but his ideas remained acceptable to the orthodox analytic groups because he did not tamper with the metapsychology in any other way.

Rado emphasized the concept of injury in his view of psychopathology. He was especially interested in the psychological and physiological processes associated with injury and the fear of threat of injury; processes such as excessive anxiety reactions to threat were subsumed under what he termed *emergency dyscontrol*. Rado's emphasis on injury gave a focus to my own thinking, and from this point on, my psychoanalytic interests were directed to investigating beliefs underlying expectations of injury, beliefs that produce fear.

Cognitive psychoanalysis reveals the beliefs underlying fears, especially those fears that do not represent reality dangers. Many such beliefs are unconscious. An impotent man, for example, would be unaware that he feared being potent; he would also be unaware of the nature of the beliefs that led to the fear that, were he to have sexual intercourse, he would be injured. His fears might be based upon a primary belief that he would be injured by a male competitor in a struggle for a desirable woman. A secondary belief might be that the acquisition of great wealth and power would extinguish impotence and defend him against any one interfering with his sexual gratification. Thus, cognitive psychoanalysis is oriented to delineating and resolving irrational beliefs that give rise to fears and to their pathological consequences. Cognitive psychoanalysis proposes that irrational beliefs associated with unfounded expectations of injury are basic elements of psychopathology. Cognitive psychoanalysis is a cognitive process and it is based upon a cognitive theory. Classical psychoanalysis is also a cognitive process but it is based upon an instinctual theory. Irrational beliefs may have their origins in childhood but I do not view any aspect of adult psychopathology as a regression to childhood organization or as a need to gratify infantile instinctual longings. Cognitive psychoanalysis differs from the behavioral therapies in a most important way: the impact of unconscious processes on attitudes and behavior is recognized and emphasized. Most primary irrational beliefs are largely unconscious, and psychoanalytic techniques, such as dream interpretation and the analysis of transference reactions, are invaluable in exposing them.

My work as represented in this volume describes cognitive psychoanalysis and explains how it developed, how it illuminates psychopathology, the therapeutic process, and the steps in therapeutic change. Affects and cognition are essential components of integrated functioning and neither modality is considered as primary.

The human activity we call work is a biosocial phenomenon subject to vicissitudes in no way less significant than sexuality. In the chapters that follow, disorders of the work function have been strongly emphasized. Freud's instinctivist theories of libido and aggression were ill-suited to explicate the psychodynamic intricacies of work disturbances. With increasing attention to ego psychology, work problems have received more psychoanalytic consideration than in the past, but work never has been assigned the theoretical importance it deserves in the genesis of psychopathology and its manifestations in psychiatric syndromes.

Several chapters had been written originally with coauthors to whom I am most grateful: Marvin Drellich, Martin Kishner, Charles Orbach, and Lilly Ottenheimer.

Throughout the years, I have been fortunate to have been able to interchange ideas with my wife, Toby. She has always given me invaluable and unstinting help in my work and contributed immeasurably to this book. I reserve a very special thanks for her.

Irving Bieber, M.D.
May 1980

PART I

Cognitive
Psychoanalysis

The papers in this first and major section bear directly on the central thesis of this book. Six chapters on psychoanalysts are followed by two specifically on the work function. Ordinarily the subject of masochism is subsumed under sexuality, but I have found that it is much more frequently associated with work dysfunction; for that reason I have placed four papers concerning masochism following two chapters on work inhibition.

Chapter 1

Psychoanalysis: A Cognitive Process

Cognition is defined in Webster as an intellectual process by which knowledge is gained about perception and ideas and as the act of knowing in the broadest sense. This is a straightforward definition and useful in its application to cognitive psychoanalysis.

The act or process of knowing may be organized as verbalizations that can be linguistically communicated or it may be organized as perceptions, ideas, and beliefs that do not become crystallized in linguistic representations. In investigating reactions to the diagnosis of malignancy at Memorial Hospital, Ohrbach and I (see chapter 14) found that some patients, without ever verbalizing it, believed that if they lived a good, moral life, serious

illness and accident would not befall them. When we con-
cretized these beliefs to them, the patients readily
acknowledged that they held such ideas and reaffirmed
them without question. Of quite a different order is
knowledge shut out of consciousness because there is a
fear of facing it. Some patients denied knowledge or even
suspicion of serious illness despite the fact that they
dreamed of loved ones dying and also had dreams indicating apprehension. Such knowledge is no less cognitive
because it is unconscious.

Psychoanalysis has developed from its very beginnings
as a cognitive method of psychiatric treatment. Any
therapeutic method that relies mainly upon interpretation
and insight is obviously cognitive. Yet Breuer and Freud,
in their original studies of hysteria (1893–1895), committed themselves to the theory of the primacy of affect
and that cognition was in the service of affect disorders.
In the editor's introduction to volume 2 of the *Standard
Edition*, James Strachey (1955) described the basic theory
as follows:

> The main theoretical position adopted by the authors
> [Freud and Breuer] . . . seems on the surface a simple
> one. They hold that in the normal course of things, if
> experience is accompanied by a large amount of affect,
> that affect is either discharged in a variety of conscious
> reflex acts or becomes gradually worn away by association
> with other conscious mental material. In the case of hys-
> terical patients, on the other hand . . . neither of these
> things happen. The affect remains in a "strangulated" state
> and the memory of the experience to which it is attached is
> cut off from consciousness. The affective memory is there-
> after manifested in hysterical symptoms which may be
> regarded as mnemic symbols — that is to say, as symbols

of the suppressed memory. [Breuer and Freud suggest] two principal reasons to explain the occurrence of this pathological outcome. One is that the original experience took place when the subject was in a particular dissociated state of mind described as hypnoid; the other is that the experience is one which the subject's ego regarded as incompatible with the self and which had therefore to be fended off. In either case, the therapeutic effectiveness of the cathartic procedure is explained on the same basis; if the original experience, along with its affect, can be brought into consciousness, the affect is, by that very fact, discharged or abreacted, the force that has maintained the symptom ceases to operate, and the symptom itself disappears.

In other words, affect, which Freud and Breuer equated with excitation, was considered to be the force behind the hysterical symptom, and cognition was represented in repressed memory. They theorized that through cognition, the original experience could be relived and the encapsulated affect abreacted, thus removing the pathogenic force. The notion of a chronically continuing excitation is, however, physiologically untenable. Let us take as an example a sexually aroused individual who is impotent. His excitation or affect is sexual and the hysterical symptom is impotence. The idea that the sexual excitation remains because the patient cannot discharge it, is patently not the case. The excitation disappears after a while and can, of course, be reevoked, perhaps again ending in impotence. But it is not as if the sexual arousal remains fixed and becomes the force behind the impotence. The impotence is a defense against sexual expression and is brought about by a fear of one kind or another. The defense does not require the constant presence of the affect; it requires only a recognition that the affect can be reevoked.

In explicating symptom formation, Freud attributed the same etiological force to various affects—sexuality, anxiety, anger, gratification—without differentiating one from another. A soldier entering a battle might experience overwhelming anxiety, and he may develop a hysterical paralysis of the legs. But it is not the anxiety that caused the hysterical paralysis. The anxiety and the paralysis are caused by the life-threatening situation. The anxiety is a physiological response to an awareness of threat and the paralysis is also a response to an awareness of threat; it serves to protect the individual from danger. As a matter of fact, hysterical paralysis can continue without experiencing anxiety and was described by Charcot as *la belle indifférence.* In both impotence and paralysis, the symptoms are not triggered by affects but rather by the *idea* of impending danger against which defenses are organized as protection.

Both Breuer and Freud were students of Ernst Brücke, a prominent member of the Helmholtz school, which held that all natural phenomena can ultimately be explained in terms of physical and chemical forces. Both men were also neurologists. Modern neurophysiology was just beginning to develop and much attention was being given to excitation and sums of excitation. By equating affect with neurophysiological excitation, a physicalist basis for a psychology could be established, thus carving a path to scientific respectability. Breuer had formulated the basic idea for the theory of constancy in neurological terms, that is, that there is a tendency to keep intracerebral excitation constant. Freud accepted this theory which had also been promulgated independently by Fechner. Freud postulated that it was the function of the mental apparatus to keep excitation at a minimum in order to prevent overloading. The pleasure principle was later derived from the constancy theory since pleasure was seen as the biproduct of the discharge of unpleasant tension (*Unlust*) and thus pleasure was thought to be motivated both by the need to reduce tension and as an incentive to reduce tension.

In further developing his theories, Freud then moved the major source of the excitation or affect from the traumatic experience to the instincts. He thought that the instincts became the source of the excitation, which derived from somatic processes in erotogenic organs. In a way he never clearly explained, the affects somehow gave rise to psychic energy that ran the mental apparatus.

In 1905, in the *Three Essays on Sexuality* Freud formulated his libido theory, a quantum theory of psychic energy. Eros was conceptualized as the sole instinct and motivating energy for all psychic processes. In 1920, in *Beyond the Pleasure Principle,* the death instinct, synonymous with the aggressive instinct, was added and it became the second instinct. After the 1905 essays, metapsychology became concerned mainly with the vicissitudes of the instincts. Affect was master; cognition was a tool for discovering and repairing the pathological manifestations of instinctual development and existence. Breuer's cognitive tool in treating Anna O was hypnosis. Freud also tried hypnosis but soon gave it up. Among other reasons, he did not think he was a good hypnotist. He next relied on exhortation and would urge his patients to remember the primary traumatic event that had encapsulated the affect. Ultimately, he came to depend on free association and dreams as a way of gaining access to the encapsulated, fixated affects. I have traced Freud's theoretical progression to demonstrate how classical psychoanalytic thought became a cognitive system in the service of the theory of affects.

COGNITION AND AFFECT

Various categories of bio-socio-psychological constellations may be classified under the general rubric of affect. I can describe at least three different categories of affect, each having in common only the fact that one component of the complex constellation is experienced as a distinct feeling. The first category includes hunger, thirst, and sexual feelings. Each such affect may arise from somatic processes independent of cognition and external stimuli. The second category is anxiety and fear, responses associated with security operations and occurring only following a perception or belief of threat. Anxiety and fear are responses to threat, responses that are integrated with cognition. As an automatic physiological response to a perception of threat, anxiety is characterized by a hypermobilization of adaptive bodily resources manifested in such phenomena as tachycardia, tachypnea, increased blood pressure, increased metabolism, etc. — the somatic mechanisms for coping with threat. Anxiety is accompanied by these complex physiological phenomena but this distressing, affecting component may be but one of many that make up a complex anxiety reaction.

Fear is a cognitive experience that reflects a belief that one will be injured by someone or something. One may be consciously aware of the fear, as in the fear of flying, or the fear may be unconscious, as often happens in fear of success. The relationship between fear and anxiety may be illustrated in the example of an individual who may be afraid to fly but does not experience anxiety unless he boards a plane or makes a decision to fly. Fear may exist without anxiety but all situations that evoke anxiety are feared.

The third category is made up of a rich repertoire of "feelings." The human is born with the potential for developing a broad range of feelings too numerous to delineate. Yet all such variegated affects are but components of more complex experiences in which cognition is always integrated with affect. In other words, affect is not endogenous. If a person is sad, he or she has a reason for feeling so, rational or irrational though it may be; and this is similarly true if a person is happy, embarrassed, or shy. And if he is depressed, he has suffered an important loss. Except for hunger, thirst, and sex, all other affects are the consequence of how one experiences and evaluates reality at any moment in personal history. Even hunger, thirst, and sexual feelings, especially in adult life, are very much part of complex behavioral patterns that involve cognition and so-called ego functioning. When one gets hungry, a decision has to be made about what, where, when, and how one should eat. Hunger does not simply trigger a reflexive gesture of pulling an apple off the nearest tree.

The rich repertoire of human affect often provides the nonverbal component of communication and, in this context, affect is in the service of cognition. A stranger who walks into a group smiling is telling the group he is friendly and safe. If he is poker-faced or angry, he will alert a defensive posture in the group. In interpreting dreams, I find I need to know the feelings the patient has experienced in the various segments of the dream.

Without such information, I generally cannot understand the dream.

The word "feeling" has two connotations. The first refers to endogenous sensations, previously discussed, and contactual sensations, important components of cognition. The second is clearly cognitive. When one says, "I feel you are right," what is being said is, "I believe you are right even though I cannot justify this belief." This cognitive connotation of "feeling" is sometimes referred to as intuition. Intuition is also cognitive. It may be defined as rapid thinking, or rapid, efficient problem solving.

Modulations in the speaking voice are affective components that accompany the verbal content of communication. These affective components are nonverbal messages. When there is a discrepancy between affective and verbal communication, it is the affective message that usually is the more convincing.

It seems apparent that affect cannot be dissociated from cognition, yet Freud did and he relegated affect to a primary role. The phrase "intellectual insight" is still heard in a pejorative sense. What is usually meant is that the patient can repeat an interpretation but does not understand it, does not believe it, or has conflict about it. Such a patient generally is neither intellectually certain about the problem at hand nor does he have insight, that is, a comprehension of the problem itself and an understanding of how it applies to him or her. When a patient shows real understanding—the "aha" response—some analysts tend to describe it as "emotional" insight, obviously assigning greater validity and value to emotion, as if insight without cognition were possible. This reminds me of a story told about the legendary Morris Raphael Cohen, professor of philosophy at City College in New York in the 1920s and

1930s. Dr. Cohen was expostulating a proposition when a student in the front row started to shake his head in apparent disagreement. Cohen paused and asked the student, "Is there something bothering you?" to which the student replied, "Professor Cohen, I feel you are wrong." Said the professor, "Is that so? Where do you feel it?" The student answered, "I just feel it in my bones." "I see," said Professor Cohen. "Well, when the feeling reaches your *head,* raise your hand."

It is of interest that some psychoanalytic dissidents who dropped most or all of the metapsychology did not altogether leave an orientation to the primacy of affect. Karen Horney (1950) has written:

> [A patient's] knowledge of himself must not remain an intellectual knowledge though it may start out this way but must become an emotional experience. . . . It is not enough to know vaguely that his anger or self-reproach is probably greater than warranted by the occasion. He must *feel* the full import of his rage or the very depth of the self-condemnation. Only then does the force of some unconscious process (and its irrationality) stare him in the face. Only then may he have an incentive to find out much more about himself.

The concept of having to recover the repressed affect is discernible in this quotation. While Freud believed that the recovery and discharge of the repressed affect was curative, Horney conceptualized this recovery as necessary for the patient's confrontation with his own irrationalities and for motivating further investigation. Yet, like Freud, she also thought that the recovery of affect was essential.

Another illustration of the emphasis on affect is the concept of primary process thinking which supposedly is a type of thinking determined or significantly influenced by the instincts or affects, as compared to secondary process thinking which is reality-bound and ego-controlled. The fact that it is called "primary process" indicates its dominant position in Freudian theory. The very nature of the term "primary process" suggests a connection with primordial instinctual forces that endow the idea with the mystique surrounding the beginnings of the universe and life itself. In my view, so-called primary process thinking is plain irrationality, no more different than other types of irrational thinking. The so-called primary process thinking of children is not irrational, nor are the mental processes in dreaming. In fact, when marked irrationality dominates the cognitive style of dreams, the dreamer is probably psychotic.

COGNITIVE PSYCHOANALYSIS

Classical psychoanalysis is a cognitive process that has an affect theory. Cognitive psychoanalysis is a cognitive process that has a cognitive theory and strategy. It is based on the assumption that therapeutic change occurs as a result of altering irrational beliefs. The theory assumes that the adverse experiences that produce psychopathology are represented as beliefs linked to expectations of injury (fears). It also assumes that many such beliefs, when carried unchanged into adult life, become nonrational and that irrational belief systems determine inappropriate affects and the maladaptive attitudes and behaviors that constitute adult psychopathology.

I have been a cognitive psychoanalyst from at least as far back as 1950. At that time, Sandor Rado presented a paper to the Society of Medical Psychoanalysts entitled, "Emergency Behavior." I was the designated discussor and the following is a quotation from my unpublished discussion:

> Many of us believe, and I think correctly, that neuroses arise from distortions and injuries in interpersonal relations, particularly in early life, but also all through life; that the convictions established in regard to the disturbances and injuries to basically important relationships are irrationally and inappropriately projected; that the perpetuation of the neurosis is based on the perpetuation of false convictions. The basis of psychoanalytic therapy rests on the realistic reorientation of irrational convictions. I believe also that the continued existence of irrational convictions results in the chronic production of false danger signals that set emergency control into operation and that emergency control will continue to respond to false signals until the perceptions of danger arising out of irrational convictions are abolished by a reorientation of these convictions.

In 1960, I presented a paper, "A Concept of Psychopathology," before the American Psychopathological Association (see chapter 3). That paper, in essence, was an exposition of cognitive analysis as I conceptualized and conducted it, and it was published in the proceedings of that organization. I defined psychopathology as the study of the nature of injury and the reaction of the individual to injury. Injury was defined as anything detrimental or perceived as detrimental to one's optimal state at any point in personal history. Injury to self could include acts of omission such as defective nurturing, inadequate stimulation, inadequate or inappropriate contact, inadequate affection, interest, and so forth. Acts of commission would include parental hostility, overcontrol, seductiveness, and so forth. Expectations of injury that no longer had a basis in reality or that were exaggerated, as in situations where injury *may* be incurred (such as driving), derive from irrational beliefs. Such beliefs may be the consequence of actual injury incurred in childhood and later projected into adult life, a time when it may no longer be reasonable to anticipate injury. Irrational beliefs may also result from indoctrination (as occurs in families with paranoid parents) or the beliefs may be linked to wishful thinking. The target of therapy is the extinction of irrational beliefs.

The paper made several other points I believe worthy of restatement. An individual with an unrealistic expectation of injury enters a situation and scans it for anticipated danger. If, for example, the expected injury is rejection, the individual will scan for rejecting people. Attention will be focused on those who may reject and thus confirm the already existing expectation of rejection. Not infrequently, individuals who are rejecting are accorded greater importance than others who are accepting. Attempts will be made to be accepted by the rejectors, attempts usually doomed to failure, which only reinforce the expectation of rejection. Such skewed interpersonal selection, and the maladaptive reparative mechanisms that follow, continue and often escalate the irrational expectations that maintain a neurosis. Irrational beliefs may coexist with realistic beliefs about the same situation. One may believe that marriage to a beloved is everything that is fine, beautiful, and much to be desired while simultaneously harboring an opposing belief, generally unconscious, that such a marriage would involve terrible, even lethal, danger. A person may be thrown into an acute psychiatric state when reality situations bring divergent beliefs into active conflict, as when a person holding conflicting beliefs, say, about marriage, decides to or actually takes the step. According to Freud's theory, in psychiatric decompensation, there is a conflict between regression to infantile impulses and reality. In my view, the conflict occurs between irrational beliefs and the pull of reality thinking and wishes. Though irrational beliefs may originate in childhood, decompensation is not a regression, a ride back, as it were, to an infantile state where early impulses may be expressed. When irrational beliefs become dominant, a decompensation occurs which may be neurotic or psychotic.

Once psychopathological organization becomes established, it operates with the automaticity of a complex conditioned reflex. The concept of psychopathology thus formulated provides a guide for psychoanalytic technique. The work of psychoanalysis involves (1) helping the patient to become insightfully aware of all convictions associated with the expectation of injury, irrational and realistic; (2) recovering the genesis of these beliefs in past experience through dreams, free associations, and analysis of transference; (3) delineating the specific defenses and reparative reactions organized along with the specific convictions or expectations of injury; (4) working out the psychodynamics of the defenses and reparative reactions.

Insight derived by a patient from such work is essential for significant improvement. Although by itself it does not either constitute or necessarily determine change, it provides the patient with the tools for deconditioning psychopathological automaticity by replacing irrational beliefs with realistic ones. An important principle in psychoanalytic technique which I have emphasized involves the delineation and analysis of basic convictions underlying expectations of injury before analyzing defenses and the reparative behaviors that are organized around these beliefs. If, for example, a patient believes that any show of self-assertiveness will result in rejection or attack, the fear of self-assertion is approached analytically before the associated defenses are brought into focus. The defenses may include drives to power, dependency on others who are self-assertive, hostile facades masking submission and so forth.

In 1974 I published a paper entitled "The Concept of Irrational Belief Systems as Primary Elements of Psychopathology" (see chapter 2). This paper more explicitly distinguished between primary and secondary irrational beliefs. Using an astronomical model, I conceptualized the primary irrational belief as the center around which rotate the secondary irrational beliefs, the derivatives of defensive and reparative dynamics. The entire complex is termed an irrational belief system. One patient who suffered from a fear of maternal abandonment had a mother who had suffered a postpartum decompensation after the birth of her second son, the patient's only sibling who was two years younger. The patient's primary irrational belief was that the mother would abandon him and replace him with his brother. The patient developed a series of defenses against such a threat. He convinced his mother and himself that he was indispensable to her welfare and survival. His need to be indispensable became a secondary irrational belief. He also developed a fierce need to be best in whatever he attempted later in life, hoping that superiority would prevent displacement by his brother and his transferential representatives. This secondary, neurotic need to be best resulted in a highly competitive, rivalrous relationship with all men and a compulsive need to produce and excel.

Psychoanalysis is the therapeutic method most suited to delineating beliefs. Such information is acquired through dreams, verbalizations, and the communication of attitudes and behavior. The analyst is led to the patient's primary irrational beliefs by tapping into work functions and sexual, romantic, and interpersonal relationships. This paper also emphasized the value of first analyzing primary irrational beliefs before engaging the secondary ones that represent defenses and mechanisms of repair. I also have stressed the idea that insight is not synonymous with change but that it is an indispensable tool for change. Fundamental changes occur in therapy only when there is a substantial change in irrational beliefs. In the working-through process, the patient learns to detect distressing affects, usually anxiety, in the actual life situation and to delineate for himself the irrational beliefs responsible for the distress. In so doing, there is a continuing and deepening conviction that the belief is, in fact, irrational, until finally, for all practical purposes, it is extinguished.

BEHAVIORAL APPROACH

A group of behaviorists, most of whom are psychologists with a special interest in cognition, for some years now have been developing their own theory and practice of cognitive therapy. Professor Marvin R. Goldfried of the State University of Stonybrook, on reading some of

my work on irrational belief systems, was impressed by
the similarity of our views, and he communicated with
me. Among his papers on the subject, one is in collaboration with A. P. Goldfine and is entitled "Cognitive
Change Methods" (1975) and another is "The Effect of
Irrational Beliefs and Emotional Arousal," with Sabicinski (1975). The titles indicate the similarity of our interests despite important differences. To my way of thinking, cognitive therapy has two major components: the
delineation of irrational beliefs and the alteration and possible extinction of such beliefs. Psychoanalysis is the ideal
method for delineating irrationalities and for determining
the psychodynamic interrelationships and processes
operative between primary and secondary irrational
beliefs.

In 1962 Albert Ellis formulated a method of treatment
he refers to as rational-emotive therapy. He designated a
group of typical irrational beliefs as the following
examples selected from a list of eleven items illustrate:

1. It is a dire necessity for an adult human being to be
loved and approved of by virtually every significant other
person in his community.

2. One should be thoroughly competent, adequate,
and achieving in all possible respects if one is to consider
oneself worthwhile.

3. One should be dependent on others and needs someone stronger than oneself to rely on.

Initially, Goldfried used the list in treating people who
had feelings of discomfort in social situations. He
assumed that at least some of the beliefs on the list had
applicability to patients' problems. More recently, he
designed a questionnaire that would reveal more specifically the irrational beliefs held by each particular patient.

The delineating techniques of the behaviorists are still in an exploratory stage, while psychoanalysis has proven its usefulness and its techniques are well established. Further, none of the items on Ellis's list deal with primary irrationalities. The need to be loved by all is generally a defense against the fear of rejection or of being treated with hostility. The behaviorists also use other familiar techniques, such as desensitization, as in the treatment of phobias, and, pragmatically, anything else that seems to work.

The psychoanalyst most identified with cognitive therapy is Aaron Beck. Although he was a practicing psychoanalyst for many years, he seems to have given up what he considers to be psychoanalysis and he differentiates cognitive therapy from psychoanalysis and behavior therapy. In agreement with other cognitive therapists, Beck asserts that in an experience, affect is determined by the operant beliefs and interpretations of the experience. He postulates that there is a conscious thought between an external event and the emotional response and that the conscious thought is the cause of the emotional response. In his volume, *Cognitive Therapy and Emotional Disorders,* he cites three situations to support his hypothesis (Beck 1976). The first is of a woman walking outdoors who suddenly realizes she is about three blocks from home and immediately feels faint. Her conscious ideas are: "I am really far away from home. If something happens to me now, I couldn't get back in time to get help. If I fell down in the street, people would just walk by—they wouldn't know me, nobody would help me." The woman's statements that purport to account for her agoraphobia and panic apparently satisfied Beck as an explanation of the woman's problem. Yet, there is nothing to explain why she anticipated illness or injury if she left her home. Beck asserts that the psychoanalytic explanation would be that this woman's unconscious wish is to be seduced or raped. This surely would not be my interpretation based on the evidence offered and I would guess that not many analysts would see it that way either. Beck gives no credence to unconscious motivation and seemingly does not consider unconscious motivation to be cognitive.

The second example: "A professional athlete consistently felt his chest constrict and his heart pound whenever he drove his automobile through a tunnel. He started to gasp for breath and his conscious thoughts were: This tunnel could collapse and I would suffocate." Beck makes no attempt to determine why the patient should think the tunnel would collapse or why he was so concerned with suffocation. The patient's statements merely delineate his conscious fears. One would have to pursue his ideational trail much further to get to the underlying irrational beliefs. If what he said about the tunnel was, in fact, his primary belief, a good engineer would be able to cure the patient in jig time simply by pointing out why the tunnel would not collapse.

The third case is that of a successful novelist who cried bitterly when he was complimented for his work. His conscious thought was, "People won't be honest with me. They *know* that I am mediocre. They just won't accept me as I really am. They keep giving me phony compliments."

These statements are more like rationalizations than irrational beliefs underlying the patient's difficulty. And there is surely a strong suggestion of problems with success. One of the best tests of fear of success is the reaction to compliments. When a compliment results in tears and depression, one can diagnose fear of success with confidence. In itself, fear of success is but an orienting interpretation. Analytic work involves a delineation of the irrational beliefs that create this fear. Beck has abandoned what he conceives of as orthodox analysis in favor of a cognitive therapy; but in cancelling out unconscious processes, he has thrown out the baby with the bathwater. His simplistic schema — external event, conscious thought, emotional response — narrows access to psychopathology that psychoanalysis had long ago revealed. An integral part of cognition is the unconscious process and the dream is still its royal road. Beck criticizes psychoanalysis as a method that gives insufficient credence to the etiological significance of *conscious* mental processes, but this is not at all so for most analysts.

There is common ground between cognitive behavioral therapists and those psychoanalysts who orient their treatment to the resolution of irrational beliefs. The behaviorists, however, lack the invaluable, time-tested and established psychoanalytic techniques for delineating these beliefs.

Chapter 2

Irrational Belief Systems: Primary Elements of Psychopathology

As I have suggested in chapter 1, an essential and invariable component of psychopathology is the belief that one has sustained or is threatened by injury, and I mean by injury any event which is considered to be inimical to one's integrity or best interests. Thus, injury may be thought of as including rejection, humiliation, loss of valued objects, physical injury, and so on. A conviction that one will be injured by certain actions or situations is another way of saying that certain actions and situations are feared. Fear is a cognitive experience that reflects a conviction about being injured. One may be consciously aware of the fear, as in fear of flying, or one may be unaware, not conscious, of the fear as often happens in fear about success.

Fear must be distinguished from anxiety which also is a response to a threat of injury. Anxiety is an automatic, physiological response to a perception of threat. Anxiety is characterized by a hypermobilization of adaptive bodily resources manifested in such phenomena as tachycardia, tachypnea, increased blood pressure, and increased metabolism — the somatic mechanisms for coping with threats of injury. The physiological phenomena are accompanied by a distressing affect we refer to as anxiety, but this affective component is but one of many that makes up the total anxiety reaction. Selye's (1947) term, "the alarm reaction," seems to me to be more accurately descriptive. The relationship between fear and anxiety may be illustrated by the example that an individual may be afraid of flying but will not experience anxiety unless he boards a plane or actually decides to fly in the near future. Hence, fear can exist without anxiety though situations that evoke anxiety are also feared.

The anticipation of injury may be an accurate appraisal of reality, as in a fear of poisonous snakes, or it may be a distortion, in which case we refer to unrealistic expectations of injury as irrational beliefs or irrational fears. Irrational beliefs associated with unfounded expectations of injury are basic elements of psychopathology. The capacity to apprehend reality as it is actually knowable at any moment in personal history is, in my view, a major criterion for assessing mental health. Psychopathology is also associated with parameters other than irrational belief systems, such as maladaptive responses to actual danger, defective development consequent upon inadequate stimulation as may occur among the disadvantaged, inadequate nurturance, defective communication patterns, defective stimulation of affect, and so forth. But even in these instances, the defective experiences are, in the main, represented cognitively as irrational beliefs. The child who has been brought up in a dour family atmosphere gets to believe that behaviors involving fun and laughter are unacceptable to others.

When a patient with psychosexual impotence comes for treatment, though the therapist may be aware that the patient has unconscious fears about being sexually effective, the patient himself will be unaware of them; he is preoccupied only with his consternation and fear of sexual failure. In psychoanalysis he may reveal irrational beliefs such as, sex is dirty and unacceptable and women do not really want it. Fear of attack by jealous male competitors is a salient dynamic in cases of impotence. Such an idea may coexist with realistic ideas to the effect that sexual effectiveness is manly, pleasurable, healthful, and so forth.

A patient's male twin was preferred by the mother who named him after her own favorite brother. The patient was the more aggressive and precocious of the two. She spoke earlier, more fluently, and talked more. Her brother repeatedly complained, "she takes my words." As a child, the patient had thought there was a fixed quantity of words; if she used more, her brother had less. The mother actively interfered with her daughter's intellectual development. She provoked guilt in oblique and direct ways: the patient was too precocious, too energetic; her talents were somehow inappropriate for her, and so on. The patient developed a severe work block stemming from her belief that her development and functioning impaired her brother. In one of her sessions she reported a dream she had had when she was about eight years old. In it she threw the book of knowledge at her brother; she hit him in the head with it and killed him.

Despite a fine intellectual endowment and artistic talent, the patient was unable to complete college. Her work inhibition was based on the irrational belief that her effectiveness would destroy her brother. In her psychoanalysis, the patient began to work through these problems. Her job required her to write reports. Initially this was difficult because of her work problems. She procrastinated and often failed to hand in requested reports. One day, as a consequence of the insight she was acquiring about her irrational beliefs regarding the dangers of work, she was able to write an unusually good report. That night she dreamed that her twin brother had suffered an epileptic attack. In the dream she had the thought that it would take at least a year before it would be safe to expose him again to her productivity. Several weeks later, she again produced a good report followed that night by a dream that her brother and daughter had died. She awakened from the dream feeling very depressed. Several months later, her brother, who was then living in another country, became seriously ill with an infectious disease. Despite her realization that her work could not possibly have affected him since he knew nothing about it, she could not completely escape the idea that in some ill-defined way, her creativity had finally injured him.

Irrational beliefs can be grouped into three major areas: (1) derivatives of actual past experience when the beliefs are congruent with reality but were then attached to situations inappropriately perceived as threatening; (2) distortions based on wishful thinking, as in the oedipus complex where a boy believes he could possess his mother if the father died; and (3) distortions based on direct misinterpretation of reality.

DEFENSES AND
REPARATIVE MECHANISMS

Defenses are ways of coping with anticipated threat; they may be organized as a way of avoiding, neutralizing, minimizing, or extinguishing a threat. Inhibition is one such defense mechanism. In sexually impotent patients, for example, the inhibition of sexual capability precludes behavior perceived as dangerous. Masochism, homosexuality, and pathologic dependency are complex constellations that may develop as major defensive adaptations.

Earlier I referred to a patient who, after the birth of a sibling, feared he would be abandoned by his mother. He developed a defensive need to be indispensable, and by adolescence he had convinced his mother that her welfare, happiness, and actual existence depended upon his superior knowledge and judgment. This shared conviction and interdigitating system of beliefs continued throughout the mother's life. As an adult, the patient harbored the conviction that he would be abandoned by transferential representatives of his mother and displaced by transferential representatives of his brother. The patient also instituted a pattern of indispensability with his wife and children, a defense that involved him in an ever increasing series of demands that were often extremely burdensome, resulting in his feeling very much exploited. To maintain his defensive posture, he developed a strong need to be best, a need that involved him in keen competitive struggles with his brother and any man seen as competent and attractive.

In the case of this patient, the primary irrational belief was that he would be abandoned. Secondary irrational beliefs then evolved from defenses against abandonment, such as the idea that his security depended upon indispensability. In an astronomical analogy, one might view psychopathology as a galaxy in which there are many primary irrational beliefs, each with its own solar system of orbiting satellites of secondary irrational beliefs derived from defensive and reparative mechanisms.

The patient who believed that her intellectual effectiveness would destroy her brother, developed work inhibitions that defended against her fear of inflicting injury upon him. Denial was another of her defenses. She denied her ability, denied that success had meaning to her and she shut out of awareness normal ambitions to fulfill her talent. She once attempted to circumvent her creative block by painting a portrait of her brother which she presented to her mother as a gift, but accompanying this creative act was a masochistic, defensive component. She used materials that were likely to soon deteriorate.

Reparative mechanisms may be realistic or irrational. Seeking competent psychiatric help is obviously realistic, as is taking a vacation when faced with exhaustion secondary to tension states, or judiciously using socially acceptable ataraxics, such as alcohol. Without psychotherapy, however, self-devised reparative techniques only occasionally accomplish a significant resolution of chronic psychopathology. Irrational reparative maneuvers add to the complexity of psychopathology and bring additional components of irrationality to irrational belief systems that already exist. An example is that of a paranoid who believes that a person or group are causing his or her troubles and unhappiness. The solution seems logical:

destroy the perceived threat, a decision that, if acted out, cancels out the possibility of realistic repair.

Magical reparative techniques are common. Amulets and potions are endowed with magical properties for healing purposes or to energize or reinstate sexual potency. Similar reparative mechanisms may be observed in homosexuality. Magical reparative mechanisms are acted out by homosexuals for whom masculinity and power are symbolized by the large penis which they seek in order to restore a damaged sense of masculinity and as a way of achieving strength in other areas of neurotic ineffectiveness. In dreams and fantasies, they sometimes castrate the large penis, the paranoid belief being that by castration they have destroyed the power of feared, aggressive men. This is a psychological theme similar to that of Delilah's destruction of Samson.

CONSIDERATIONS OF TREATMENT

Therapeutic strategy consists initially of delineating the patient's irrational beliefs as they become apparent, emphasizing in particular the primary ones, and then analyzing secondary beliefs derived from defensive and reparative integrations. While the therapeutic aim is the extinction of irrational beliefs, it is most difficult to alter and resolve beliefs associated with an expectation of injury. The difference between giving up an irrational belief that is associated with an expectation of injury and one that is not, may be illustrated by the discovery that the earth is round. An astronomer of the fifteenth century would not likely have been resistive to accepting the new-found knowledge, but a seaman who was convinced that sailing in the same direction would eventually bring his ship to the earth's edge, where it would topple into an abyss, would be much less likely to readily change his views; his belief that the earth was flat would be associated with certain death. A contemporary example is of a patient who must go abroad on a crucial business matter but is extremely afraid to fly. His psychiatrist tells him, "I have a pill that will totally extinguish your fear of flying. Will you take it?" "No, no," says the patient. "I won't take a pill like that. If I take it, I won't be afraid to fly; so I'll take a plane; it will crash and I'll get killed."

Fundamental changes occur in treatment only when irrational beliefs are dispelled. Such beliefs are exposed by the patient's productions, associations, dreams, and so forth. A useful technique for uncovering primary irrational beliefs is to survey the major functions: work, sexuality, interpersonal relations, and quality of affect. If a patient is functioning below potential or is unable to sustain the level of performance of which he is capable, or if a patient is uncreative in all spheres, or if he is unable to have his creativity shown to others, the patient undoubtedly has fears about successful work performance.

If a person suffers from sexual inadequacy of one type or another, cannot fall in love, cannot maintain a love relationship, or cannot marry, there are usually irrational beliefs of injury for fulfilling such sexual goals. In the broad realm of interpersonal relationships — an inclusive category by itself — if a person fears closeness with others, or fears it only with people of the same sex, or opposite sex, the reasons for the fears must be established. Ordinarily, this is not especially difficult. The therapeutic challenge is how to convince patients that the irrational beliefs they hold are, in fact, irrational and have something to do with their anxieties and inhibitions. In the case of the patient with severe work inhibitions, it soon became clear to her that her fear of successful work was based on the belief that it would injure her brother. In cases of impotence, it is very difficult for such patients to be convinced that their symptom is based on unrealistic fears related to having successful intercourse. It is usually necessary to accumulate impressive evidence and to present it time and time again as it appears in dreams, fantasies, and interpersonal transactions. It sometimes may take a year or more before a patient is convinced that he or she is harboring an irrational belief. The patient who believed he would be abandoned by a desirable woman and displaced by another man, spent a long time in analysis before he was able to see clearly that he was holding such an idea. The realization that one is host to an irrational belief with deleterious effects is the first necessary step in its extinction.

I shall not dilate upon the need to establish a solid therapeutic alliance and all that it implies such as trust, respect, and confidence. But not infrequently it is necessary to analyze irrational beliefs about the analyst that relate to mistrust, fear of closeness, fear of financial exploitation, and so forth—in brief, the analysis of negative transference.

The second step is to convince the patient that a primary irrational belief actually is irrational. This aspect of analysis is the most difficult part for most, if not all, patients. Not only is it very hard to give up the belief that one will be injured, it is especially difficult to relinquish defenses that have been organized to prevent or ameliorate expected injury. The patient who thought her creativity would hurt her brother seemed completely convinced, after years of treatment, that this belief was irrational. Yet she had a brief setback when he became seriously ill at a time she was doing her most effective work.

Establishing the conviction that a belief is irrational is accomplished through nonverbal as well as verbal analytic experiences. On a verbal level, the analyst must demonstrate not only that a belief is irrational, but why it is so and what the reality surrounding the belief actually is. Toward this end, patients must exercise all faculties of reasoning that promote resolution. Concurrently, nonverbal experiences with the analyst also help resolve irrationalities. Patients who are convinced that their parents are cold, hostile, and inconsiderate and who transferentially expect the analyst to conform to the parental pattern, may have a different attitude after a continuity of experience with a warm, concerned, interested analyst who does not match preconceived notions about parental figures.

Outside the analytic situation, patients tend to become involved in various testing maneuvers related either to reinforcing or relinquishing an irrational belief. In steps one and two, irrational beliefs are delineated and patients, hopefully, become convinced that their beliefs should be given up. I view these steps as the "working out" phase of therapy. These steps proceed concurrently though they may be sequential. Step three is the "working through" phase. Patients come to identify the operations of their beliefs in the circumstances of their life situations and in interpersonal transactions. If the analysis proceeds well, this phase will see the extinction of symptoms and an alteration from neurotic, or maladaptive, to appropriate attitudes and behavior.

When he began treatment, the patient who believed he would be displaced by other men had reacted with anxiety when he met a man who, in some way, consciously or not, reminded him of his brother. If the patient felt he had met his intellectual superior, he responded with avoidance or attack. In working through, he had to become consciously aware of anxiety when meeting transferential rivals and he had to recognize, then and there, that the other man was not a realistic threat and could not displace him. Only by establishing new convictions was he relieved of anxiety and able to relate to others rationally. Over and over again, the patient had to go through the process of identifying his fear consciously, recognize its irrationality, and then alter his intended neurotic behavior. Working through is the application in the life situation of the working-out phase.

I have been discussing operations of primary irrational beliefs. Secondary beliefs, that is, those organized in defensive and reparative arrangements, must also be dealt with. Wilhelm Reich (1945) in *Character Analysis* pursued an onion layer model, advocating peeling away defenses in order to get at the underlying pathology. This therapeutic strategy resulted in unnecessarily turbulent therapy and is, in fact, dangerous in borderline and psychotic types of pathology. Primary irrational beliefs can be delineated without assaulting defenses. A basic principle of my technique is to postpone the analysis of secondary beliefs until the patient has arrived at an awareness of his primary beliefs. If a patient fears displacement by others, I clarify this fear before analyzing the defenses against being displaced. Such defenses may consist of hostility, competitiveness, exaggerated needs for attention, needs for indispensability, and so forth. If a defense, say, hostility, is pointed out before the patient knows where such behavior fits into his psychological world, he is apt to suffer increased feelings of guilt and unacceptability which may escalate into depression. When a primary belief becomes clear, the patient is then able to comprehend and integrate the analysis of secondary beliefs. In my experience, this technique avoids a stressful, stormy course of treatment and it avoids iatrogenic resistances. Though distressing subjects may be explored, it is the theme, the memories, the responses that may be painful; the analysis itself need not be.

Exceptions to this therapeutic strategy sometimes occur when secondary irrationalities constitute a resistance to the analysis. The basic principle — analysis of resistance — then takes precedence. A competitive need to prove the analyst wrong may lead the patient to deny interpretations or shut them out. Such defenses are, of course, a threat to the analysis. But even in these situations, the analysis may be salvaged if the patient is shown that the resistance is integrated with a primary belief that it is necessary, for whatever reason, to win out over authority and defeat the analyst — a self-destructive, unrealistic solution.

In summary, irrational beliefs associated with expectations of injury are basic components of psychopathology. Primary irrational beliefs may be differentiated from secondary ones which have become part of defensive and reparative mechanisms. Primary beliefs with its satellite secondary beliefs make up the irrational belief systems of psychopathology. This therapeutic schema conforms to the data that patients bring into treatment and it illuminates the analytic process.

Chapter 3

A Concept of Psychopathology

All schools of psychoanalytic thought have concerned themselves with the relation of injury to psychopathology. Freud studied the relationship within the framework of instinct; Sullivan used the framework of interpersonal relationships. Rado's emphasis on injury and adaptation to it gave initial direction to my own orientation, in which the concept of injury constitutes the framework for the study of psychopathology.

The variegated and complex interrelationships in the constellation of conditions and events in which injury has occurred may be subsumed under the nature of the injury. An analogy to tuberculosis can be drawn. The injurious agent in tuberculosis includes more than the tubercle bacillus. Components in the study of tuberculosis include the biosocial conditions which bring the bacillus and the host together, the conditions that determine susceptibility of the host, and the psychobiologic responses of the patient. Similarly, a study of psychological injury includes all pertinent knowledge about the individual experiencing the injury, all pertinent knowledge about the conditions giving rise to the injury, and the delineation of the individual's responses to it. Thus defined, psychopathology can be viewed as the study of the nature of injury and the reaction of the individual to the injury.

Whenever an injury or the possibility of injury is perceived, defensive reactions are automatically set into operation. There are three basic biologic defensive reactions to the perception of injury: (1) anxiety, (2) inhibition, and (3) rage.

1. Anxiety is an acute excitatory reaction involving the hypermobilization of all physiologic resources preparatory to meeting a threat. It is an indiscriminate reaction occurring with any type of threat. The estimation of the extent of danger represents an equation between the nature of the threat and the perceived capacity to master it. The intensity of the reaction reflects the estimation of the degree of danger. If the intensity of the anxiety reaction is above the tolerance threshold of the organism, disorganization in cerebral integration may occur. If anxiety is prolonged beyond tolerable limits, somatic exhaustion may occur. The organism, therefore, requires defenses to the anxiety response itself. Where the threat is not removed or cannot be removed, the physiologic defenses to anxiety involve (a) an increasing refractoriness to the stimulus, (b) inhibition of the perception of the threat, and (c) physiologic inhibition of the anxiety reaction

itself. Where the threat is removable, biologic defenses also include flight and avoidance reactions. The individual's perception of the existence of anxiety alerts him to the existence of a threat, even though he may not be able to recognize or locate the threat. Thus, as Freud has pointed out, the anxiety reaction may have a signalling effect.

2. Inhibition, the second basic biologic defense, operates in the direction of terminating all action or excitation which is perceived as causing or maintaining the threat. Because inhibition is automatic and may paralyze important adaptive resources, it may itself produce anxiety.

3. The rage reaction is a more highly organized excitatory response which may serve to eliminate threat through bluff or attack. The three basic biologic defenses described above are involved in what Rado has called "emergency control." He has termed the maladaptive reactions to threat "emergency dyscontrol." The concept of emergency dyscontrol raises important questions yet to be answered. Are there constitutional variations in the biologic equipment which mediate the basic defensive reactions? Are there individuals who overreact to threatening stimuli on the basis of constitutional variations? Do cerebral mechanisms vary in their capacity for handling massive excitation? Do some individuals decompensate under anxiety more easily than others because of constitutional determinants? Answers to these questions are fundamental to a comprehensive understanding of psychopathology and remain subjects for research.

As the adaptive potential of the organism increases with advancing age and development, there is an increased capacity for devising more varied and intricate defenses. Defenses become increasingly more discriminate and related to specific threats. All resources of the organism at all levels of integration are potentially available throughout life for defensive organization against threat. When adaptive functioning becomes impaired because of psychopathology, as it always does, reparative behavior appears. Reparative techniques, which will be referred to later, can be dominantly realistic or unrealistic.

Freud initially divided the sources of anxiety into two major categories: (*a*) those connected with the inner or instinctual impulses, which he called "neurotic anxieties," and (*b*) those arising from external threats and apparently unconnected to the instinctual impulses, which he called "real anxieties." Although this division had certain merit, it was confusing. In the last analysis, the source of all danger, excluding certain types of illness, is referable to the outside world. Because he considered neurotic only the psychopathology connected to the instinctual impulses, Freud found himself unable to explain the traumatic neuroses of World War I. When he reformulated the libido theory in *Beyond the Pleasure Principle* (1920), he incorporated the self-preservative "ego instinct" into the libido. In this way, all threats to the organism became instinctually related. The merit in Freud's original classification lay in the differentiation between threat from the environment and threat perceived to be internally generated. Impulses are part of the self system and cannot be avoided as can external threats. The perception of the sexual impulse offers a good example. If the overt expression of sexual impulses is perceived as dangerous, any stirring of sexual excitation may be perceived and reacted to as a threat. The ubiquity of sexual stimuli in the environment and the nature of neuroendocrine organization may unpredictably create sexual excitation at any given moment.

To meet this response, special defenses emerge. Excitation is channeled to the executive apparatuses of other excitatory processes which occurs in displacement. To insure stable adaptive functioning, defenses against sudden sexual impulses must attain predictable automaticity. Isolation from others may defend against most external threats, but it is not a guarantee against felt sexual impulses. Hence, inhibition becomes a major defense against the expression of unacceptable and frightening impulses.

I have categorized psychopathology into two broad cognitive areas, not mutually exclusive, according to whether a perception of injury or threatened injury is realistic or not. Misperceptions of threat resulting from unrealistic expectations of injury are, in the main, the consequence of actual injury in past experience, displaced to a current situation where the beliefs are no longer appropriate; or, anticipated threat may be an erroneous interpretation of past events. An individual brought up in a repressive environment may continue to believe that all people in a position of authority are repressive; he or she will be unusually alert to repressive cues and will selectively concentrate attention on those authority figures who are, in fact, repressive. In such instances, the perceptions may be accurate but selectively distort the total reality since nonauthoritarian figures are excluded from the frame of reference. This mechanism of selectivity and reaffirmation of irrational convictions plays an important role in maintaining the chronicity of psychopathology. A child who burned her finger on an electric heater became afraid to touch anything colored red. An unpreferred child came to believe that, if he could excel over a preferred sibling it would be displaced in parental affections. The continuity of such a belief in adult life tends to be expressed in destructive, pathologic competitiveness.

The many defenses organized around irrational beliefs of injury complicate and increase psychopathology. Most defenses are based upon fallacies and become sources for additional conflict which, in turn, induce new defenses against the existing ones, and so on. The individual whose fear of authority is defended against by submissive attitudes and behavior may develop a drive for power and domination as a defense against submission. The drive to power then brings with it destructively competitive attitudes toward peers and feared authority figures which only intensify conflicts and further disturb interpersonal relationships. The complex network of defenses often overburdens adaptive capacities and increases decompensatory trends. Although reparative maneuvers are basically manifestations of a drive toward health, unrealistic reparative behavior exacerbates psychopathology. A sexually inhibited woman may attempt a breakthrough by resorting to kinky sex and multiple partners, activities that may involve her in a sordid life style and in an inability to form self-enhancing, meaningful sexual relationships. Reparative behavior for such a woman would be finding competent psychiatric treatment and entering into situations that realistically negated the irrational beliefs underlying her sexual inhibitions.

Irrational expectations of injury may coexist with more realistic beliefs relevant to the same situation. A common irrational belief about marriage, not generally conscious, is that marriage to a valued and loved person is dangerous. Such a belief derives, in part, from the childhood situation in which a parent prohibits and inhibits sexuality, resulting to some extent in feelings of sexual unaccepta- bility. In the main, however, I have found that the fears associated with heterosexuality are linked to the oedipus complex. Traceable directly to this triangular conflict is the irrational, unconscious but easily demonstrable belief that a love relationship with a valued person will invoke hostile reactions from all or most members of the same sex, in particular, parentlike figures. The expectations of same-sex hostility may become the nucleus around which important defenses and reparative reactions are orga- nized. The resulting psychopathology may coexist with conscious and realistic aspirations about marriage. The individual who consciously values sexuality, especially in marriage, who thinks one should marry for love — that marriage is desirable, fulfilling, etc. — at the same time may unconsciously entertain an opposite set of attitudes and beliefs. The two opposing systems of belief about marriage may coexist in a dynamic interrelationship and there may be a constant shifting in the weight that each system exerts on the individual's dominant adaptation at any one time. Dreams are an excellent clinical guide to an understanding of the predominating, ongoing dynamics.

The conflict between irrational and realistic beliefs about the same situation is an essential aspect of psycho- pathology. Irrational beliefs and its attendant psycho- pathology may form part of character and relatively stable behavior that may find expression in daily life. In some people, irrational beliefs remain quiescent, being over- shadowed, though not eliminated, by appropriate reality beliefs. Irrationalities may reemerge upon entering a new situation, such as marriage; they may also become reacti- vated when an injury or series of injuries confirm old beliefs. In such an instance, psychopathological episodes may be acted out in a personality who previously had appeared to be fairly stable.

This formulation differs from Freud's concept of psychopathology which postulates conflict between the reemerging infantile instinctual impulses on the one hand, and reality on the other. Both formulations have in common the assumption that much of adult psychopathology has its roots in childhood experience, but they differ in the conceptualization of the underlying content that reemerges in the psychopathological state.

Conflicting patterns of adaptation constitute another aspect of psychopathology. One can construct a hierarchy of adaptive patterns ranging from the optimal and most effective to the least optimal and least effective. One musician may successfully concertize; another, equally gifted, may give up music entirely and watch television all day. Downward movement does not occur without experiencing conflict; it is perceived and reacted to as a threat to self. Anxiety states during homosexual panic derive, in part, from a sense of injury that a less effective adaptation may supplant a more effective one.

Psychopathology falls into two broad diagnostic categories — neuroses and psychoses. A patient's sense of reality is a salient criterion for differentiation. When irrationality dominates the major adaptation or when past history indicates a tendency toward developing states of irrationality, psychosis is diagnosed. Nonpsychotic psychopathology is usually diagnosed as neurosis. In the neurosis, irrationalities are organized and integrated with such seeming plausibility that cognitive flaws may not be immediately apparent. In the psychoses, the internal logic of systems of thinking tends to be inconsistent, contradictory, and obviously irrational. Even in well-systematized delusions, careful scrutiny and evaluation reveal gross distortions of logic and judgment. Certain concepts from cardiology may be usefully borrowed. The neurotic personality can be said to be "compensated." In the psychosis, adaptive functioning is in "failure" and the personality is "decompensated." Adaptive failure and decompensation may prevail in vital areas of function. In extreme failure, there is more or less total disorganization of effective functioning. Actions may be purposeless and meaningless; the ego is "fibrillating." Behavior that is a manifestation of disorganized functioning cannot reasonably be assigned meaning as in some types of urinary and bowel incontinence seen in deteriorating schizophrenics. The classical view of psychotic behavior as regressive implies a return to earlier stages of organization. The psychotic behavior seen in severe decompensatory states may have little or no relationship to integrated behavior at any stage of development; it is, rather, a manifestation of disintegration. Regression is a poor concept. Its usage has produced a distorted picture of the dynamics of psychotic behavior. Motivational theories of human behavior, of which the libido theory is one, can properly assign motivation *only* to organized functioning.

When psychopathological organization becomes established, it acquires a patterned automaticity. The concept of psychopathology thus formulated provides a guide for psychoanalytic technique. The work of cognitive psychoanalysis involves helping the patient to become insightfully aware of (1) all convictions associated with an expectation of injury, irrational and realistic; (2) recovering the genesis of these beliefs in past experience through dreams, free association, and analysis of transference; (3) delineating the specific defenses and reparative reactions; and (4) working out the psychodynamics of the defenses and reparative reactions. Insight derived from such work is essential for significant improvement, although, by itself, it does not necessarily determine change. It provides the patient with a method for deconditioning psychopathological automaticity by replacing irrational beliefs with realistic ones. I have emphasized a principle in cognitive psychoanalysis that involves the delineation and analysis of basic convictions underlying expectations of injury before analyzing defenses and reparative behaviors. If a patient believes that any show of self-assertiveness will invite rejection or attack, the fear of self-assertion is approached analytically before the associated defenses are brought into focus. The defenses may include drives to power, dependency on others who are self-assertive, overt hostility masking submission, etc. The subject order that first takes up the analysis of defenses and unrealistic reparative techniques is often traumatic for the patient and tends to elicit unnecessary resistances. When defensive and unrealistic reparative techniques are analyzed, I delineate for the patient how the defenses are integrated with the underlying expectations of injury that created the need for the defenses in the first place.

Sexual problems arising from prohibitive mores and from the dynamics of the oedipus complex constitute major determinants of psychopathology. The relationship of sexuality to psychopathology has been well documented in psychoanalytic literature and requires no further comment. For reasons beyond the scope of this chapter, I shall not detail my disagreement with the libido theory except to state that I do not regard as sexual the need to satisfy hunger, or the needs for nurturance, affection, contact, stimulation, etc., which are ordinarily assigned to the oral stage of development as outlined by Freud. The frustration of these needs tends to create in the child the problems that can be broadly classed as fears of rejection. Fears of unacceptability with accompanying fears of rejection usually occupy central interest in treatment. Inadequate parental response to a child's needs for acceptance, however, only partially contributes to this problem. Social stratification and ethnic and class bias also create and maintain the fear of rejection. No society has yet evolved that has guaranteed fulfillment of all basic needs to all its members — adequate food supply, housing, medical care, opportunities for the development and expression of individual potential, and the recognition of the dignity of each individual and the subgroup to which he or she belongs. Social stratification guarantees satisfaction of basic needs to its privileged groups, thus promulgating a preoccupation with status and prestige and encouraging competitive drives and fears of rejection. To the extent that a society fails to meet the needs of all its people, it is pathogenic and its pathogenic social conditions exert a potent force in determining psychopathology in the individual.

Personality and psychopathology are highly dynamic and keep evolving throughout life. New threats of injury alter established psychopathology by reconfirming old expectations of injury and create the need to adapt to the new threats. In a study of cancer patients (chapter 14), Ohrbach and I have described their reactions to the disease and to surgery. The reality threat to life and uncertainty about acceptance by others in a new adaptational context of illness, produced in some patients psychopathological reactions not identifiable in their preoperative personalities. Conversely, good life situations tend to militate toward the resolution of psychopathology.

In conclusion, the cognitive method of psychoanalysis I have conducted is based upon the concept of injury, realistic and misperceived. In this formulation, psychopathology is characterized by (1) all the irrational beliefs associated with injury, including defensive and reparative reactions organized around such beliefs; (2) maladaptive responses to threat (emergency dyscontrol); (3) the symptomatic manifestations of disintegrating adaptive functioning.

Chapter 4

Biosocial Determinants
of the Neuroses

What is meant by mental illness or, conversely, mental health? Freud, at least initially, defined neurosis rather simply. Dynamically, it was seen as the conflict between instinctual drives and social demands; diagnosis was symptom-oriented, and patients consulted a neuro-psychiatrist for the treatment of anxiety, neurosthenia, phobias, obsessions, compulsions, hallucinations, and so forth. Only those with symptomatic complaints were considered to be neurotic or psychotic. Freud's paper on anal character in 1908 and Reich's subsequent elabora-tion of character defenses extended the psychopathological sphere well beyond symptomatic borders, while the development of psychosomatic medicine extended the symptomatic borders themselves. New parameters were introduced with ego psychology, which stressed personality or ego functioning. The evaluation of ego "strength" became one way of evaluating mental health — the stronger the ego, the healthier the individual; the weaker the ego, the sicker the individual. Strength of ego was evaluated largely by the capacity to cope with stress and by the psychiatrist's estimate of the extent of effective functioning relative to the patient's potential.

René Spitz (1965) introduced an original concept, *psychopathogenesis*: failure in development of inborn potential behavior patterns as a consequence of the absence of appropriate stimulation. Sandor Rado offered another concept, "emergency dyscontrol," in which responses to threatening stimuli are inadequate or inappropriate in preventing psychologic injury or in repairing injury once sustained. In amplifying Rado's concept of emergency dyscontrol, I include dysfunction of the alarm reaction itself. The genesis of this dysfunction may be experiential in that children reared by overanxious parents learn to react too sensitively and with overintense affect to threatening stimuli. A metabolic defect may also be involved in the neurophysiological and neurochemical aspects of the alarm reaction itself.

In the high-powered fields of their psychomicroscopy, Freud, Reich, Spitz, Rado, and such psychosomaticists as Dunbar, Alexander, French, and others focused on the individual. These authors were oriented to the individual's relatedness and adaptation to his environment. Their emphasis was on the study of individual systematics in the context of as many aspects of the relationship between the individual and the environment as could be observed or determined theoretically. Harry Stack

Sullivan, however, pioneered in studying behavioral disorders in the context of the interactional systems operant between individuals, using the dyadic therapeutic relationship as a model.

A profile of the mentally "healthy" individual may be assembled even from these briefly discussed conceptualizations. He appears to be free of psychogenic symptoms such as "neurotic" anxiety and of the symptoms previously referred to. When exposed to reality threat, he will react appropriately, commensurate with emergency control. His potential for effective functioning will have been adequately and appropriately stimulated to permit its fullest development, and he will have an unimpeded capacity for its expression. He will have the capacity to marry a loved one with whom he sustains a consistent, affectionate, sexually orgastic, and companionate relationship. He will be a loving, constructive parent. Finally, he will be an individual who relates to his fellows in a consistently warm, meaningful, cooperative, and assertive way.

This profile of the mentally "healthy" man or woman fits no one whom I know — at least personally — yet it is based on the important guideposts in personality study made possible by the contributions of psychoanalysis. To the extent an individual deviates from this profile, there may be evidence of a personality defect or disorder. Now the mentally "healthy" individual should be distinguished from the so-called "normal" one. On the one hand, the concept of normalcy is statistically derived and refers to the average, the usual; on the other, "normalcy" is intended to describe a state of health — a hygienic analogue. Because of its dualistic meaning, the term "normal" should be restricted to its statistical usage. I shall not differentiate here between neurosis and psychosis since I view the biosocial determinants of psychopathology to be operant in both conditions.

THE FAMILY

The nuclear family is the biosocial unit of our social structure; the taproot of personality is grounded in this unit. The adjustments within a family represent the nature of the interrelationships and reciprocal interactions of its members. Within the family system, each member influences the personality development of every other. The flow of interchange within a family will vary, change its course from time to time, and fluctuate with the give and take of daily life. But at any point in time, the family has coherence, role assignments, and a system of relationships characterized by subtle but well-defined interpersonal alignments. Shifts in pattern occur as new members come and old ones leave. These rearrangements may create revolutionary shifts in family relationships or they may be smoothly integrated into the forward movement of growth and change. The parents are the architects of family structure and fundamentally determine the ongoing processes. Personality maladaptation is the objective manifestation of dysfunction in the family and the development of a severe personality disorder in the child is almost always evidence of the pervasive effects of parental psychopathology. The extent of pathogenic influence varies depending on parental interaction with each specific child. In some families, one child may bear the brunt; in others, most or all may be seriously affected. Psychopathologic responses differ in each child depending upon how a multiplicity of factors — sex, rank order, physical and intellectual endowment — articulate with parental needs, attitudes and values.

An outstanding advance in understanding the determinants and dynamics of neuroses has been the growing recognition of the role that the family plays in the genesis of psychopathology by transmitting parental psychopathology to the offspring, howsoever this is communicated and established. This is not to assign blame since parental psychopathology, in its turn, is determined by the psychopathology of grandparents within the framework of psychopathogenic elements in the environment of origin. Even postulating a set of ideal parents, can we anticipate that the offspring will be free of psychopathology? It would seem that parents can only relatively protect children from pathogenic influences. Parents cannot fully forestall neurotic conflicts that accompany certain phases of development, though much can be done to effect a resolution of such conflicts. Yet two generalizations can be made. First, the earlier in personal history psychopathology emerges, the more directly traceable it is to parental influences. Second, the more severe the child's difficulties are, the more directly connected it is to parental psychopathology.

Each infant requires fulfillment of needs common to all infants and from birth on will also manifest differences from other infants. Since infantile needs require the ministrations of at least one other person, human needs are biosocial from the start. As the child develops, his requirements become increasingly more complex, differentiated, and personally styled. The parental capacity for meeting a child's needs appropriately determines in large measure whether optimal development will occur.

Parental Transference Reactions

Unrealistic parental attitudes include a wide range of responses, some that have the characteristics of transference. Parental transference involves the irrational identification of a child with significant persons in the parent's life history, including self. Not infrequently, parents relate to a child as though he or she were an extension of themselves. The child is a unique and separate individual whose requirements in a biosocial context we term "needs" and in a sociopolitical context we term "rights." Any parental attitude that is dissociated from the reality of the child's individuality is, by definition, unrealistic, as are all concepts, attitudes, and behavior deriving from beliefs that the child is an exteriorization of the parental self. Parental transference results in a distorted image of the child and tends toward inappropriate relatedness to his or her needs and rights. Such distortions in perception, and consequently in parenting behavior, become pathogenic influences.

It must be emphasized that the cognitive aspects of parental transference may not be organized at a level of conscious awareness and may coexist with more realistic, conscious concepts. When a mother identifies her son with her own father, consciously or unconsciously she may be attempting to replicate with her child selected aspects of her relationship with her father. Such a transference may be associated with anxiety and guilt, particularly those affective responses that had sexual overtones or reflected rivalrous attitudes for exclusive possession of the father. Responses of this type disturb the mother-son relationship, usually in the direction of her withdrawal from him or in defective contact. Or there may be an overcloseness and overprotectiveness as a defense against the fear of being robbed of the child. There may be alternating phases of both types of attitudes and behavior. Or the mother may identify her son with a brother, an uncle, or other significant male and then behave inappropriately. A mother may identify her daughter with her own mother, transferring a complex set of attitudes including pathologic dependency and competitive attitudes. A mother may also identify her daughter with a sister, grandmother, and so forth. Transference reactions in fathers are also commonly observed.

The transference from self is a special kind of parental transference. Here the essential irrationality is that the child is not a separate individual but extends from and adorns the self. Parental behavior deriving from such a transference is usually proprietary, controlling, and exploitative. In such cases, the child is viewed as more likely to fulfill a range of frustrated wishes than is the actual self. In families with more than one child, different facets of self may be transferred to each child, with a special role identity assigned to each. While such parents condition all their children to orient themselves primarily to parental gratification as a primary responsibility, one child may be singled out and groomed for success and fame in a particular endeavor; a second child may be groomed as companion and entertainer for the parents, and so on. Assigning a child the role of a loser as a way of indirectly acting out parental masochism is not uncommon. A transference maneuver from a split self-image where one child is identified with the "good self" and another child with the "bad self" may be observed in the psychoanalyses of patients who are parents.

In general, parental transference reactions are admixtures of transferences from significant persons and from aspects of self. Preference for one child over another is always an expression of neurosis manifested in a transference reaction. Preferential attitudes are important determinants of serious psychopathology for preferred and nonpreferred children alike, although their adaptive patterns and psychopathologic reactions may differ. In psychoanalyzing adults, I am usually able to reconstruct the salient transference formations of parents toward the patient, and to relate these transferences to specific aspects of the patient's psychopathology. Insights gained through this type of analytic pursuit are highly effective in promoting therapeutic progress.

Parental Beliefs

The orientation of the child to social reality and the interpretation and definition of this reality is a major parental function. How parents interpret reality depends, of course, upon their social values and beliefs and how they communicate them through verbally and non-verbally expressed attitudes and behavior. Where a conflicting set of beliefs is communicated, the child is more likely to trust nonverbal cues. If a mother verbally approves of her young daughter's masturbating but expresses an attitudinal revulsion at witnessing it, the child is more likely to be influenced by the affective response. Beliefs are pathogenic that do not reflect the nature of reality as it is currently knowable and which conflict with the child's needs.

The variegated beliefs one holds may be ordered according to systems, for example, dominance-submission, cooperation-competition, aggression-pacifism. The acceptance-rejection polarity is one such important system. In general, self-esteem reflects a sense of confidence in one's acceptability to others. Acceptance by others is a biosocial need; it assures the gratification of a range of requirements only other humans can fulfill—security, communication, sexuality, etc. Behavior that ensures personal acceptance begins in early life. Behavioral techniques and value systems are learned and continually reinforced by parental and surrogate approval, affection, reward or their opposites.

Parents who inculcate unrealistic beliefs about acceptability disturb sexual, assertive, affiliative and other maturational processes. The child who is encouraged to believe that, to be acceptable to the parents and to others, he or she must be "best," is propelled into intense competition with peers, a situation that seriously interferes with feeling accepted in the peer group. Disturbances in assertiveness and creativity develop in children whose parents believe that acceptance is assured through conformity, submission, and self-sacrifice. Parental beliefs that are not congruent with reality dislocate the child's potential for optimal development and appropriate social relatedness, even when the parents are oriented to furthering the best interests of the child.

The Instincts

Modern man has good reason to be dissatisfied with his mammalian heritage. We inherited a type of alarm reaction to threat more suited to meeting the physical dangers to which primitive man was exposed than those met with today. The massive hypermobilization of physiological resources, characterizing the alarm or anxiety reaction, serves little useful function in modern life. Anxiety causes suffering, often interferes with appropriate behavior, and is an important factor in psychosomatic illness. We might be better off with a much quieter alarm response. While waiting for the proper mutation to appear, we have discovered alcohol, alkaloids, and the ataraxic drugs — each designed to diminish the intensity of the anxiety reaction. We also could do quite well with a much subdued rage reaction, which constitutes a type of biologically patterned response adapted to physical combat. For the most part, violence is an atavistic way of dealing with human problems, although man has achieved the technological facility to make it the final solution.

The relationship of instinct to neurosis must, of course, emphasize sexuality. Freud, noting the frequency of sexual symptomatology and disturbances in sexual functioning, constructed a theory of neurosis based on the primacy of libidinal and aggressive instincts. In the genesis of psychopathology, sexual development plays a major role. Psychopathologenic factors related to sexual development fall into two categories: the *prohibitive* and the *competitive.*

Under the rubric of prohibitions are the power-linked influences, parental and other, which interfere with sexual behavior at various stages of maturation. These include interference with infantile genital manipulation, which begins during the first year of life; interference with masturbation, sexual curiosity, and sexual play in childhood; and, after puberty, proscription of premarital intercourse. Although the apparent rationale for these restrictions is to produce a monogamous adult capable of fulfilling sexual needs in marriage, the more usual outcome is a sexually inhibited adult whose difficulties interfere with sexual fulfillment in and out of marriage. Restrictive parental and societal attitudes toward childhood sexuality and premarital sexual relations surround it with an aura of shame and unacceptability. The psychopathologic consequences are numerous, complex, and familiar.

Sexually competitive attitudes and behavior begin in childhood and are an integral part of the oedipus complex, which begins somewhere between the third and fifth year. The first manifestation of what I consider to be sexually determined object relations is a specific type of orientation toward heterosexual individuals. I have termed it the *stage of heterosexual orientation*. In "Olfaction in Sexual Development and Adult Sexual Organization," I reported (Bieber 1959) on the observations which led me to the hypothesis that the initial heterosexual phase is set off by the child's beginning capacity to react sexually to heterosexual odors. In the first stage of sexual orientation to the parent of the opposite sex, competitive attitudes and behavior toward the same-sex parent first becomes observable. Whether competitive behavior follows heterosexual orientation, or appears simultaneously with it, is undetermined. Whether early sexually competitive behavior is biologically patterned and part of our mammalian heritage is also undetermined, but the frequency of combative behavior for sexual partners in infrahuman mammals suggests a biologically determined pattern. In "The Role of Olfaction in Sexual Development," Kalogerakis (1963) reported observations on a male child who expressed negative reactions to his father's odor even many hours following parental intercourse. The obviously negative olfactory response was also accompanied by competitive behavior. Kalogerakis hypothesized that olfaction is the modality that ushers in sexual competition. Whether or not competitive reactions are biologically patterned or learned, rivalrous reactions are among the early vicissitudes of the very young and may constitute a stumbling block in later development. The long period of biosocial maturation necessitates prolonged dependency upon parents. Between the second and fifth year, the emergence of sexual feelings for the heterosexual parent and the associated competitive feelings toward the same-sex parent — the oedipus complex — contribute toward disturbing the child's relationship with both parents during a period when he requires a filial bond uncomplicated by conflict. Neurotic symptomatology and specific phobias frequently begin during the oedipal phase.

In my view, the so-called "latency" period involves repression or attempts at repression of incestuous and competitive feelings. It is a period during which the child attempts to reinstate a nonconflictual relationship with both parents made necessary by a growing (though unconscious) awareness of a need for continued dependency. The sexual repression remains incomplete, however; substitutive techniques for sexual behavior as well as for expressing sexual competition are usually in evidence.

Parental reactions to the child's emerging sexuality in large part determine the nature of the resolution of the oedipus complex. Parents who accept and respond in positive ways to the child's heterosexual behavior, who are not competitive or threatened by the hostility accompanying the child's competitive attitudes, and parents who promote the appropriate sexual identification of the child help in the resolution of the oedipus complex. It is my impression that complete resolution of the oedipus complex is rarely achieved. In patients whom I have psychoanalyzed, derivatives of the psychopathology noted have been traceable to the oedipus complex.

The development of the oedipal conflict may be inevitable, but its solution does not seem to rest upon redesigning family structure as we know it. The family fulfills profound emotional needs, provides the opportunity for the development of a rich, deeply experienced relatedness to others, and becomes the emotional base for monogamy. Identification with an esteemed same-sex figure appears to be essential in resolving competitive problems and in providing reality testing for extinguishing retaliatory expectations accompanying rivalrous feelings.

Competition is one adaptive technique for coping with scarcity; no one competes for the plentiful. When an individual's resourcefulness is inhibited in goal achievement, the goal may be perceived as scarce despite its adequate representation in the environment. A belief that desirable heterosexual objects are scarce is associated with sexual inhibition, further sharpening sexually competitive attitudes.

SOCIETY

Psychoanalysts as a group have given considerably less attention to the broader societal determinants of neurosis than to either family or instinctual determinants. The data necessary to evaluate societal determinants are not immediately available to the individual psychoanalyst in private practice and the patient samples are too small for this type of research unless one collaborates with other analysts. Even then it becomes necessary to collaborate with social scientists in order to explore the multifaceted complexities of the problem fully and systematically. Social scientists have an equally difficult problem. They must enter the clinical area to investigate societal determinants of personality disorder or mental illness. The collaboration between the clinician and the social scientist appears to be essential and points to the increasing need for interdisciplinary research. In a paper entitled "Cultural Anthropology and Social Psychiatry," Marvin K. Opler (1956) discusses the enormous difficulties facing social scientists who are investigating this problem. "It may indeed be arduous to describe in any psychodynamic detail the stamping into physiological manifestations and emotional economy, of environmental experience. Until this is done, however, there will be neither advancement in social psychiatry, nor a valid cross-cultural science of culture and personality."

Cultural anthropologists have demonstrated that variations in cultural patterns are associated with variations in personality traits. Since culture and personality are related variables, personality disorders and patterns of culture may also be considered as related variables. Referring to the personality profile I have offered as a standard for mental health, the greater the deviation from this standard among the general population of any culture, the greater the convergence between cultural traits and personality disorder. Maternal rejection and frustration are pathogenic in our own society. In the Balinese studies of Bateson and Mead (1942), where maternal frustration was observed to be an institutionalized technique of child-rearing, there is a tendency for the society to produce a withdrawn, schizoid individual.

The generalization that cultural traits provide a social matrix for personality disorder points up the problems which still challenge behavioral scientists. What types of psychopathology are socially determined? What factors in social structure and process are pathogenic? How do pathogenic social processes become transformed into psychopathologic processes? The psychoanalyst, on the basis of his expertness in psychopathology, may contribute in the search for answers by formulating relevant hypotheses and problems which may then be investigated systematically.

First, he may hypothesize that those aspects of structure and process in a society which lead to feelings of rejection among its members or to differential social acceptance and status of groups are pathogenic. Data are available to him which support the formulation that rejection — whether it occurs within the family setting or outside of it — is pathogenic. I have psychoanalyzed many members of minority groups and of groups accorded inferior social status. Feelings of unacceptability and inferiority associated with membership in these groups have been observed in all such patients. To be sure, such attitudes toward self varied as to intensity and salience in different patients, depending upon how such attitudes articulated with feelings of unacceptability and inferiority derived from other interpersonal sources. The intensity of these feelings varied also with the social distance between the group with which the patient was affiliated and groups having higher status and social acceptance. For example, the level of self-acceptance derived from the affiliate group seems to be lower among Blacks than among Jews, at least in my own experience with patients from these minorities. Psychoanalysts may advance the general principle that social forces promoting and maintaining inferior status for a subgroup tend to produce psychopathology in its individual members. This psychopathology will tend to be more immediately observable in members of very low-status groups, though psychopathology will not be confined to them. Studies of prejudice indicate that antiminority attitudes are not restricted to particular groups and classes. Since prejudice is irrational, it is psychopathologic whether on the basis of class, race, religion, or other factors. While psychoanalysts deal with the data which link prejudice to psychopathology and psychopathogenic influences, the social scientist must illuminate the broader societal forces that create and maintain prejudice.

Second, the psychoanalyst may hypothesize that forces tending to alienate people and to disturb cooperative and affectional relationships are pathogenic. As pointed out earlier, actual scarcity or an erroneous belief in scarcity of elements thought to be necessary to optimal welfare can lead to competitive — and thus alienating — interpersonal relationships. That which is regarded as necessary to optimal welfare may rationally include adequate food, housing, medical care, and equal opportunity for the development and expression of individual potential. Irrationally, the possession of a Cadillac may be regarded as social "oxygen."

Another societal factor leading to disturbances in cooperative relationships is authoritarianism. Outstanding work in this area has been contributed by Adorno in studies on the authoritarian personality (Adorno et al. 1950). In the psychoanalysis of patients, we can observe evidences of reactions to members of primary groups — familial, occupational, and social. Where an authoritarian has power in the group, the patient reports a type of response that appears to parallel the behavior of individuals living under authoritarian-repressive political conditions — fear and mistrust of authority, mutual suspicion, and dominance-submission patterns of behavior. It can be demonstrated psychoanalytically that authoritarianism is a powerful alienating influence and, therefore, psychopathogenic. As a corollary, it may be proposed that the more strongly developed is democracy in a society and in its subgroups, fewer are the social determinants of mental illness.

Chapter 5

Psychoanalysis and Psychoanalytically Oriented Psychotherapy

Classical psychoanalysis draws a clear distinction between analysis and psychotherapy. The use of the couch and no fewer than four sessions a week are deemed essential if treatment is to be considered psychoanalytic. The theory underlying these prerequisites is that the development of transference, transference neurosis, and the analysis of these psychological states require the technique as prescribed by Freud. The psychoanalytic tradition does not, however, offer a well-defined structure for psychotherapy, other than a general concept of psychodynamics and, implicitly, common sense.

Cognitive psychoanalysis is concerned with substantive issues, not with technical aids. If there is a delineation and working-through of irrational beliefs, and if defensive and reparative maneuvers are analyzed, then there is no clinical difference between psychoanalysis and psychoanalytically oriented psychotherapy.

TECHNICAL AND STRATEGIC CONSIDERATIONS

The Couch

Freud first described the use of the couch in his early publication, "The Psychotherapy of Hysteria" (Breuer and Freud 1893–1895). Convinced that the neurotic symptom was linked to a memory of an antecedent, relevant, and traumatic event, Freud would ask the patient to lie down and then would insist that the patient recall such an event. When this did not turn out to be particularly productive, Freud would apply manual pressure to the patient's forehead which, he wrote, "invariably worked." In his paper "On Beginning the Treatment" (1913) he stated:

> Before I wind up these remarks on beginning analytic treatment, I must say a word about a certain ceremonial which concerns the position in which the treatment is carried out. I hold to the plan of getting the patient to lie on a sofa while I sit behind him out of his sight. This arrangement has a historical basis. It is the remnant of the hypnotic method out of which psychoanalysis evolved. But it deserves to be maintained for many reasons. The first is a personal motive but one which others may share with me. I cannot put up with being stared at by other people for eight hours a day or more. Since, while I am listening to the patient, I, too, give myself over to the current of my unconscious thoughts, I do not wish my expressions of

face to give the patient material for interpretations or to influence me in what he tells me. I insist on this procedure, however, for its purpose and result are to prevent the transference from mingling with the patient's associations imperceptably, to isolate the transference, and to allow it to come forward in true course sharply defined as a resistance. (p. 133)

Transference and Transference Neurosis

Four basic concepts constitute the theoretical underpinnings for the use of the couch: transference, transference neurosis, regression, and free association. Freud's first mention of transference appears in *Studies on Hysteria,* published between 1893 and 1895. In it, Freud talked of a young lady who had experienced a wish for a certain man to "boldly take her in his arms and give her a kiss." The wish, uttered in a therapeutic session, was directed to Freud, who interpreted it as a transference from the antecedent situation. He did not propose an alternate hypothesis — that this sexually frustrated woman who was too inhibited to assert her own sexual wishes, entertained a modified rape fantasy that could be evoked by men she found attractive — in this situation, her analyst.

Transference next appears in *The Interpretation of Dreams* (1900) where it has a somewhat different connotation, yet exposes and reveals the basic assumptions underlying transference and transference neurosis. According to Freud, unconscious, unfulfilled instinctual wishes, like animals trapped in a cage, are constantly seeking a way out. The way out for an instinct is to connect itself to a conscious idea that has access to the motor apparatus, so that the wishes can become gratified through action.

Thus, as a wood tick lying in wait for an unsuspecting victim, these unconscious impulses find a suitable conscious idea to attach to and then transfer or cathect the idea with instinctual energy. The idea may then seek expression in a neurotic act or symptom. One can infer from Freud's writings on transference that, somewhere along the way, he came to believe that the analytic situation was an ideal locus for the latching on of unconscious and instinctual wishes both as to object, the analyst, and to the various aims that derive from the libidinal stages and phases that are described in the analysis itself.

In his lecture on transference, Freud (1917) states:

> When . . . the treatment has obtained mastery over the patient, what happens is that the whole of his illness is concentrated upon a single point — his relationship to the doctor . . . . When the transference has risen to this significance, work upon the patient's memories retreats far into the background. Thereafter, it is not incorrect to say that we are no longer concerned with the patient's earlier illness but with a newly created and transformed neurosis which has taken the former's place. We have followed this new edition of the old disorder from the start. We have observed its origin and growth and we are especially well able to find our way about it, since, as its object, we are situated at its very center. All the patient's symptoms have abandoned their original meaning and have taken on a new sense which lies in relationship to the transference where only such symptoms have persisted as are capable of undergoing such a transformation. But the mastery of this new artificial neurosis coincides with getting rid of the illness which was originally brought to the treatment with the accomplishment of our therapeutic task. A person who has become normal and free from the

operation of a repressed instinctual impulse in his relationship to the doctor, will remain so in his own life after the doctor has once more withdrawn from it. (p. 444)

Shortly thereafter, Freud (1917, p. 447) wrote, "This *transference*, alike in its positive and negative form, is used as a weapon by the resistance; but in the hands of the physician, it becomes the most powerful therapeutic instrument and it plays a part scarcely to be overestimated in the dynamics of the process of cure."

I do not hold with Freud that an old neurosis can be converted into a new one, that it is located in the transference and that it can be resolved by the analysis of an artificially constructed transference neurosis. If, in fact, an old illness could be transformed into a new one in which the analyst is the central figure, then, indeed, it is logical that analysis of the transference neurosis became the central technique of classical theory. The couch is deemed to be essential in this undertaking because the analyst must remain impersonal and unseen so that he can serve as a blank screen onto which transference objects, as experienced in childhood, can be projected. Further, the analysis must be conducted in an atmosphere of relative privation since satisfaction of an instinctual wish removes the motive force for therapy.

All this sounds organized and systematic, but it does not work as theorized. The totality of a patient's psychopathology, or a major part of it, is not transferable to the analyst; that it can transmigrate and become a new illness is hypothetical rather than real, and it is a phenomenon that I have never observed. I do not encourage transference neurosis; it is neither desirable nor inevitable. Patients differ one from another and technique may vary from time to time, depending on therapeutic needs. As to transference itself, if it is defined as a replica of aspects of an antecedent relationship, then transference to the analyst always occurs. If, however, analytic transference is restricted to the *irrational* components of replicated reactions, then transference may also include spouse, children, employer, friends and so forth. In the wide spectrum of possible transference reactions, a single analyst can elicit only a segment, albeit an important segment, and each analyst evokes different transference reactions from different patients. One who expresses warmth may evoke anxiety about intimacy. Male and female patients respond differently to male and female analysts (see chapter 6). Freud was well aware of this phenomenon and said so in his paper, "Observations on Transference Love" (1915b, p. 154) and in his lecture on transference (1917, p. 443). In the former paper, Freud spoke of the erotic transference of the female patient to a male analyst, that is, her "falling in love with him." "This phenomenon occurs without fail which as we know is one of the foundations of psychoanalytic theory."

In the forty or more years in which I have been practicing psychoanalysis, many women patients have developed some sort of sexual feelings toward me but these feelings did not constitute a "falling in love" or a transferential problem. Only a handful of women developed a significant erotic transference and, with one exception, all of these patients have either been "borderline" or schizophrenic. When generalizations are made, they must rest upon the vast majority of cases, not upon exceptions. Freud also postulated that the positive transference of a male patient to a male analyst was basically erotic, although he did not use the phrase "falling in love." He stressed the hostile transference of the male patient to the male analyst, recognizing the oedipal basis for the difference.

Of historic as well as clinical interest is the anecdote communicated to me personally by Abram Kardiner, who had been analyzed by Freud. Kardiner stated that, at least in his own case, transference was never analyzed. Freud concentrated almost entirely upon latent homosexuality and the oedipus complex. Roy Grinker Sr. once described an incident which strongly suggests that the sanctity of transference neurosis was not quite as Freud wrote about it. During a session, Grinker complained that he could not find a good cigar in Vienna. Freud rose from his chair, took a cigar from his humidor and presented it to his analysand. (Grinker never smoked it; he kept it as a treasured memento until it crumbled with age.) Another anecdote Grinker told is about Freud's dog, Yufi, who would be let in and out of the consulting room. When the dog left the room one day, Freud said, "You see, Yufi isn't interested." Later, when he let the dog in again, he said, "Yufi will give you another chance."

As to technique, I interpret transference to me only when I am clearly and convincingly the object either in dreams, attitudes, fantasies, or behavior. I do not assume that I am present in every dream or that I am the central concern of every session though I am always aware of the presence of transference and I interpret negative transference as soon as it is discerned or when it constitutes a resistance. The patient's distortions and irrational beliefs are expressed and acted out vis-à-vis the many persons encountered in everyday life. I use the realities of individual relationships and situations as the bases for analyzing transferences. Distortions and irrationalities may be identified as they occur and thus I focus on that instead of concentrating on a patient's transference to me. This technique has important advantages. First, it considers what the patient is talking about and what he or she can readily understand. When a patient is talking about parents, spouse, lover, employer, or friend, he or she is talking about them, not about the analyst. Good contact is maintained in the context of the productions; the patient is spared being presented with some obscure, speculative connection with the analyst which may be submissively accepted but not understood. Second, the therapeutic alliance is not disturbed so that an uncluttered working atmosphere may facilitate the exploration of irrational transferences as they are acted out in the patient's real life, without obfuscation by unnecessary examination of the analyst-patient relationship.

An illustration of the importance of working out primary irrational beliefs before they appear as analytic resistances was demonstrated in a patient who was treated by a student some years ago. The student was analyzing a woman who was approximately his own age. The patient had a brother who was clearly the mother's favorite. The patient's relationship to her brother was characteristic of that of a nonpreferred to a preferred child, and, in this case, also included a corrosive hostility. The student had failed to work out this aspect of the patient's psychopathology in the early phases of treatment. When it appeared in the analytic transference, needless to say, it was accompanied by highly negative resistance, punctuated by an alienating hostility. Her hostility interfered with the cognitive clarity necessary to resolve the irrational aspects of her reaction, and prevented her from accepting any analytic interpretations. With this impasse, the patient terminated treatment.

Thus, the analyst not only must be aware of transference, but what the transference is likely to involve also must be anticipated. If the analyst is a male, significantly older than the patient, a father transference is likely to be evoked; if the analyst is female, significantly older than the patient, a mother transference is likely. If the analyst is about the same age as the patient, a sibling or peer transference may be evoked, and if the patient is significantly older than the analyst, a son or daughter transference will likely be evoked. The interpretation of the analytic transference, however, is not of minor consequence. For some patients, the concrete experience of analytic transference and its continued interpretation is absolutely necessary in order to work through fears of the parents, older siblings, and so forth. I have had women patients who insisted on being treated by a male therapist but who finally required the concrete experience of a relationship with a woman analyst. These women would not have accepted referral to a woman to begin with. That would have been much too threatening. It took years of analysis with a man before their fears could be sufficiently attenuated to permit analysis with a woman. Ideally, this type of patient should have an analyst of each sex, starting with one of the opposite sex.

As has already been indicated, it is usually the more disturbed patients who develop prolonged, intense transferences. When meaningful and intense transferences do develop, be they erotic or hostile, they occur just as readily with the patient sitting up as lying down. I also have found that negative transferences are more easily and rapidly resolved when patient and analyst are face to face.

As noted previously, my work with analytic transference varies from patient to patient and with the same patient from time to time. Yet, if the amount of time spent analyzing the transference to the analyst is any criterion, then such transference analysis occupies a relatively small part of my work with most patients.

Regression

Regression is conceived of as a process in which the patient retraces developmental steps, picks up scattered repressed instinctual impulses, makes them conscious, and with the help of the analyst, extinguishes anachronistic wishes. The term itself has come to have several connotations, such as a pathological relapse, falling back to attitudes and behavior that were once appropriate but are no longer, and the appearance of disturbed or bizarre behavior, so-called primitive thinking. Freud, however, had a very specific construct in mind. The libido developed in stages; each had its phases with specific aims and objects. In the oral-receptive phase, the object was the mother and the aim was oral gratification through sucking her breast or through participating in other oral activity related to the mother such as eating, or its affectional equivalent, love. In the oral-active or cannibalistic phase, the aim was to exercise oral mastery on objects. After 1920 and the formulation of the death instinct, the active phase of libidinal development was identified partly with the aggressive instinct and partly with ego mastery functions. Although never explicitly stated, the father was the object of the anal phase, particularly in boys. Freud postulated that the psychic representation of every libidinal phase remained intact, as if used stage sets of various plays, each depicting a developmental phase, were lodged in one big theater with all the players in place, each unit capable of being relit and reanimated by the proper triggering device, namely, regressive tendencies. Anachronistic phases could be recathected by regression when an instinctual impulse in a more advanced libidinal phase, such as the genital, was blocked or frustrated. The impulse would then seek gratification by returning to an earlier libidinal phase where it had once been successfully gratified. Regression could also occur when there was a fixation at a libidinal phase caused by frustration or, conversely, by overindulgence at that phase.

In my view, behaviors that are generally interpreted to be regressive are attempts to reinstate a previously adaptive technique. An example is that of a five-year-old who reverts to the bottle and to baby talk upon the birth of a sibling. The earlier behavior is being reinstated but in a new and different context and for a different purpose. In infancy, he or she nursed a bottle and talked baby talk because it was consonant with the appropriate level of neurophysiological development. Now the child is reverting to this behavior as a defense against the threat of loss of parental support, interest, and love. If a single component in a complex behavioral constellation is extrapolated from its meaning and context, comprehension of the total behavioral integration is lost. The use of a component — that is, baby talk and bottle nursing — as evidence that a five-year-old has regressed to an early level of personality organization with a return of infantile aims and objects, assigns fictitious and erroneous meaning to behavior whose realistic meaning in a realistic context is already known. A very young child who talks baby talk and takes a bottle is not the developmental or psychological equal of a five-year-old who is reinstating such behavior defensively. Each subsequent stage of organization, though deriving from its antecedent, alters that antecedent irreversibly; though there may be identifiable components that remain, the early state as such is gone. One cannot retrieve the acorn from the oak. I once watched a colleague who is both an analyst and a hypnotist regress an adult under hypnosis to the preverbal period and then bring him back by verbal instruction. The analyst saw no contradiction in this procedure.

The concept of regression may also lead to false conclusions. In a clinical discussion, a student interpreted a particular patient's behavior as regressive because when he was angry he shook his arms in rage as a child would. The student concluded that the reasons for the patient's rage were therefore childish and immature. When the situation was described more fully, the reasons for the rage were understandable, appropriate, and reflected nothing childish or immature. My analytic vocabulary for adults does not include such words as infantile, childish, adolescent, or immature. Such descriptions are inaccurate, analogically incorrect, and their intent is almost always pejorative.

Regression is also thought to occur when an individual in a state of helplessness becomes pathologically dependent on one or more others, giving the impression of a return to a child-parent type of relationship. Actually, pathological dependency is associated with an inflation of the image of the one who is helping and with magical expectations of protection and assistance. Such a posture is a reinstatement of an adaptational coping maneuver, that is, dependency in the face of helplessness. The pathology and the problem are concerned with the factors that created the state of helplessness, not with the secondary adaptational dependency, though the latter may contribute to the psychopathology. If regression and dependency are viewed as the primary sources of psychopathology, the emphasis is misplaced on the supporting crutch when concern should be focused upon the fractured limb that created the helplessness.

Free Association

Free association replaced Breuer's cathartic method as a technique for tapping unconscious material. The golden rule was for the patient to say whatever came to mind. Any break in the flow of free association was assumed to be a resistance; no consideration was given to other reasons for a break, such as fatigue or a pause when a newly-remembered idea came into consciousness. Even if breaks in free association were resistances, however, they were not necessarily what Freud later interpreted them to be. As he further developed his ideas on transference, he came to the conclusion that a break in free association always heralded the beginning of transference resistance. He assumed that the patient had come across material that he or she did not want to reveal and that the concealed idea contained an instinctual wish, either libidinal or aggressive, that was directed toward the analyst. Also excluded was the possibility that the patient might be fearful of opening up a situation he or she was not ready to face, either with the analyst or alone. In one case, a patient became extremely resistive when intense hostility to one of his sons and the consequent destructive paternal behavior could no longer be denied.

Free association has two connotations. If it refers to a patient's verbalizing uninterruptedly so that the analyst can follow themes within an organized train of thought, then it is not only valuable but an indispensable part of the analytic process. On the other hand, I have never found free association that consists of a series of verbalized disconnected thoughts to be of value in illuminating unconscious psychodynamics. Generally, each session has at least one major theme; some have several. If patients are not interrupted, this theme will be established in the first five or ten minutes of the session. As in a dream, a reality situation usually determines the theme. If the theme is one of rejection, the likelihood is that the patient has experienced, or believes that he or she has experienced, a recent rejection and will give an account of it. If I think that the patient's inferences are unreasonable, or the reaction maladaptive, he or she is encouraged to remember a similar circumstance. Such associations are oriented toward establishing the psychogenetic bases for the patient's beliefs about rejection. Productions of this kind are just as easily obtained with the patient sitting up.

I direct patients to associate to their dreams and lead them to those parts of the manifest content most likely to be productive. This type of dream association also does not depend on the recumbent position. If the patient becomes blocked or runs out of material, I do not say that he or she is resisting, nor do I assume that this is transference resistance. Silent periods, where the patient sweats it out uncomfortably, are also avoided. I do not favor the technique where the analyst says nothing or at regular intervals asks, "What are you thinking about?" If the patient cannot talk, I do. I ask relevant questions about the theme of the session, elicit additional past history, or, if necessary, talk about something that interests the patient, thus stimulating verbalization. This avoids the torturous experiences many patients have with silent periods, and it avoids the secondary iatrogenic resistances engrafted upon the ones that interfere with analytic verbalizations in the first place.

Dreams are my major access to the patient's irrational belief systems, conscious and unconscious. Dreams are, indeed, the royal road to unconscious processes; therefore, I see no reason to place major reliance on secondary paths. Patients are encouraged to write down all dreams, date and keep them after presenting them in session. If there is any question about how often patients omit significant aspects of a dream that was remembered upon awakening, one has only to ask that the dream be related again, first from memory, then read what had been written. As expected, what is omitted is often the most telling part of the dream. When patients are not urged to write down dreams as part of the analytic program, the analyst may be unwittingly collaborating in a patient's resistance. By keeping the notes of the dreams, patients are able to retain a good record of their analysis. When a particular subject comes up that deserves scrupulous attention, the patient is reminded to survey old dreams dealing with that subject. One patient dreamed of teeth from time to time. I requested that all previous dreams in which teeth appeared be brought into the next session. This review illuminated the meaning of the old dreams as well as the new.

Before terminating, most patients are able to analyze their own dreams. It becomes an important aspect of the continuing analytic work that should follow formal termination. A few patients do not bring in many dreams. The analysis of such individuals is still possible, though it is difficult and presents a greater challenge to one's therapeutic creativity.

CONCEPTS OF PSYCHOPATHOLOGY AND PSYCHOANALYSIS

In 1950, Sandor Rado addressed the Society of Medical Psychoanalysts on the subject of emergency behavior. As the designated discussor, I made the following remarks:

> Dr. Rado has made profound contributions to a theory of psychoanalysis and, as my teacher, he has played a determining role in the development of my psychoanalytic thinking. The concept that injury or the perception of threat of injury is a cardinal point in the understanding of the psychopathology of neurosis, has been advanced by him for many years. As a consequence of this contribution, he then became interested in the somatic and psychological defensive adaptations to injury or threatened injury which he has grouped together under the title, "emergency control." Dr. Rado has developed his ideas of emergency control to the point where he believes that "failures of emergency adjustment" are of paramount importance and that they are the basic factors in the etiological psychodynamics of all forms of disordered behavior.

Rado viewed parental and authoritative indoctrination and prohibitions as the source of the fears underlying emergency control. The child's relationship to power and authority formed the conceptual model on which he elaborated his ideas on adaptational modes—submission, defiance, and guilt. He tended, however, to underemphasize other important sources of pathology within the child-parent relationship: affectional deprivation, inadequate contact and stimulation, and defective communication. The role of sibling and peer relations was also under-emphasized. In explicating psychopathology, Rado's central ideas moved to "emergency control" while mine emphasized "irrational belief systems." In further response to Rado's address, I said the following:

> The neuroses arise from distortions and injuries in interpersonal relations, not only in early life, but through-out life. Irrational beliefs and belief systems become established consequent to the distortions and injuries that ensue from basic relationships that are destructive. The irrationalities are unrealistically projected to new situations so that the perpetuation of neuroses is based on the perpetuation of erroneous convictions. Psychoanalytic therapy rests upon the correction of irrational convictions toward the end that ideas and idea systems become consonant with reality. I believe that the continuity of irrational convictions has the effect of chronically tripping false danger signals that set emergency control into operation. Emergency control continues to respond to false signals until unrealistic perceptions of danger arising out of false convictions are abolished.

This quotation contains my basic concepts of psycho-pathology. I view psychopathology as the consequence of adverse interpersonal experiences, beginning with defective and disturbed parent-child relationships, sibling relationships, and pathogenic extrafamilial relationships.

Adverse experiences and the individual's idiosyncratic adaptation to adverse experiences are represented in the adult by fears, symptoms, disturbances in functioning, defenses, and mechanisms of repair. Fear is another way of saying that one believes that one will be hurt. Thus, fear of flying indicates that there is a belief that injury will result from going aloft. I define injury as any event or interaction that is perceived to be inimical to one's best interests, such as rejection, humiliation, physical injury, and so forth. In sum, psychopathology consists, basically, of irrational expectations of injury — expectations that become integrated with defenses and mechanisms of repair. These concepts have nothing to do with regression to infantile states or repressed instinctual impulses wanting out. Such ideas, in my opinion, have seriously confused psychiatry and psychoanalysis.

Any type of therapy that is oriented toward delineating the neurotic fears or irrational beliefs about injury, which tracks down the genesis of such beliefs and delineates the defenses and reparative mechanisms relating to the fears in order to resolve them, is psychoanalysis. These delineations make up its *strategy*. The ways in which these goals are accomplished are the *techniques*. The use of the couch or the frequency of visits is technical, not strategic. An emphasis on transference, transference neurosis, and so forth, is also a technical aspect. The differences between psychoanalysis and psychoanalytically oriented psychotherapy are merely technical, not strategic. Since the patient does not use the couch in psychoanalytically oriented psychotherapy, this supposedly alters the nature of analytic transference and prevents a transference neurosis from developing. I have already detailed why I believe that these assumptions are not valid.

The face-to-face technique has many advantages over the use of the couch. It allows the analyst to be more active, and tends to encourage more activity on the part of the patient. The couch tends to assign to the patient major responsibility for conducting the therapy. Face-to-face sessions require fewer weekly visits to achieve progress than do the classical four and preferably five sessions a week on the couch. My own quota is generally two or three sessions a week, depending on the patient's ability to use these frequencies productively. Once a week is acceptable and entirely compatible with a successful analytic outcome. Success or failure in the analysis does not depend on frequency of sessions. This is a very important consideration in view of the financial limitations of so many for whom a reconstructive type of therapy is indicated.

It is high time that we got over the idea that psychoanalytically oriented psychotherapy is second-best or a kind of poor man's psychoanalysis. Many years ago the late Sidney Tarachow, a classical analyst, told me, with some bewilderment, that his results in psychotherapy were often better than those he achieved in psychoanalysis. I think that for most patients, what we call psychoanalytic psychotherapy is superior to classical psychoanalysis. I do not argue against using those techniques believed to be most helpful in attaining therapeutic objectives. I, too, invite patients to use the couch when it is deemed to be an advantage. What I object to are the claims of those analysts who confuse the reconstructive goals of analysis with technical aids and insist that a therapy is not analytic unless it includes the use of the couch, primary emphasis on analytic transference, four or five sessions a week, and so forth.

When I first became a psychiatrist, I was theoretically naive. By good fortune, I chose both an analyst and a control analyst who at that early date had already discarded the metapsychology but who were still developing their ideas. For a beginner, the absence of an established theoretical replacement was most uncomfortable. My colleague, Meyer Maskin, and I would kid each other that our ideas were subject to change without notice and that we should put such a sign in our waiting room. Yet, we were much better off in having struggled to find our conceptual way than to have been entrapped in the illogic of metapsychology so early in our careers.

Chapter 6

Transference and the
Sex of the Psychoanalyst

It has become a psychoanalytic commonplace that a patient's search for help from the analyst structures a situation that promotes a parental transference. But whether the demand-satisfaction parameter is sufficient to produce parental transference invariably, has not been systematically tested. Do patients of young analysts make parental transferences as frequently as do young patients of older analysts? Recently, a young analyst who was treating a much older woman confided that her central transference to him was that of an ambitious mother to a favored son. Does the personality and appearance of the

In collaboration with Lilly Ottenheimer, M.D.

analyst affect transference and if so, how? We have found
that not all our patients make parental transferences to
us. For many years, patient transference to Bieber has
generally been that of father, uncle, or older brother;
patients do not develop mother or sister transferences;
while Ottenheimer elicits transferences involving mother,
older sister, or aunt. Classically, it has been assumed that
the patient, in pursuit of infantile gratification and the
need to work through unresolved problems, makes multiple transferences to the analyst. In order to encourage
working through, the analyst remains passive and impersonal so that transference will be facilitated. In this way,
the analyst can best serve as object for parental, sibling,
and other transferences depending upon the patient's
changing perceptual, conceptual, affective, attitudinal,
and behavioral responses.

Transference itself consists of identifying one individual with another familiar figure in personal history where
salient aspects of the prior relationship are unconsciously
carried over. The projections involved in transference,
however, must be differentiated from adaptational techniques. Behavioral devices may develop in a boy as a way
of coping with mother or sister but he may also behave in
a similar way with other boys without developing a
mother transference toward his playmates. A boy may
develop techniques of charm to defend himself against his
mother or to control her. He may also find that such
behavior is effective with older men without perceiving
them as mother figures. An ambitious mother may condition her child to believe that superior performance is a
prerequisite for acceptance and love. In relating to an
analyst of either sex, such a patient may feel that the analyst's respect and acceptance are predicated upon unusual

performance within and outside the analysis. It may be argued that the resurgence of such expectations is evidence of a mother transference. If this formulation is correct then Bieber has been a mother figure to such patients and Ottenheimer has at times been perceived as a father.

We think the essential characteristic of transference is the identification of one or several individuals with the analyst. The evidence of such identification may appear in dreams, parapraxes, other unconscious productions or in conscious reporting that must be carefully evaluated. One might infer that a patient has developed a mother transference because the male analyst is portrayed as a female in a dream. A male patient who is hostile to a male analyst may depict an attack upon a female in a dream, yet, on probe, the female figure may represent the therapist — a disguise of the actual object of attack.

Sex is a basic part of one's sense of identity and most patients do not become confused about sexually defined boundaries. The male analyst is perceived as a male figure; the female analyst, a female figure. As to sexual responsiveness, Bieber does not observe erotic responses to him by male patients, including male homosexuals; rather, as among heterosexuals, the response is as to a male competitor — father, brother, and so forth. In contrast, female patients may develop sexual responses to him, albeit anxiety-laden. In dreams, the mother figure often appears as the threatening intruder. Ottenheimer finds that the most frequently expressed sexual anxiety among her female patients is fear of her as an authoritative, competitive woman who is jealous of her power and which she may use should the patient make independent, assertive moves — particularly if the moves are sexually assertive. Such apprehensions are not observed in her male patients.

Male patients in treatment with a male analyst may, through analysis of transference, work out the stressful, competitive problems they had with their father and male siblings, and the neurotic sequelae of rejection, detachment, and hostility from males. Male patients have been more likely rejected by fathers than mothers; female patients have been more likely rejected by their mothers. But even where patients have not experienced parental rejection, the dynamics of the oedipus complex determine the competitive relationship of male to male and female to female, and it appears as transference phenomena in the psychoanalytic situation. When a female is in treatment with a male analyst, problems linked to maternal rejection, hostility, and competitive reactions to the mother cannot be worked through directly through transference; instead, the patient must depend upon cognitive, reconstructive insight. A woman who is afraid of aggressive women must become aware of her expectations of attack from them in much the same way that one becomes aware of danger without actually experiencing it. One may become aware of a fear of falling from a great height without having to jump to prove it. For most patients, this type of cognitive enterprise is sufficient to work through irrational expectations of injury from the mother or other women; living through the direct experience of transference with a woman analyst is not essential. For the more disturbed patient, however, particularly in borderline states or among schizophrenics, the cognitive, imaginative process is usually inadequate. Such women require the concreteness of an actual relationship with a female therapist for immediate reality testing and for negating irrational fears of women.

Thus far the points we have made conflict with classical assumptions about transference neurosis in that the presumably "healthier" patients are said to develop transference neuroses and are therefore amenable to analysis. Psychotics, who have so-called narcissistic neuroses, are said not to develop transference neuroses and hence are not amenable to analysis. In our experience, excluding disorganized psychotics, it is among the most disturbed patients that transference assumes great prominence. This type of patient may become obsessively preoccupied with the analyst, develop intense erotic responses and paranoid formations, and may require more analytic work on transference reactions than do less disturbed patients who tend to concern themselves more with their life situations and less with the analyst. Some female patients are even too fearful of women to undertake analysis with a woman. They are the very ones who ultimately require analysis with a woman so that they may have the opportunity to work through their fears directly. Most patients probably would resolve more of their problems more fully if given the opportunity to work with analysts of both sexes.

Clinical Examples

During Bieber's military service, he initiated a project in which patients were simultaneously treated by a male and a female therapist (1948). Although the longest period of treatment in that situation was three months, the results obtained were very encouraging even under the precarious conditions of war.

The project was conducted in an Army hospital in an overseas theater by a team consisting of a woman psychiatric social worker, a serviceman-artist who conducted an art class, and Bieber. After the initial psychiatric interview, all "open-ward" patients who wished to could join the class and were told they were free to consult with any member of the team. If either the social worker or Bieber were selected, regular therapeutic sessions were arranged.

Private Larry was admitted for observation after he confided to his sergeant that he had engaged in homosexual activities prior to induction. On admission he was tense and frightened, complaining of increasing anxiety since entering the army. He had been eating and sleeping poorly and was no longer able to carry out assignments effectively. He denied having had any homosexual experiences after induction, yet was afraid he would be dishonorably discharged.

Larry was the youngest of seven siblings. The father, an unstable, irritable, impulsive, and irresponsible man, had been physically cruel to his children. The mother was an obese, passive woman whom the father dominated. The family was always in precarious financial circumstances and Larry had supported himself after the age of fourteen. He managed, nevertheless, to complete high school and prior to induction was employed as a clerk-receptionist to a psychiatrist.

After several sessions with Bieber, Larry was told about the therapeutic project. He evinced interest and joined the class. He chose the social worker as his therapist and they met five times a week. In his initial session with her, he criticized the exaggerated emphasis placed on sex by the army. After several interviews, consumed in talking about the length of his hospitalization and his discomfort in being on a neuropsychiatric ward, he said he had run out of material and decided to discontinue the sessions. He attended drawing classes for the next two weeks without making any effort to see the psychiatrist or social worker. He then asked to renew his sessions. He said he had been feeling very "jittery," even more so than on admission, and recognized he had been more comfortable when in daily contact with his therapist.

The resumption of his sessions corresponded with the end of his first month in the hospital. During this period his art work had been relatively unproductive. He had made a drawing containing bombs, a noose, a swing suspended over water, and other fearsome objects. This precipitated considerable anxiety. It was the first subject he had discussed on his return. He had dreamt about it and requested interpretation. Larry then confided his anxiety about receiving help from a woman and stated he was becoming increasingly aware of his affection for her. As treatment proceeded, however, his anxiety about his positive feelings for his therapist abated. He also began to recognize that the fonder he became of his therapist, the fonder he became of the artist. He was delighted with the progress he was making in the way he felt and behaved and in his art work. On one occasion, he joined the team in the drawing conference and felt comfortable discussing his associations to his drawings. To the frequent portrayals of water in his early drawings, he associated his enuresis present up to the age of twelve, a fact he had not previously mentioned. His pictures began to have unity, color, and flexibility of theme. He became more comfortable with the other patients and ward personnel. After seven weeks of treatment, he wrote to his family; he had been unable to do this for several months.

At the end of his second month of treatment, Larry's therapist took a twelve-day leave. During this period he did little drawing and was rather depressed. When she returned, he again became productive. He mentioned at this time that he was interested in a girl and was corresponding with her. After three months of this type of therapy, in which the patient had the opportunity to work out specific difficulties he had with both sexes, he was evacuated to the States. He had had the opportunity to move from one team member to the other when the major problem presenting itself demanded either a man or a woman.

The following case started analysis with Bieber and completed it with Ottenheimer.

The patient was thirty-eight at the beginning of her analysis. She entered treatment suffering from a postpartum depression after the birth of her fourth child. The first three children were male, the last, female. The patient had experienced a postpartum depression following the birth of her last two male children which she had rationalized on the basis of not having had a daughter which, presumably, she longed for. Her rationalization no longer held when she suffered a postpartum depression following the birth of her daughter.

The patient was the youngest of three children and the only daughter. Her father, a professional man, had a close, devoted relationship with her. She was clearly his favorite. The mother, detached and hostile, made the patient think that she was awkward and clumsy despite her unusual beauty and talent as a dancer. The eldest son was the mother's favorite. He followed his father's profession. This brother was condescending to the patient and paid little attention to her. Her transference to Bieber was alternately that of the father and older brother who, incidentally, bore the same first name as the analyst. In the initial phase, the salient transference was to a protective, strong, male figure. Her dreams consistently reflected fears that she would be robbed of her child by a powerful female. In some dreams, she would renounce her children, and then reconstitute a large family of adopted children. The birth of her first child had not been followed by a postpartum depression. Her first son was born when her husband was overseas during World War II. At that time she was living with her parents and she shared the care of the child with her mother.

As the analysis proceeded, the positive features of the father transference changed to that of the father who took for himself the desired mother. The patient's mother had catered to the father's every whim. The older brother had also been given special, privileged treatment. The patient's sense of inferiority to men, coupled with a desire for their acceptance and respect, became as clearly apparent as her competitive resentment. The following dream is illustrative. The patient had entered a contest. It is extremely important to her that she win first prize — a large breast. Her older brother is eligible to enter the contest, which he confidently indicates he can win; however, he is utterly disinterested in the prize. The patient's own preference for her sons reinforced her belief that mothers prefer their sons, though the patient did not reject her own daughter who was a much valued child.

The patient went through an intense and disturbing erotic transference. She was aware of her sexual feelings which were associated with guilt toward her husband. She began to feel disinclined to have sexual relations that heretofore had been satisfactory. When she did have intercourse, the image of the analyst appeared before her and interfered with orgasm. At one point, she considered terminating treatment since she held the analyst responsible for intruding upon and threatening to destroy her marriage. Although conscious guilt was directed toward her husband, the patient developed a symptom that was exceedingly disturbing to her and that revealed her guilt toward her mother. Wherever she went, she thought she saw the analyst's wife. This symptom was neither hallucinatory nor delusional but had the characteristic of *deja vú*. After taking a second look, she would always know that she had been mistaken. Despite the obvious association between this symptom and her erotic feelings toward her analyst, the patient still found it difficult to accept the idea that she felt competitive and guilty toward his wife. It was also during this phase that she criticized the office decor which she believed had been done by the analyst's wife. One day she sent in a large ceramic plaque depicting mother and child. In this instance, she acted out an unconscious wish to have a child with her analyst as the father, while expressing a competitive wish to replace his wife. It was during this phase of erotic transference that she dreamed that a woman with a knife entered the patient's bedroom at night to kill her. The intruder turned out to be a maternal aunt.

As time went on progress was made in resolving her oedipal problems, although her competitive attitudes toward, and fears arising from sexual competitiveness and expectations of hostility from women were still easily activated even after five years of treatment. Her dreams and behavior revealed her continuing wish to repair her sense of feminine inadequacy which had its roots in her disturbed relationship with her mother. The patient kept indicating a wish for a relationship with a maternal figure as well as a need to act out a maternal role, particularly with other women. Her submissive tendency to renounce her heterosexuality in order to win the love of a rejecting mother—a homosexual dynamic—had been worked out, though at no time was there evidence of an erotic response as such to women. When Ottenheimer agreed to continue the analysis, the patient reacted with apprehension and some tendency toward flight, but her relationship with Bieber was too trustful to support any rationalizations about being rejected by him. She accepted the advice to transfer, but about a month elapsed before Ottenheimer's schedule permitted her to continue with the patient.

In the initial phase of treatment with her new analyst, the patient was openly hostile. She explained her hostility as a consequence of feeling unwanted since she had had to wait a month. Her first dream confirmed the hostility but the dream also suggested other determinants of her reaction. In this dream, Ottenheimer was teaching the patient how to iron. She then took the iron from the analyst, placed her on an ironing board and flattened her out with the hot iron. The dream depicts the analyst teaching the patient a feminine task, an experience the patient never had shared with her mother who, in fact, had been defeminizing. In the dream, the patient accepts a symbol of femininity from the analyst—a clothes iron—but then destroys her with it. The dynamics indicate hatred toward the mother for failing to promote the patient's femininity and it reveals sexual competitiveness intensified to a murderous pitch toward a castrating mother.

The patient's belief that heterosexuality was incompatible with receiving affection from helpful women is

illustrated by another dream which also reveals her conflict between renouncing either wished-for affection from
women or heterosexuality. In the dream, the patient is
with a female gynecologist who informs her that the result
of her checkup is very satisfactory, but the patient pays
little attention to the report. She is preoccupied with the
fact that the gynecologist is conveying this information in
a manner, though not unfriendly, which is nevertheless
clearly professional. In relating the dream, the patient
commented that she would have been satisfied with a less
favorable report had the gynecologist shown her special
warmth. In other words, despite growing confidence and
strength as a woman, improvement meant little if she
could not have her mother's love. Her first productions in
this analysis were concerned with the idea that she might
gain her mother's love if she refrained from growing up
and becoming a sexually expressive woman.

In her work with Ottenheimer, the patient had the
opportunity to see for herself that her heterosexuality held
no threat and sexual renunciation had no value to the
analyst. Direct reality testing with a woman analyst made
it clear that the patient could be accepted, admired, and
warmly treated by a maternal figure, a therapeutic relationship that significantly contributed to a further resolution of her oedipal problems. It was also necessary for her
to have the experience of working with a woman whom
she could, in turn, respect and admire. Apart from her
rivalry, the patient had always thought of women as
second-raters, an idea fostered by her mother's servile
adulation of the father and older brother. Learning to
trust another woman and to work with her on an emotional, intellectual and professional basis encouraged
greater self-acceptance as an individual and as a woman.

After two years, she was able to terminate her analysis, having resolved problems that she had only partially worked through with a male analyst.

A second patient, who was also treated by both authors, had a similar therapeutic experience. This patient, too, was the only daughter of a doting father and a detached mother who preferred her son, the patient's younger and only sibling. Ottenheimer has treated three other patients who originally were analyzed by male therapists. In each case, the patient developed a mother transference; in none, a father or other male transference. Whenever any of the patients referred to her previous analyst, the transference was that of father. None of the five women developed an erotic transference to Ottenheimer though each reported having had erotic feelings toward her previous male analyst. As each of these analyses unfolded, the patient would compare analysts to the disadvantage of one or the other. As a technical consideration, Ottenheimer would, during the same session, analyze these productions. The comparison would usually turn out to be a divisive maneuver—a replication of the wish to separate the parents.

In sum, the sex of the analyst is a salient determinant of the type of transference made. Men do not, in general, develop mother or sister transferences when treated by a man; they do not develop father or brother transferences when treated by a woman. Conversely, women do not transfer male figures to women analysts. Certain types of patients who, in consultation, are strongly insistent upon referral to an analyst on the basis of sex preference are likely candidates for the type of terminal analysis we have described. Further, in cases where a therapeutic plateau has become established after years of productive work, transfer to an analyst of the sex opposite to the therapist may be indicated. Finally, in our view, it would be advantageous for all patients to experience analysis with both a male and female therapist.

Chapter 7

Disorders of
the Work Function

Love and work were said by Freud to be the mainspring of human existence. He described man's major life problems as *Lieben und Arbeiten,* yet he gave minimal attention to *Arbeiten,* focusing his interest mainly on sexual psychopathology and symptoms.

In a review of psychoanalytic concepts of the meaning of work, Neff (1965) stated, "Freud's remarks on work are scattered very sparsely through his writings and are typically encountered as asides set down as incidental observations. His evaluation of the importance of work in man's psychological economy is ambivalent. On the one hand, he argues that work is one of the two great spheres of human activity . . . on the other hand, Freud obviously saw work not as a pleasurable activity to be sought but as a painful burden to be endured."

Popular definitions of work also emphasize stress, exertion, and the absence of pleasure. Webster's *Third International* defines work as "activity in which one exerts strength of faculties to do or perform: a. sustained physical or mental effort valued as it overcomes obstacles and achieves an objective or result . . . ; b. the labor, task or duty that affords one his accustomed means of livelihood . . . ; c. strenuous activity marked by the presence of difficulty and exertion and absence of pleasure . . . ." Lacking entirely in this definition is the notion that work can be conflict-free, that it may flow without undue strain, that work under normal conditions is pleasurable, and that pleasure may increase as it taps larger reservoirs of developed personal resources.

To Freud, work seemed to be compelled by external necessities, and it followed the reality principle rather than the pleasure principle (1920). "Human beings exhibit an inborn tendency to carelessness, irregularity and unreliability in their work. Laborious training is needed before they can learn to follow the example of their celestial models." With the development of ego psychology, however, the significance of work was given greater emphasis as a function and as a means of providing affective satisfaction. Following the life and death instincts, a third instinct, the mastery instinct, was postulated by Ives Hendrick to account for the pleasure experienced in work. Lantos (1943) distinguished between the pleasure of playing, which she thought derived from the activity itself, and the gratification of working, which she thought derived from the achievement of goals. To the gratification of play, she assigned the autoerotic instincts of childhood; to those of working, she assigned the self-preservative instincts of adulthood, while Erikson (1959, 1963) assigned the establishment of attitudes to work and achievement to the latency period. Pleasure in work had a place in the new ego psychology of classical psychoanalysis, but to maintain a theoretical structure consistent with the pleasure principle, work had to become a means to an instinctual end. I prefer a nonmetapsychological view: the pleasure in work is an appropriate, affective component of integrated functioning; the work itself may be multimotivated.

The inability to work or to take pleasure in it, the reality situation permitting, is always a symptom of psychopathology, a symptom I have termed "work inhibition." Conversely, I define optimum work functioning as the maximum development of interest and skill in a chosen field. Personal resources should be consistently and effectively available without anxiety, inhibition or other manifestations of neurotic reactions, and with an ability to enjoy appropriate feelings of gratification during work and upon its completion. One should also be able to exhibit to others the products of work and creativity. Not many people, in or out of analysis, completely fulfill these criteria. Most people have some sort of problem about work which may range from unimportant, transient lay-off periods, to chronic work inhibition; however, people who are dedicated to work of personal choice, find it pleasurable despite occasional disappointments, pitfalls, and obstacles. In their own idiom, the young refer to a commitment to performance of personal choice as "doing your own thing," the work-related equivalent of sexual liberation.

The absence of conscious pleasure in effective work and achievement is a symptom of work-connected anxiety. Karl Menninger (1942) stated, "Three fourths of the patients who come to psychiatrists are suffering from an incapacity of their satisfaction in work or their inability to work. In many, it is their chief complaint." I have found that the work difficulties of patients are as pervasive as their sexual difficulties and to many are even more prominent and distressing. It is not unusual for patients to be orgastically effective and to have a good relationship with their sex partner, yet to suffer keenly from the most profound work inhibitions. I have interviewed many an occupational and school drop-out who was virile as a lover, but totally impotent as a worker. In general, psychoanalytic researchers and writers have taken an oblique and elitist interest in problems of work, concentrating their attention on the subject of creativity, a kind of high-echelon category for work, while neglecting the day-to-day struggles about work.

In our society, work as we know it begins with schooling. Upon entering the first grade, the child's world becomes structured around new tasks and expectations that must now be fulfilled outside the family milieu and among peers. But before a child enters school, a great deal has already happened that may maximize or minimize chances for success in this untried enterprise.

Each normal newborn has a developmental potential for organizing an extensive, complex, intellectual repertoire. Depending upon the quality of parenting and cultural setting, potentialities can be stimulated, even overstimulated, or natural interest and curiosity may be neglected and inhibited to the point where exploratory behavior, creativity, and interest in the environment are practically extinguished. For most of the underprivileged, black and white, the culture of poverty has constricting effects on individual potentialities, aspirations, and the pursuit of curiosity. A substantial number of children arrive at the first grade suffering from the effects of understimulation and profound disturbances in the ability to communicate. They may already be so intellectually impaired that they are unable to learn to read or comprehend with even passable proficiency. According to authoritative anecdotal information, if a child has not developed basic learning skills by the third grade, the disabilities may be irreversible. In order to forestall such eventualities, special prekindergarten programs have been instituted in some disadvantaged areas. Bruno Bettelheim has suggested that there be a radical change in the total life style of the culturally deprived child and his family. Bettelheim's idea is to form Israeli-type kibbutzim for disadvantaged parents and their children as a practical and promising way of overcoming educational defects.

From their earliest grades, some children are unable to keep up academically with their peers because they are dyslexic or have some other learning disability. Such youngsters develop depressive reactions often manifested in behavior disorders, apathy, daydreaming, or feelings of boredom. These indications of learning problems are often misunderstood, misinterpreted or overlooked. For most children, however, learning difficulties are psychological in origin and stem from a defective home situation. In large part, it is the educators who are assigned the enormous responsibilities of coping and coming up with meaningful solutions. The challenges faced by contemporary educators involve much more than teaching, in itself never a simple task. The educational arena has

broadened to include the vast array of learning and social-
ization problems met with in the classroom that have been
determined mostly in the family.

Individual psychopathology is no longer dissociated
from family pathology and, more broadly, social pathology such as class, race, and gender discrimination, war,
and so forth. These societal, cultural, and institutional
influences also account, in part, for the ubiquity of work
disorders; however, the family and its members remain
the operational unit for psychoanalytic study and treatment. In this context, work inhibitions derive mainly from
two major sources: disturbed oedipal maturational
development induced by the psychopathology of parents,
and sibling rivalry reinforced by parental rejection or
preference for one child over another. Children are often
inculcated with irrational beliefs about competition by parents who foster a dog-eat-dog concept of interpersonal
relationships. The antisocial attitudes learned in the family dislocate relationships with peers and promote expectations of hostility for achievement. Consequently, effective work becomes imbued with anxiety and inhibition.

The first sign of a work problem is a drop in performance level. Children who are identified as underachievers
have already hit a developmental or psychological snag
and have become work-inhibited. A child's learning difficulties may be developmental, perceptual, or psychological, but whatever the determinants, the situation
signals trouble and must be accounted for. Occasionally,
a dissonant child-teacher relationship is the barrier, but,
in most cases, the child's problems are psychological.

Once past the early grades, work dysfunction may next
become apparent at adolescence. New beginnings and
completions tend to mark the onset of work inhibitions.

Performance difficulties may surface in the first year of junior high school, or the last year of high school; the first year of college and upon completion of college. In professional and graduate school, difficulties occur most frequently in the first half of the course, peaking again in the last year. The well-known stumbling block for doctoral candidates is the thesis, where students complete all other requirements but that. The ubiquitous signs of their work block are loss of interest, difficulties in concentration, avoidance of study tasks and feelings of boredom.

In initial interviews, when I tap into work and school history, I routinely ask the patient what he or she wanted to be as a child. By the age of ten or eleven, children whose curiosity has not become constricted have already established areas of individual interest. Some have a special interest in art; others want to be a teacher, doctor, athlete, actor, and so on. Upon reaching college, some students still have no idea of a general area of interest, no thoughts about a future occupation or profession—a situation often explained away as being part of the dilemma of youth or the need to "find" oneself. Actually, such young people are significantly work-inhibited. A lack of direction is associated with a lack of interest; a lack of interest is associated with a lack of ambition. Ambition is a normal attribute. It is the motivational aspect of planning and represents the direction of personal growth and development.

Work problems may first become apparent when formal education has been completed and the graduate enters the "adult" world. Employment may then be postponed, or there may be frequent job changes, lack of interest, absenteeism, undue anticipation of work-free weekends and holidays, and feelings of anxiety when on the job. In interviews, I ask patients, "What is the longest time you held one job?" and "What was the highest salary you earned?" A wide discrepancy between ability and education and the patient's current employment suggests psychopathology involving work.

In the method of cognitive psychoanalysis that I conduct, patients are oriented to the dynamics of their work problems by having two psychodynamic constellations outlined: fears about failure and fears about success, though such fears are not mutually exclusive. Most patients experience both types of fear. They readily comprehend the nature of their fears about failure. They know they fear rejection and humiliation; they know what it feels like to lose a sense of self-esteem. The less sophisticated, especially, find it difficult to understand their fears of success. Success, they protest, is exactly what they are after. It is hard to accept the idea that one fears to achieve what one profoundly desires. Yet, it is the fear of success, particularly among the more educated and talented, that most often determines work inhibitions.

Freud first drew attention to the fear of success in "Some Character Types Met with in Psycho-analytic Work" (1916). In the section, "Those Wrecked by Success," he described two cases: one, a woman who had a psychotic breakdown when a marriage she had wished for became possible; the other, a man who, when offered a position he had long aspired to, fell into a depression and remained depressed for many years. Freud traced these patients' fears to guilt feelings which he related to the oedipus complex. Oddly enough, his observations received little, if any, attention.

In 1951, I first elaborated the psychodynamics of fears of success, emphasizing the prominent and regular occurrence of such fears in work inhibitions. By itself, fear of success is simply a headline that orients the patient to the source of the difficulties. The specific irrational beliefs underlying the fears of success require detailed analysis. The belief that achievement will antagonize or evoke jealousy in rivals, particularly power figures who will retaliate by attack, needs to be delineated and traced to its origins. Pathologically dependent individuals may harbor the fear that success will evoke the wrath of those depended upon and that they will withdraw support, a threatening idea. Others may fear that success will result in isolation; that it will lose friends and the affection of loved ones, especially family members, and especially if success is associated with upward mobility and entry into a higher social stratum. Such fears need not be irrational. Sometimes family and friends do discourage the initiatives and success of intimates for fear of losing them. Conformity to tradition is a way of defending the family and community against the threat of disruption, but if group standards are not those of excellence, creativity, and achievement, the guilt and fear of antagonizing one's fellows by superseding them become powerful deterrents.

Other determinants of work inhibition include antisocial aims, such as the wish to exploit or dominate others. If aspirations encompass hostile intentions to belittle and defeat others, then personal resources and the goal itself will be perceived as antisocial; work efforts will then be accompanied by anxiety and inhibition. Fear of being in the limelight may also account for the avoidance of achievement where exposure to the attention of others is felt as a threat.

In families where there are child preference patterns, the preferred child usually develops deep-seated guilt feelings. The guilt is based on the idea that the unfavored sibling has been deprived of a rightful share of affection and privilege (see chapter 13). The favorite may become inhibited and masochistically renounce attributes and skills. This type of inhibition is, in part, an altruistic attempt to equalize competition and, in part, a defense against hostility and retaliation from the less favored one. Where a son is preferred by his mother over other siblings, and especially if he is preferred over the father, a situation develops that not only engenders anxiety about work but also about sexual success. The grandiosity instilled in a preferred son is accompanied by the belief that his sexual success will deprive other men of the love of a desirable woman. Sexual difficulties may ensue, ranging from impotence to resistance to a meaningful relationship. These symptoms also promote depressions that tend to become more severe over time. Similar dynamics may be observed in daughters who have been preferred by the father over the mother or other daughters.

From its original meaning as a sexual aberration, the term *masochism* has evolved as a description of self-defeating behavior. Masochism may play a role at all levels of performance, from initial stages of interest and motivation, to completion. In various combinations and permutations, objectives may be blocked, the work itself sabotaged, and monetary or prestige rewards minimized or destroyed. The term *loser* has come to be used to describe the individual who undermines potentialities and opportunities. Work-related masochism may be acted out in lateness, procrastination of tasks, forgetting appointments, making foolish, inappropriate errors, minimizing accomplishments, getting into accidents, psychosomatic complaints that interfere with work, and so on. Not infrequently, educational and occupational failures may be traced to masochistic defenses against fears of success.

Masochism is also a central dynamic in drug abuse, the excessive use of alcohol, and even in excessive smoking, where unconscious attempts are made to undermine the health and vigor needed to work effectively and consistently.

In a contrasting category are the compulsive workers, the so-called "workaholics" who are driven to seek relief from anxiety in the shelter of their occupation. They are unable to have fun or relate adequately to spouse, children, and friends, and attempt to achieve global satisfactions through work. Some work-driven people are motivated by the fear of being outclassed by rivals, while others may be profoundly influenced by the Puritan ethic and feel guilty and uncomfortable unless they are unremittingly involved in purposeful work. An individual's drive to work compulsively does not preclude work inhibition. Some may so occupy themselves with routine tasks that no time is left for creative work, which is avoided because they have fears about it.

Compulsive workers are driven by anxiety and must be differentiated from prodigious workers whose curiosity and pleasure in their work is unobstructed by neurotic difficulties. They are the fortunate ones who have a passionate and abiding interest in their work, prefer it to any other occupation, and are productive, effective and happy in their pursuits.

WORK INHIBITION AND DEPRESSION

Most people who work below their abilities are aware of it. Consciously or unconsciously, they know they do not put forth the effort needed to achieve the goals they aspire to. They recognize that others with no greater talent are more successful. The awareness of constricted work performance generates feelings of depression. In my view, depression is a reaction to loss or threatened loss of something or someone highly valued, such as a loved one, body part, an ability, self-esteem, money, an artifact, or a *function,* such as work. The common denominators of all depressions are the high value placed upon the loss — the belief that the loss is irreplaceable and irretrievable, and the general sense of hopelessness accompanying these beliefs.

There are two types of depressive reactions: the first concerns the individual's conscious or unconscious belief that he or she has been responsible for the loss in some way and should have prevented it. The second is a grief reaction, associated particularly with the loss of a loved one. Pure grief is not accompanied by guilt or hostility toward the lost one. Most depressive reactions met with in clinical practice concern cases where the patient has a guilt-ridden belief that he or she has played some part in a loss or threatened loss. A major depression stemming from other sources may itself inhibit the work function; however, I have noted that in most patients, their depressions are induced by the sense of loss associated with work inhibition. The greater the discrepancy between talent and the capacity to use it, the greater the depressive reaction. Paranoid characters may project their psychologically rooted failures onto external situations — discrimination, bad luck, and so on. As they move into their middle years, however, the growing awareness of the intractibility of their work problems and the unlikelihood of their achieving career aims put such people at risk for a significant clinical depression.

More often than not, menopausal depression occurs in women who are disappointed in the way their lives have turned out. Such a depressive episode may follow when the last child leaves to attend college, marries, and so forth. The chronic constriction of personal resources and an inability to mobilize other interests presages such a depression. The middle-life crisis in men, the so-called "male menopause," is also a syndrome of depression and is based on psychodynamic constellations similar to those in women.

Among the most profoundly work-inhibited people I have ever examined are heroin addicts. In an unpublished study (referred to in Bieber 1970), S. Foster and I interviewed fifty consecutive cases of heroin addicts who were admitted for detoxification at Metropolitan Hospital in New York City. We obtained careful school and work histories and in each case we noted a sharp drop in performance somewhere between a year and a half to two years before the beginning of the addiction. Symptoms noted were loss of interest in school work or job, an inability to concentrate, and feelings of boredom and restlessness. If the patients had been attending school, they began to cut classes and ultimately dropped out. As a group, this sample of addicts was above average in intelligence and ability. To support their habit, they stole or otherwise illegally obtained between $50,000 to $100,000 annually without getting caught—a way of life that requires resourcefulness and intelligence. After detoxification, many addicts made a renewed attempt at work. Often, their abilities were soon recognized by their employer, leading to promotion or an increase in salary.

Predictably, there was a return to the use of heroin within a matter of weeks. Addiction masks an underlying depression and all addicts suffer from depressions. They attempt to replace gratification lost through inhibition and, by the use of drugs, narcotize the pain of failure. The frequent suicides among them attest to the severity of their depressions.

Even an apparently benign work disorder may activate untoward consequences in other areas of personality and behavior. One such patient was a forty-two-year-old associate professor in a medical school. His routine work was effective and satisfactory to the chairman of the department. The patient had original ideas but could not bring himself to publish. He would become inhibited when faced with exposing his creativity. He had a history of occasionally wearing feminine apparel during intercourse with his wife; otherwise, he had a relatively stable adaptation. When a new chairman was appointed, trouble began; he insisted that the faculty publish their work. The patient was unable to surmount his writing block and he became progressively more depressed. He then developed a delusion that if he were a woman, he would be free from the work demands he could not meet. In pursuit of his delusion, he sought and obtained transsexual surgery. His depressions, however, continued and within the next two years he suffered a series of very severe depressions. Finally, he committed suicide.

In sum, the belief that successful work poses a threat to self and others brings about work inhibition. Inhibition itself is a biological defense against action perceived as dangerous. Psychiatric symptoms and disabilities, particularly depressive syndromes, follow in the wake of work inhibition. A clinical picture and an evaluation of prognosis and appropriate treatment remain inconclusive without a careful review of work effectiveness. The specific psychodynamics underlying work inhibitions are illuminated by probing fears of failure and success. Such data delineate the specificity and history of the irrational fears unique to each patient. Treatment involves the analysis of the irrational beliefs of injury associated with effective work, the method that I term cognitive analysis.

Chapter 8

Pathological
Boredom and Inertia

Boredom can be roughly classified as normal and pathological. Normal boredom may arise when one is compelled to work at stereotyped tasks with requirements far below one's work potential, or when work offers no opportunity for initiative or creative application. This paper is concerned with the problem of pathological boredom and inertia, the by-products of fear.

Pathological boredom and inertia are manifestations of inhibition, the inability to act in some important area of life. In extreme reactions, such as those clinically termed "depressions," the inhibition of the capacity for action involves most of the areas of functioning. Depressed patients are those who have lost interest in the world around them; they are, among other things, intensely bored. They are restless and uncomfortable in their inactivity and have the desire to do something, but they do not know what it is. Suggestions for activity are rejected; attempts at guidance into action are, as a rule, repulsed. The depressed patient is deeply afraid of action and undertakes it only with great effort; it is an effort that is necessary to override the fear and, consequently, the inertia the fear produces.

These are extremes of inhibition. More commonly seen is boredom related to the inhibition of more localized areas of action. Many people are bored with free time. They may be reasonably comfortable in their daily work but look forward to evenings, weekends, vacations, and all other periods of fun and relaxation with attitudes varying from displeasure to outright fear. These individuals are afraid to have fun and feel severe pleasure inhibitions. When exposed to an atmosphere of gaiety, such individuals feel bored, tend to separate themselves from the group, and look for a kindred spirit to engage in a conversation about more serious matters. Individuals with pleasure inhibitions frequently immerse themselves in work and seek out assignments that preclude free time. Their work is often diffuse in character, noncreative, and not goal-directed; it is designed to kill free time. Many such people, lacking in insight, complain bitterly about how hard they work and how they never have time for fun and relaxation.

Let us now turn to another type of boredom, the boredom with work. In this category are individuals who are afraid of work, particularly gainful work. The gains may be monetary, or in prestige, or, more subtly, those which promote personality growth. This fear of work leads to varying degrees of work inhibition. Work inhibitions are widespread. In extreme cases the fear of work leads to a total inability to perform gainful work. Such individuals are compelled by their anxieties to loaf about and to putter around rather than work consistently and with interest. In general, this group is concerned with finding ways of dissipating time. They form the "drop-out" fringe of society. Wealthy men of this fringe are called "playboys" or, with the women joining in, form the "jet set." Such activities are really not ones of choice. The anxieties involved in work inhibitions are manifestations of a profound personality disturbance. The playboy or jet-setter is only slightly freer in play than in work. Boredom is the rule and gradual deterioration of personality is not unusual. The unfortunate consequences are not the wages of sin but the results of severe constriction in a capacity for action.

Closely related to the type of person who is unable to perform gainful work are those who frequently change jobs and occupations. New jobs or occupations are undertaken with enthusiasm, interest, and great hope. After a period of time, depending on individual pattern, anxiety about work appears either as such, or in one of many peripheral manifestations. Loss of interest in work with accompanying boredom is common. Anxiety and work inhibition mount to the point where the individual either leaves his work or creates a situation that precipitates being discharged. The reasons given for leaving are, as a rule, rationalizations: the work was uninteresting, too difficult, unsuitable, and so forth. In a paranoid individual, the cause for discharge is attributed to the employer or other workers and the cycle is repeated. This is a mechanism that may be identified in the so-called dilettante. A dilettante follows an interest to the point of inhibition, then takes up some other interest.

A much larger group is in a less extreme position in the spectrum of work inhibitions. These people are able to work, but they work with considerable anxiety, little interest, or both. They look forward to evenings, weekends, and holidays but do not necessarily expect pleasure from their free time. Work inhibitions are also associated with pleasure inhibitions. People with such problems seek free time essentially for relief from the anxiety that accompanies work. The anxiety is either felt as such or is concealed in a cluster of symptoms, one of which is boredom. Less severe though incapacitating manifestations of work inhibitions are suffered by individuals in whom periods of productive work are accompanied by enthusiasm and interest but then fluctuate with periods of lassitude, indifferent performance, and boredom. When the inhibited periods are restricted to one or a few days, they tend to be thought of as "off-days." If these periods last longer, they are often explained away with the idea that one is tired and overworked and in need of a vacation. Actually, these periods are characteristic of minor depressions. These fluctuations in productivity seem to be the rule rather than the exception. There is cause for serious concern when off-days stretch into weeks or months or when they recur at frequent intervals.

Another type of work anxiety expresses itself not so much in the incapacity to work as in the attitude toward the gains derived from work. Gains may be dissipated or denied, or if they are monetary, the money is frequently squandered. Individuals with this inhibitory syndrome cannot save and are usually in debt, despite, in many cases, relatively large incomes. If the gains lie in prestige, the individual may indulge in activities to undermine it.

A brief comment about original or creative work. Too often creative work is considered to be the sole property of the arts and sciences. Creativity is an attribute of all persons, not of a discipline. Each time we discover or invent something new to us, we are creative, no matter how often this discovery has been made by others, and we experience the excitement and gratification which are the concomitants of creative activity. Inhibition of creativity is a serious loss and is a salient factor in creating a feeling of boredom.

THE CONCEPT OF INHIBITION

Inhibition is a biological, defensive reaction that protects the organism from danger. Anticipated injury need not be of a physical order; it may be rejection or humiliation — in short, anything considered harmful to one's interest. The threat of injury need not be realistic. But as long as one believes there is a threat, he will react, and if the threat is severe enough, action will be inhibited. When sexual intercourse is perceived as dangerous, impotence is a usual consequence. The inhibition is automatic and beyond control or, at best, under fragmentary volitional control. The perception of danger may be conscious or unconscious, but in either case action is inhibited. Sexually impotent individuals state honestly that, as far as they are aware, they are not afraid of sexual relations; but dreams and free associations establish terror of such an act. People who suffer from severe sexual anxiety may not even be aware of sexual desire. Similarly, those with severe work anxiety may not know what kind of work interests them. Although the wish to work may be recognized, they have difficulty in initiating action. In such instances, the individual knows what he would like to do but never gets around to doing it. Procrastination is an overt symptom. If the inertia associated with beginning action is overcome, inhibition may subsequently interrupt it. There are also those who can carry action almost to completion but cannot finish. Frequently they end projects without really completing them or they finish with a weak ending. This is more likely to happen when the individual does not experience the gratification and pleasure that normally accompanies completed action. With these considerations as a background, let us proceed to a discussion of the psychodynamics of pleasure and work inhibitions, the two major contributors to the feeling of boredom.

Pleasure Inhibition

Normal, healthy children are happy children. Only the human laughs. Laughter and gaiety are part of the progressive humanization of the child. The infant first develops the ability to laugh when it is about three months old, but only in response to parental laughter and external stimulation. All normal children are born with the potential for laughter, but it appears only as a response to stimulation. Many years ago, René Spitz (1945) reported a study of a group of infants brought up in nurseries in Europe during World War II. Because of a shortage of personnel due to wartime conditions, only the physical needs of these infants could be met. Normal stimulation and play with the children were not possible. These children never learned to laugh nor respond properly to human warmth and affection. After the sixth month, they gradually began to deteriorate physically and mentally and most of these babies were dead by the end of their second year. In testing the children for deterioration, Spitz used a nodding and smiling gesture in order to elicit a smiling response which is apparently essential for normal human development.

Pleasure difficulties can begin in the cradle, but for those who suffer from difficulties in feeling and expressing pleasure, they begin somewhat later in childhood. Such problems occur among children who are inculcated with the idea that anything they may wish for themselves is selfish and base. Such indoctrination is accomplished by exploitative, usually overambitious parents — more precisely, ambition-frustrated parents — who delude themselves and their children into thinking that in this way the best interests of the child are served. When brought up with such ideas, such children become guilt-ridden about enjoying any activity or acquisition that carries with it pleasure only for themselves. Consequently, they feel compelled to share all pleasures with others, or they derive pleasure only from doing things for other people. In many, the desire for simple, straightforward gratification is immediately transformed into a compulsive need to fulfill some duty, or to give pleasure to another person. Action arising from such compulsive needs is never spontaneous and is always accompanied by resentment at some level of consciousness.

One patient spent a month of her analysis working through anxieties surrounding her desire to purchase a print she admired. The picture was very reasonably priced so that the money involved was no problem. During this month she indulged in all manner of expiatory behavior, including the purchase of significantly more expensive gifts for her friends.

Pleasure difficulties can also arise under circumstances, not rare, when the child is called upon to help support the family—reality imposes upon the child's right to play and pursue normal interests. But even under such circumstances, constructive parents who do not wish to exploit such a situation by impressing upon the child's pleasure needs a stigma of guilt, do not foster pleasure inhibitions. Not infrequently, parents of a child prodigy who has achieved success secure their reflected glory and their income by interfering with activities thought to be unrelated to the child's career. As a consequence, resentment toward work develops, as well as anxiety about pleasure, with subsequent inhibition in both areas.

An attitudinal blend deriving from the harsh realities of life in the old country and the vestiges of the puritanical mores associated with the work ethic in this country, have dominated the attitudes toward pleasure for almost three centuries of our history. The idea that the pursuit of pleasure, laughter, and fun is sinful—qualities now regarded as signs of mental health—had its roots in religious ideology. Righteousness was identified with the inhibition of pleasure; the concept of goodness was in large part a negative one. People were praised for what they did not do. The "good" man was one who left wine, women and song to the devil; the "good" woman left behind even more. Such mores were particularly detrimental to women. The prototype of a lady was of one whose virtue increased with her physical and emotional immobility. Even the pleasure of eating had to be controlled and concealed; the highborn lady should never reveal a hearty appetite. The attitudes were involved with sexual behavior as well, which was regarded as especially sinful. Sexual frigidity has now come to be recognized as a psychiatric symptom and not a virtue. For the revolutionary change in attitudes and behavior about sexuality, a great deal of credit goes to Freud and his co-workers, who disregarded the conventions of their time and scientifically pursued the facts about human motivation and behavior.

No discussion of pleasure inhibitions can avoid a consideration of child-rearing patterns that concern sexual development. Although attitudes toward adult sexual activity have undergone radical changes, the same does not yet apply to childhood sexuality. Many parents still communicate the idea that sex is bad and dirty, but also expect the child will somehow believe upon reaching adolescence and maturity that sex is romantic and beautiful. Faulty early indoctrination seriously interferes with comfortable social relations with the opposite sex, with good marital relationships, and with certain activities not directly sexual: inhibitions in dancing, singing, and even creative writing are rooted in such a background.

Psychodynamics of Work Inhibitions

Essential for understanding problems of work inhibition is a familiarity with the problem of competition, and some knowledge of the genesis of competitive attitudes in children. The two major sources of competitive problems in children are sibling rivalry and the oedipus complex.

Sibling rivalry is the competition among children for parental affection. It occurs in all children who have brothers and sisters. It is frequently, but not always, more intense in the older child's feelings toward the younger one. Competitive feelings arising out of sibling rivalry are by no means gentle. They are intense and often murderous. Children recognize that parental disapproval will be incurred and so the direct expression and conversion into action of such impulses are usually inhibited. Parental preference for individual children tends to intensify rivalry feelings in the child preferred and in the ones excluded. Preference is never an indication of a selected child's superiority; it is always an indication of the neurosis of the parent. Children soon learn the values their parents live by, and as part of the learning, developmental process, and by seeking parental affection, adopt their parents' values. In many families, intelligence, achievement, and success are highly valued. School work is likely to become the battleground on which sibling rivalry is fought out. Since an important motive for excellent work may be preferential parental affection, working may become enmeshed with guilt and anxiety. Success is then identified with injury to a sibling, and this idea produces guilt feelings in relation to the sibling, giving rise to fear of parental disapproval. Paradoxically, the success sought as a way of winning parental affection is seen as potentially alienating it. This is particularly true for the nonpreferred child who perceives, often accurately, that the parent does not want him in the home; transferred to the schoolroom, the child reacts to the teacher and schoolmates in large measure as he does to his parents and siblings. Many school problems are the consequence of sibling rivalry. Frequently, children with such problems function below their capacities; some bright children fail in their grades on the basis of sibling conflicts. These attitudes and problems do not disappear as childhood is left behind. They become an integral part of adult personality and experience but rarely are the problems completely resolved. We live in a sharply competitive society and competition anxieties are often aggravated and perpetuated by life experience. What has been noted about schoolwork also applies to other endeavors and pursuits motivated by competitive feelings arising from sibling rivalry.

The second major source of competitive feelings is the oedipus complex. Within the structure of the oedipus complex, the father becomes a son's hated rival and, at the same time, remains a loved and respected figure, one from whom love is also sought and desired. Pursuing the idea that if he becomes better than the father he will be accepted by the mother, the son becomes competitive with his father. To exclude him, however, means to antagonize this powerful figure, with the danger of retaliation and the danger of losing the rich positive elements of their relationship. For these reasons, the child feels obliged to conceal his hostile wishes, and any sphere in which they find expression is fraught with anxiety. Hence, all work in childhood and adult life that incorporates competitive feelings toward the father or father substitutes is laden with anxiety and weighted with inhibition. It is not a coincidence that many sons refuse to follow in the footsteps of their father. They avoid the same occupation for fear of beating the father at his own game. The sons who do choose or who are compelled to undertake the same pursuits rarely excel over their father, not because of inferior ability, but because of the guilt and fear incurred by superior performance. Where the parents are competitive with their children—fathers with sons, mothers with daughters—the entire problem is seriously aggravated.

Attitudes toward the father become transferred to other men; sometimes to all men, more often to certain types of men, such as men in authority and men who look like the father, and so forth. What has been said of men applies equally to women in their relationship with their mother. Competitive attitudes toward the mother are later transferred to other women.

All work and activity motivated by antisocial wishes are accompanied by anxiety and easily lead to inhibition. Thus, any activity that has as its goal the domination of others carries with it the burden of anxiety. If work in such a psychological gear is accomplished, it is accomplished despite fear and tends to be accompanied by a host of psychosomatic symptoms. Moreover, the work is achieved at the expense of good human relationships. No one dominated by antisocial wishes can have good human relationships.

We are now in a better position to understand a type of commonly experienced and deeply rooted fear: the fear of success. We hear a great deal about fear of failure but relatively little about fear of success. Yet the fear of failure is, in most instances, secondary. The individual who has fear of failure is afraid not because of a lack of personal resources needed for the task, but because of an inability to use them. He is inhibited by fear. We have seen how success is perceived as a weapon of aggression. The irrational notion that success is hurtful can exist even in situations where the work is socially constructive and valuable. Yet it can be inhibited by the fear that it may hurt others. A grown person may be completely thwarted in a work effort by ideas stemming from childhood conflicts based on unresolved sibling rivalry or on oedipal conflicts. The adage, "one man's gain is another man's sorrow," expresses a social attitude that does little to dispel irrational ideas of the sort we are discussing. The fear that one's success may elicit envy and hostility instead of warmth and friendship does much to inhibit successful performance.

A common manifestation of the fear of success is an inability to accept compliments without embarrassment or self-minimizing retorts. Some people immediately respond to the comment, "How well you look," by a description of how bad they feel. Others conceal their abilities behind a facade of mediocrity though they may be richly endowed with talent. The fear of success causes many to sabotage their own efforts as in the case of athletes who are clearly in the lead, then suddenly falter and lose to less able players.

So much for competition as a determinant of work difficulties. It is by far the most important factor but two others must also be considered: the fear of making mistakes and fear of the limelight. Fear of making mistakes is related to attitudes toward authority. This fear cuts deeply into spontaneity and freedom of action. Authoritarian, overdemanding, perfectionistic parents and teachers who inflict humiliation and punishment upon children for their errors produce in many a fear of being assertive. Originality, creativity, and spontaneity are particularly affected. It has been said, and correctly, that those who never make a mistake do nothing. Individuals who are painfully afraid of being wrong, who shy away from action, who undertake everything with indecision and reluctance, are most comfortable when their proficiency is beyond question with routine tasks. The very routine that promotes comfort, however, also promotes boredom. Such individuals tend to avoid anything new, different, and interesting.

The fear of being wrong leads to perfectionistic trends and to an inability to tolerate criticism. Every test, including examinations by physicians, becomes a trial difficult to bear. Making a mistake or being wrong is tantamount to revealing what is felt to be unacceptable in one's self. This includes feelings of hostility or any other attitudes sensed as antimoral or antisocial. The depth of the fear of making mistakes may be seen in the irritated response of self-conscious people to such bits of advice as, "Don't be afraid of making mistakes, everybody makes them." Fear of possibly exposing what is felt to be unacceptable turns many people away from attention-getting situations. They avoid the limelight and shy away from central positions. They are more comfortable in the shadows but are then left with feelings of having been overlooked.

Ways of circumventing boredom are as numerous as boredom is extensive. The use of drugs, notably alcohol, is widespread. Marijuana is used, often specifically, as a drug to escape from work and circumvent boredom. This is not to imply that relief of boredom is the only reason people drink, but it is certainly one use to which it is put. When this is the case, alcohol is used as an anesthetic or for somatic gratification to replace the gratification lost through inhibited action. A person may sit around and drink because he can do nothing better. Some use food in this way—the so-called "foodaholics." Others may engage in sexual activity, not especially for the satisfaction of sexual desire, but as a technique for spending time. Sex, when so motivated, may itself become boring. Social gatherings, too, may be sought to avoid boredom; the interest in such gatherings may hinge simply on a need to be with people rather than a way of enjoying active interpersonal exchange or sharing common interests. Some seek out clubs or organizations without having a primary interest in the objectives of the group. Many look for thrills and excitement as a way out of the boredom trap and try to find "kicks" in gambling and fanciful adventures. Some even hope for war. An exciting catastrophe is relished as an event that lifts one out of boredom and a humdrum existence. Movies and television are common means of circumventing boredom. There is nothing pathological about watching television or going to a movie, but it is a symptom of psychological difficulties when it replaces an activity that one would prefer doing but is forced to abandon because of anxiety and inhibition.

THE PSYCHOTHERAPY OF BOREDOM

The common-sense approach to the therapy of pathological boredom consists largely in advising a patient to undertake a hobby. Since the inhibitions that produce pathological boredom soon interfere with the pursuit of hobbies, this advice is of little value. Attics and cellars are filled with the by-products of burnt-out hobbies. Therapies based on the principle of leadership-initiated activity such as occupational therapy, art, music therapy, and so forth, are also of limited value. The psychotherapy of pathological boredom should be oriented toward investigating the underlying psychodynamic processes that give rise to the inhibition and boredom. Pathological boredom is a symptomatic manifestation of a deep-seated personality disorder. For this reason, the treatment of choice is psychoanalytic therapy.

Chapter 9

The Meaning
of Masochism

Masochism has been a core problem in psychoanalysis for many years; it is central in the dynamics of psychopathology. A short review of Freud's thinking on the subject will point the way to the main section of this chapter which is concerned with my own observations, theoretical orientation, and conclusions.

In *Three Contributions to the Theory of Sex* (1905a) Freud stated,

> The tendency to cause pain to the sexual object and its opposite, the most frequent and most significant of all perversions, was designated in its two forms by Krafft-Ebing as sadism for the active form and masochism for

the passive form. Other authors prefer the narrower term algolagnia which emphasizes the pleasure in pain and cruelty, whereas the terms selected by Krafft-Ebing place the pleasure secured in all kinds of humility and submission in the foreground. The roots of sadism can be readily demonstrated in normal individuals. The sexuality of most men shows an admixture of aggression, of a desire to subdue, the biological significance of which lies in the necessity for overcoming the resistance of the sexual object by actions other than mere courting. Sadism would then correspond to an aggressive component of the sexual instinct which has become independent and exaggerated and has been brought to the foreground by displacement. The concept of sadism fluctuates in every-day speech from a mere active or impetuous attitude toward the sexual object to an absolute attachment of the gratification to the subjection and maltreatment of the object. Strictly speaking, only the last extreme case can claim the name of perversion. Similarly, the designation masochism comprises all passive attitudes to the sexual life and to the sexual object; in its most extreme form, the gratification is connected with suffering of physical or mental pain at the hands of the sexual object. Masochism as a perversion seems further removed from the normal sexual goal than its opposite. It may even be doubted whether it ever is primary and whether it does not more often originate through transformation from sadism. It can often be recognized that masochism is nothing but a continuation of sadism directed at one's person in which the latter at first takes the place of the sexual object.

This was Freud's early position on sadism and masochism. It rested on several relatively simple though unproven assumptions: (1) that there is a resistance to sexual intercourse in women which has to be overcome by men — an assumption that is highly questionable in the human and other species; (2) that the male sexual impulse is, therefore, normally endowed with an aggressive component to overcome resistance in the female; (3) that this aggressive component can be detached from the sexual impulse to lead an autonomous existence as sadism — though the "how" and "why" for such detachment is not explained; (4) that the sadism can be turned against the self if an identification with the sexual object develops, and it thus may become masochism; (5) though not specifically stated, it is implied that the woman is the object of the man's sadism and she must have a corresponding masochism to facilitate her overcoming resistance to intercourse.

By 1924, Freud had materially altered his views on masochism. He departed from his initial position of doubt as to whether masochism was ever primary and proceeded to elaborate a theory of masochism based on the assumption of its primary and instinctual character. In his paper, "The Economic Problem in Masochism" (1924b), he pursued this theory to the following conclusions: (1) that masochism is part of the death instinct or Nirvana principle whose function it is to reduce the relatively unstable activities of organic life to the more peaceful and stable qualities of inorganic life; and (2) that masochism presents itself in three forms:

> It comes under our observation in three shapes: as a condition under which sexual excitation may be roused; as an expression of feminine nature, and as a norm of behavior. According to this, one may distinguish an erotogenic, a feminine and a moral type of masochism. The first, the erotogenic masochism, the lust of pain, is

also to be found at bottom in the other forms; the concept of it can be supported on biological and constitutional ground; it remains incomprehensible unless one can bring oneself to make certain assumptions about matters that are wrapt in obscurity. The third, in certain respects the most important form in which masochism appears, has only lately been properly appreciated by psychoanalysis as a sense of guilt that is for the most part unconscious; it admits, however, of *full* explanation and co-ordination into our previous knowledge. Feminine masochism, on the other hand, is the form foremost accessible to observation, least mysterious, and is comprehensible in *all* its relations. (pp. 257–258, italics mine)

The above quotation demonstrates Freud's tendency, common to other mortals, to become most dogmatic where he felt least assured. He proceeds from the comparatively modest and ambiguous statement about erotogenic masochism, that "it remains incomprehensible unless one can bring oneself to make certain assumptions about matters that are wrapt in obscurity," to the remark that moral masochism admits of *full* explanation, and that feminine masochism is least mysterious and comprehensible in *all* its relations.

When he further discusses feminine masochism, however, he cannot decide whether this is feminine or just plain childish. "The obvious interpretation which is easily arrived at is that the masochist wants to be treated like a little, helpless, dependent child, but especially as a naughty child" (1924b). He concludes his discussion on feminine masochism by stating, "The feminine type of masochism described is based entirely on the primary eroto-genic type, the lust for pain which cannot be explained without going very far back."

About moral masochism he concludes that it is based on the man's sexual wish to be beaten by his father. Thus Freud finally integrates masochism into his libido theory — masochism is a primary erotogenic impulse, a "lust for pain." He sets the basis in this paper for linking dependency and helplessness with masochism, and dependent and passive longings with the instinctual apparatus. By and large, the views enunciated by Freud in "The Economic Problem in Masochism" remain the theoretical base for current orthodox psychoanalytic thinking on this subject.

From the viewpoint of cognitive psychoanalysis, masochism can best be understood as an adaptation, not an instinctual drive. In the main, masochistic acts and attitudes are in the service of defensive techniques in order to protect the self from greater and more painful injury, no matter how realistically injurious the masochistic act itself may be. It is a matter of choosing the lesser evil. It is an unrealistic choice since the masochist brings upon the self real injury as protection from an illusory danger. Had Freud not been so heavily committed to his libido theory, he would have himself recognized this meaning of masochism, for he wrote:

> Castration, or the blinding which represents it, often leaves a negative trace in these fantasies by the condition that just the genitals or the eyes are not to be injured in any way. (Incidentally, masochistic tortures seldom convey an impression of such seriousness as the brutalities — fantasied or actual — of sadists.) Moreover, in the manifest content of masochistic fantasies, a feeling of guilt comes to expression, it being assumed that the subject has committed some crime which is to be expiated by his undergoing pain and torture. (1924b, p. 259)

Freud indicates, and accurately, that masochistic injury is less than castration (or its equivalent, blindness) and that the pain suffered in expiation for a "crime" is less than that which, in the patient's view, would have been inflicted by the offended authority.

MASOCHISM AS A DEFENSE

Masochism was originally observed and described in relation to sexuality. This is understandable because of the dramatic and incongruous connection between painful activity and sexuality, a basic, pleasurable function. Masochistic defenses are also prominent in other areas but, because of the historical background, I shall begin with masochism in sexuality.

For the large majority of people, sexuality is interfered with from infancy to adult life. The earliest expression of sexual activity identified by the parents, particularly by the mother, is generally the infant's manipulation of the genitals. It becomes established as directed and purposeful behavior somewhere between the fifth and ninth month. As a rule, this behavior is prevented by always keeping the genital area diapered, precluding manual contact, and by persistently removing the infant's hands from the genitals whenever such contact is made. I recall observing a mother diapering a male infant of about nine months whose hands went to his genitals as soon as they were accessible. Each such movement was immediately followed by the mother pushing the hands from the genitals. This sequence of events occurred five or six times. Some minutes later, I asked the mother whether she had ever noticed the child manipulating his genitals. She quite honestly answered that she had not. She was totally unaware of the entire experience. As with infantile masturbation, all other sexual behavior meets with prohibitive and frequently punitive parental responses. This includes sexual exploration — visual, tactile, and other — sexual play with other children, and any sexual activity directed toward the cross-sex parent. Prohibitive and punitive responses to childhood sexuality are not confined to parents; teachers, and other adult authorities, in general, may also communicate antisexual attitudes and behavior. These influences, derived from the mores of our society, constitute the basis for the component of sexual anxiety that I refer to as the prohibitive component.

The second major component of sexual activity derives from the oedipus complex. This component is not unrelated to the prohibitive component; the children of restrictive parents enter the oedipal phase with an already injured sexuality. In the oedipal phase, a sexually rejecting same-sex parent and a competitive cross-sex parent promote in the child severe sexual anxiety. Since most people are exposed to sexual restrictions and go through an oedipal phase, almost all come to adult life with at least some sexual anxiety. Among the more neurotic, the sexual impulse becomes fused with an expectation of injury, so that sexual excitation is accompanied by anxiety, inhibition, or defensiveness. The more severe the sexual injury, the greater the anxiety. During sexual activity many individuals have sensations that combine sexual excitement and anxiety, but they are unaware that anxiety is a component of what they are feeling. They interpret the sensations as sexual excitement, and assume that their tremulousness and consequent fatigue are a natural part of sexual experience. When such persons resolve significant aspects of their sexual fears, they begin to recognize how much their sexual feelings had been admixed with anxiety. One patient, in a slip of the tongue, coined the word *anxirement* — a combination of anxiety, desire, and excitement. This condensation tells the story.

Some individuals experience nothing but anxiety in sexual situations; others cannot function sexually without resorting to defensive techniques. The sexual masochist cannot perform, or cannot perform with pleasure, unless the act is accompanied by masochistic activity. Masochism subserves the function of localizing and identifying both the anticipated injury and the injurer. In effect, the masochist says, "I cannot function sexually. I am too frightened of the punishment I will sustain for behaving in a sexual way. I am therefore making you, my sexual partner, the source of the injury because I know you and know that you will hurt me. I also know you will not hurt me too severely." By localizing the anticipated injury as to source and extent, the masochist can then perform sexually. That the masochist wants pain only partially explicates the dynamics. He *must* have it to function. In analysis, when sexual anxiety diminishes, the masochistic behavior disappears.

In sexual masochism, the pain may be physical or psychological — humiliation, rejection, etc. Whatever the character of the pain, its defensive purpose is to localize and delimit the anticipated injury so that the sexual activity can be carried out.

Sexual sadism, closely related to masochism, involves a similar defensive technique. The sadist also identifies the potential danger, but by inflicting the pain, dominates and punishes the "threatening" person, that is, the sexual partner. Neither masochism nor sadism is ever part of normal sexual behavior. Freud's concept that sadism was a normal component of masculine sexuality and masochism, of feminine sexuality, came from his idea that sadomasochism was instinctual and that the male was dominant.

Masochistic defenses appear in many areas of behavior, particularly competitive behavior where the goals are not only sexual. The fear of antagonizing competitors by successful performance, and of arousing their hostility, leads many individuals to sabotage their efforts, which results in diminished effectiveness or failure. It is an invariable concomitant of work inhibitions. Self-sabotage may involve any aspect of functioning including physical appearance, where the individual presents himself or herself far less attractively than personal resources allow. Such behavior is purposely self-destructive and, therefore, masochistic. Its function is defensive and a way of warding off attack from a feared competitor. To emphasize: self-injury is not sought for the pleasure it provides. Masochistic injury is an irrational way of seeking protection against a greater injury from a hostile rival. Masochistic maneuvers to avoid success or dissipate its rewards may be understood in this context.

A simple test to determine the extent to which an analytic patient has resolved masochistic defenses is to comment on how well he or she is doing in the analysis or to extend a compliment for work well done. If the patient responds by complaining how poorly he or she feels, or that the work was really badly done, or unimportant, or by wasting the next few sessions, then the patient still has a way to go in the analysis. One patient was compelled, after each productive session, to sabotage the next one in purposeless meanderings. He improved to the point where he wasted only part of the next hour. One day after a productive session involving an important dream, he returned with repetitive, unproductive material. When I suggested that we go back to the dream, he replied, "Look, I've got to waste five minutes telling you this and if you interrupt, I'll waste ten minutes."

Feelings of Inadequacy

A frequently noted dynamic as a masochistic defense are feelings of inadequacy. Such feelings are generally expressed in terms of physical, intellectual, or social inadequacy; the patient will report feeling unattractive, sexually unwanted, stupid, or uninteresting. The pathognomic test is the patient's response to the analyst's disagreement. If the analyst says that the patient really is attractive and the patient responds with irritation and denial, pointing out that the left ear sticks out too far, or the nose is too big, an alleged inadequacy is being used as a defense.

Some years ago, I analyzed a handsome man who kept repeating how unattractive he was because he was short. He was five foot ten. Another case, a model, thought her feet were so unattractive, she would not go to a public beach. Neither her feet nor any part of her anatomy could be considered as unattractive by any rational observer. There are, of course, many determinants for feelings of inadequacy, but I am emphasizing that its role in masochism further perpetuates these feelings. In the analysis of the model, we established that a determinant for the antipathy she felt toward her feet was a displacement for guilt about masturbation which involved her hands. Even after the anxiety about masturbation greatly diminished, the symptom did not disappear until the need to use it masochistically was also resolved. Both patients were very much afraid of accepting their natural endowments. They were, in effect, saying to their feared competitors, "Don't be jealous of me. I'm nothing, nobody, an ugly creature." The same dynamic is often noted among patients who are very bright, even brilliant, but who insist that they are unintelligent or dull. When their accomplishments are pointed out, they protest that they have fooled everybody, or merely have good memories, or are really idiot-savants.

There are two major therapeutic considerations in approaching feelings of inadequacy as related to defensive masochism. First, inasmuch as a cardinal principle of my cognitive analytic technique is to leave a defense undisturbed until the patient understands the underlying fears that require the defense, I do not generally respond to a patient's protestations of inadequacy. The one exception to this principle is the depressed patient who needs me to recognize his or her value. Second, when the salient anxieties underlying a defense have been worked out, the patient's use of feelings of inadequacy must then be integrated with the underlying anxieties and, in so doing, demonstrate that the feelings of inadequacy are, in large part, a segment of the patient's masochistic defenses.

Another common determinant of masochistic behavior is turning upon one's self hostile and destructive impulses that cannot be expressed outwardly. Here again, masochism is a defense that protects the self from the greater injury of retaliative attack, were the hostile and destructive impulses to be directed outward.

Some patients fear being in a good state of health and vigor. They associate the idea of health and energy with effectiveness, with sexual and assertive behavior, and, in general, with freedom. Because they fear being assertive, they defensively and unconsciously keep themselves in a state of lowered vitality. This is accomplished through masochistic acts, such as getting insufficient sleep, eating inadequately, drinking and smoking excessively, exhausting oneself, etc. One patient had to keep himself awake until 3:00 or 4:00 A.M. every day and consequently was chronically fatigued. If he retired at a reasonable hour and turned on the radio, he invariably fell asleep within a few minutes, and felt rested and energetic the next day. Despite this, he continued his masochistic behavior, rationalizing that it was too dull to go to bed early. His associations to good health were "virility" and "masculinity." This patient was frequently beset with a psychosomatic complaint, so that he rarely felt well. He was afraid of the sensation of well-being and of appearing as a healthy man.

Similar to this type are those patients who need to have a feeling of anxiety and tension, or to obsessively worry in order to feel reasonably comfortable. That one requires discomfort to feel somewhat comfortable seems paradoxical, but there are individuals who are chronically defensive and otherwise feel disarmed and in danger. Analysis of such patients reveals that they cannot let down their defenses lest they express feared impulses or expose themselves to attack by aggressive competitors. It is of interest that pain and illness may serve as a substitute for anxiety and obsessiveness. Many such patients report that they are free from anxiety and feel relaxed, a rare experience for them, when they are ill or suffering from a painful condition. It is a well-known observation that severely obsessive-compulsive people improve in times of extreme stress, as in war or concentration camp confinement — an adaptation related to defensive masochism. Some people under severe anxiety bite their lips or tongue or indulge in painful scratching or skin-picking, activities that apparently relieve anxiety and demonstrably slow the tachycardia accompanying the anxiety.

Pain and painful affects may function as a spur that triggers activity or controls behavior. Painful affects such as self-loathing, self-contempt, and even feelings of guilt, may have as their aim, at least in part, a change in the behavior that prompted these feelings. Similar dynamics are involved in head-banging, severe nail-biting, self-flagellation, etc. — self-inflicted pain and injury that are masochistic techniques to ward off anticipated greater injury. Some patients require pain or painful affects to stimulate motivation to achieve desired goals and gratifications, as illustrated by those who have to do unpleasant tasks before they can enjoy themselves. Compulsively performing "necessary" chores is the painful payment that earns the pleasure. A more complex adaptation may be noted among individuals who compulsively strive for money, power, and prestige. Many such people have to maintain a constant state of stress and tension to help drive them on. Relaxation is perceived as straying from their ambitions and responsibilities and sets off intense anxiety. Yet, the painful feelings of tension are resented, and resentment is often projected to the work itself or to subordinates and others involved in it. Like a hot traveller through a desert who uses his thirst to propel him to an oasis at journey's end, this type of individual hopes vainly and irrationally that the struggle for success will bring achievement and the surcease of pain. The self-generated painful affects are masochistic defenses as is the goal itself.

Two closely connected types of reactions deserve mention. First, for reasons beyond the scope of this chapter, the fear of coming too close or getting affection from others: when a relationship promises to become intimate, warm, or even friendly, some individuals act in such a way as to destroy the relationship. This clearly is masochistic because its aim is self-deprivation and the act by which the sabotage is carried out is usually self-derogatory. Second, a profound fear of rejection may compulsively drive some people into self-sacrificing activities oriented toward winning and preserving the love of significant others. The self-exploitation and submission may become so onerous that it generates impulses to kick over the traces — to destroy the personal resources that are thought to attract affection and acceptance of others, and to undermine in some way the love itself, thus to be freed from the compulsive self-enslavement. These dynamics are masochistic and, if acted out, are realistically self-destructive.

Masochism in Dependent Adaptations

Masochistic defenses play an important role in a dependency constellation. The subject of dependency has been given exhaustive treatment not only by psychoanalysts; the social work literature, for obvious reasons, abounds in references to dependency. Yet its meaning and dynamics have not been satisfactorily clarified. The behavior of adults and children are described in quasi-instinctual terms such as passive longing, innate desires to be dependent, wishes to be taken care of, yearnings to be a baby, and so forth, without distinguishing between normal expectation of help and pathological dependency. Often, pathological dependency in adults is confused with the physiobiologic dependency of children. Interdependence and mutual aid are a part of social living. Normal adults have no wishes to be taken care of, no passive longings, no desires to be infantile. Pathological dependency in adults is a defensive adaptation in which an individual who possesses the resources to mediate a function cannot use them because of anxiety and inhibition; therefore, gratification or fulfillment of the function is sought through the resources of another.

Pathologically dependent individuals perceive those depended upon to be supermen and superwomen. The need to endow them with magical power arises in part from the belief that no ordinary mortal, such as the depender, can solve the problems or do the things that he or she is too inhibited to do. Inflating the endowments of those depended upon may also be an attempt to re-create a mother or father figure in order to act out or work out problems originally related to these figures. This dynamic is a paranoid mechanism where the source of personal problems is imputed to one individual or group, as in a man, for instance, who relates to another man as to a father and then hopes to solve his problems by dominating, even killing him. Whatever the motives for endowing others with magical power, the dynamics necessarily involve self-depreciation. No adult can perceive another adult as omnipotent except through self-diminution.

The difference in the potential resources of normally intelligent people is not so great as to permit the perception of another as superhuman. Such a perception is achieved and maintained through the inhibition of personal resources and constriction of affect. The greater the unrealistic enhancement of another person's image, the greater the inhibition with accompanying attitudes of awe and reverence, instead of appropriate respect. So long as a need exists to endow others with superhuman power, there is a coexisting need for masochistic self-depreciation and self-destructiveness. In treating such patients, I have observed that they rarely, some never, permit themselves to experience a sense of completion, fulfillment, or high self-esteem; such feelings destroy the image of magical power in others. Pathologically dependent individuals cannot accept a status of equality with the objects of their dependency for this, too, would destroy the needed image of magical human power. The analyst's offer of equality to this type of patient stimulates anxiety and resistance. The need to maintain an inflated image of others is one of the basic sources of anxiety in the dependency constellation.

Masochism as a Cause for Anxiety

Normally, anxiety is a response to a realistic threat of danger or injury, whether internal or external, and resources are mobilized for defense. Masochism is an irrational response to threat, always hurtful to the self, and it always sets off anxiety commensurate with the extent of the self-sustained injury. Masochistic impulses and acts, though in themselves defensive in purpose, account for a significantly high share of the anxiety experienced in psychopathologic states and of the secondary defenses against the anxiety.

The dynamics of masochism are built into the pathological dependency constellation and form an integral part of it. Masochistic defenses cannot possibly have reparative effects; instead, they heighten anxiety, add materially to furthering injury to the personality, and broaden symptoms.

Masochism as an Automatic Response

Some children are habitually exposed to a parenting pattern in which love and attention are given only during illness or after hostile treatment; thus, love and attention come to be associated with painful affects and illness. These children grow up to be adults who have learned to resort to masochistic maneuvers when they fail to get the affection they seek. They may resort to provocative behavior to elicit hostility, guilt, and expiatory feelings of love from those whose affection is sought. I have found that patients may behave this way when more direct and constructive means of eliciting love are inhibited for neurotic reasons.

Masochism as a Circumventive Technique

In "A Child is Being Beaten" (1919) Freud described in an adult a consciously erotic fantasy of a child being beaten on the naked buttocks, a fantasy he believed was more common in women than men. An exercise in imagination, it reveals as it conceals the sexual nature of the fantasy. The idea of being beaten passes censorship and, at the same time, includes punishment for a prohibited sexual act, thus covering up the unacceptable sexual thoughts and reactions. It is similar to the childhood game of playing doctor, which places prohibited sexual activity in the framework of blameless make-believe.

Freud (1919) viewed the fantasy of being beaten as masochistic, but he also stated,

This phantasy—a child is being beaten—was invariably cathected with a high degree of pleasure and had its issue in an act of pleasurable auto-erotic satisfaction. It might therefore be expected that the sight of another child being beaten at school would also be a source of similar enjoyment. But as a matter of fact this was never so. The experience of real scenes of beating at school produced in the child who witnessed them a peculiarly excited feeling which was probably of a mixed character and in which repugnance had a large share. In a few cases the real experience of the scenes of beating was felt to be intolerable. Moreover, it was always a condition of the more sophisticated phantasies of later years that the punishment should do the children no serious injury. (p. 180)

Other examples of masochism could be offered but they would not further elaborate the concept. Masochism is not an instinct; it is an adaptational contrivance. The pain, or its equivalents, is not sought or self-inflicted for the pleasure in the pain per se. People with pronounced masochistic tendencies may superficially create the impression that they are enjoying the pain or humiliation. Analysis reveals that the apparent pleasure is a facade to cover up the intense, underlying hostility consequent to the masochistic act, and an attempt to convince one's self that the sustained injury is not painful but even pleasurable — a distortion to prevent expressing hostility. Hostility always accompanies a masochistic act and is directed against the feared person from whom injury is anticipated and for whom the defensive masochistic act is being performed. Since the hostility frequently cannot be openly expressed, it feeds back by being turned inward and increases the masochism.

HANDLING MASOCHISTIC DEFENSES

As I have emphasized throughout, I do not interpret defenses before the underlying anxieties are understood and can be integrated with the analysis of the defense. Obviously, this technique applies to the analysis of masochism, an important defense. It is the analyst's task to interpret reality for a patient whose perceptions are unclear or distorted. If a patient believes that sexuality is dirty or hurtful, the analyst must convey the reality that sexuality is pleasurable and not hurtful. This may appear as simple reassurance or permissiveness, but only because replacing irrational thinking by reality *is* reassuring, and liberating a patient from oppressive ideas seems permissive. As to masochistic motives or acts, however, the analyst must take care that he or she is neither reassuring nor permissive. Support of a patient's masochistic act, analytically expressed or tacitly implied by not pointing out its masochistic purpose, intensifies anxiety and leads to mistrust of the analyst. For example, a patient is contemplating marriage but becomes overwhelmed with anxiety about commitment, and takes flight into promiscuous sexual relationships. If the analyst has the mistaken idea that he must be sexually permissive and tells the patient, "Sex is perfectly normal and it is fine to have relations with anyone you like," he would be supporting the patient's masochism and losing the opportunity to work on the real source of his fears. The promiscuity in this case does not serve to bring sexual fulfillment; it is a masochistic technique to destroy an important relationship because of irrational fear of the consequences. If the analyst interprets the situation correctly, the patient cannot then assume that his self-destructiveness is being condoned. After underlying anxieties have been discerned, masochistic acts should be brought to the patient's attention; he should then be helped to understand what the acts were calculated to defend against in specific situations.

Masochism Defined

Masochism consists of acts and attitudes, conscious or unconscious, that are oriented toward bringing about pain or setting up situations that are realistically destructive to the self. Masochistic acts and attitudes have an adaptational, defensive function inasmuch as they are motivated toward preserving the self from what is perceived to be greater pain or injury. The perception of greater injury must be unrealistic for a defense to be masochistic; when an apparently self-injurious act actually preserves the individual from a greater danger, the act is not masochistic (e.g., a man who cuts off a finger which had been bitten by a poisonous snake).

This chapter has emphasized the role of masochism in psychopathology; however, not all neurotic acts that are self-injurious are masochistic. Neurotic behavior is, in one way or another, hurtful to the self, but it need not be masochistic. Much of the harm people do to themselves by their neurotic behavior is a by-product, not the purpose of the behavior. For an act to be masochistic, it must have as its *aim,* consciously or unconsciously, the infliction of pain or injury upon the self.

Sadism and Masochism

The terms "sadism" and "masochism" were first introduced into psychiatric literature by Krafft-Ebing in 1882. His extensive clinical descriptions are still well known, but his theoretical explanations became obscured by the great range, brilliance, and ingenuity of Freud's explorations of human motivation. Krafft-Ebing borrowed the term "sadism" from the French novelists of his time, who had come to use it to describe the perversion about which the notorious Marquis de Sade wrote vividly in his novels associating sex and cruelty; and he named as "masochism" the perversion described by the writer Sacher-Masoch, whose romances and novels centered around the association of sex and pain.

SEXUAL INTERPRETATIONS

In *Psychopathia Sexualis* (Krafft-Ebing 1892a) three categories of sadism were identified: (a) sadistic acts following coitus that gave inadequate gratification; (b) sadistic acts by individuals with diminished virility in attempts to enhance sexual desire; (c) sadistic acts calculated to induce orgasm without intercourse in cases of total impotence. Sadism was defined as "the experience of sexually pleasurable sensations (including orgasm) produced by acts of cruelty, bodily punishment, afflicted by one's own person or when witnessed in others, be they animals or human beings. It may also consist of an innate desire to humiliate, hurt, wound or even destroy others in order thereby to create sexual pleasure in one's self" (p. 80). The extensive case descriptions of sadism were grouped into nine categories: (1) lust-murder,[1] (2) mutilation of corpses, (3) injury to women (stabbing, flagellation, and the like), (4) defilement of women, (5) other attacks on females — symbolic sadism, (6) ideal sadism (in the ideational sense — it included fantasies of sadistic activities), (7) sadism with any other object, for example, whipping of boys, (8) sadistic acts with animals, (9) sadism in women.

Krafft-Ebing attempted to explain sadism (1892b) by two major formulations. First, sadism was considered to be a pathological elaboration of the aggressive component of male sexuality:

1. A dramatic example of lust-murder was the history of Marschalls Gilles de Rays, who was executed in 1440 because of the mutilation and murder he had practiced for eight years on more than 800 children. "This inhuman wretch confessed that in the commission of these acts he enjoyed inexpressible pleasure" (p. 42).

In the intercourse of the sexes the active or aggressive *role* belongs to the man; woman remains passive-defensive. It affords a man great pleasure to win a woman, to conquer her; and in the *ars amandi* the modesty of a woman who keeps herself on the defensive until the moment of surrender is an element of great psychological significance and importance. Under normal conditions a man meets obstacles which it is his part to overcome and for which nature has given him an aggressive character. This aggressive character, however, under pathological conditions may likewise be excessively developed, and express itself in an impulse to subdue absolutely the object of desire, even to destroy or kill it. (p. 44)

Second, Krafft-Ebing proposed that in sadism there was a spilling over of behavioral fragments from one excitatory constellation to another: "It is necessary to return to a consideration of the quasi physiological cases in which at the moment of most intense lust very excitable individuals who are otherwise normal commit such acts as biting and scratching which are usually the result of anger" (p. 43). The concept that components of the attack constellation of behavior can be incorporated into sexual organization has been supported by relatively recent ethological studies of animals (Thorpe and Zangwill 1961). Krafft-Ebing also advanced the idea that, once the association between sexuality and cruelty had become established, each was capable of activating the other: "When the association of lust and cruelty is present, not only does the lustful emotion awaken the impulse to cruelty, but vice versa. Cruel acts and ideas cause sexual excitement" (p. 45).

Krafft-Ebing's view of sadism in general was that "it is an excessive and pathological intensification of phenomena which accompany the psychical *vita sexualis* particularly in males" (p. 45). But he was unable to account for the pathological state that predisposed to psychical degeneracy. He cautioned, however, against regarding all cruelty as sadistic or sexual, pointing out that such motivations as vengeance and a desire for power might lead to cruelty.

Krafft-Ebing (1892a) described masochism as the association of passively endured cruelty and violence with lust:

> Masochism is the opposite of sadism. While the latter is the desire to cause pain and use force, the former is the wish to suffer pain and be subjected to force. By masochism I understand a peculiar perversion of the *vita sexualis* in which the individual affected, in sexual feelings and thoughts, is controlled by the idea of being completely and unconditionally subject to the will of the person as by a master, humiliated and abused. This idea is colored by lustful feelings. . . . The essential and common element in all these cases is the fact that the sexual instinct is directed to ideas of subjugation and abuse by the opposite sex. (p. 131)

He recognized the self-imposed limits in masochistic behavior, in contrast to sadism, which can go on to murder: "The extreme consequences of masochism are checked by the instinct of self-preservation and therefore murder and serious injury which may be committed in sadistic excitement have here in reality, as far as is known, no passive equivalent" (1892b). He used the term *moral masochism* (1892a) for the behavior and affect not immediately associated with sexual excitation; it provided "a moral satisfaction from the idea of enslavement."[2]

2. In the seventh edition (1892b) this is spoken of as "moral satisfaction," in contrast to "sensually colored masochism" (p. 88). In the twelfth edition, the term has become "moral masochism."

When masochistic experiences were restricted to fantasy, the term *ideal masochism* was used.

With only three exceptions, Krafft-Ebing's case reports described masochism in males and included being bound, flagellated, and degraded. As for masochism in women, he stated (1892b):

> In women voluntary subjection to the opposite sex is a physiological phenomenon. Owing to her passive *role* in procreation and long existent social conditions, ideas of subjection are, in women, normally connected with the idea of sexual relations. They form, so to speak, the harmonics which determine the tone quality of feminine feeling. (p. 33)

The three female cases of masochism were in the *ideal* category and involved fantasies of flagellation by men or submission to them.

In sum, Krafft-Ebing's conclusions about the psychodynamics of masochism contained three central concepts. First, the basic element in masochism was a desire for complete subjugation and tyranny. The submission was seen as a response to abnormal dependence on the sexual object in order to guarantee a continuation of love and sexual gratification. Abnormal dependence was termed "sexual bondage." Second, a sexualization of submission occurred as the consequence of a long-standing association of submission to a love object: *"When the idea of being tyrannized is for a long time closely associated with a lustful thought of the beloved person the lustful emotion is finally transferred to the tyranny itself and the transformation to perversion is completed"* (1892b, p. 141). Third, certain individuals had a "pathological intensification of lust" and required painful stimuli to reinforce the more usual types of sexual stimuli. He did not account for this oversexed condition, which he called "hyperesthesia sexualis," other than to observe that it frequently occurred in "mentally abnormal" individuals. Hyperesthesia sexualis was interpreted as the basic psychical substratum required for the development of sadism and masochism. It now appears that the hyperesthesia sexualis he referred to is a combination of sexual inhibition and a compulsive attempt to overcome it through esoteric, compulsive, or other such adaptive maneuvers as may be observed among nymphomaniacs and prostitutes.

Freud's initial formulation of sadism (1905b) was essentially the same as that of Krafft-Ebing; he considered sadism to be an exaggeration of the normal aggressive component of the masculine sexual instinct. Freud added the notion that the sadistic component could become independent and "by displacement usurp the leading position" (p. 158). Clearly derivative was the equation of sadism with masculinity and activity and of masochism with femininity and passivity. As a basic innovation, Freud linked masochistic pain to disgust and shame, a force interfering with the expression of the sexual instinct, but one that is overriden by the masochistic acceptance of the pain. Thus, without stating it explicitly, Freud identified masochism as a defense. Each author, however, related sadism to masochism in a unity of opposites in such a way that no explanation inapplicable to both perversions was believed to be adequate.

Freud first formulated masochism as a transformation of sadism. He rather doubted the existence of a primary masochism, although he spoke of an "original passive sexual attitude . . . exaggerated and fixated by a great number of factors such as the castration complex and the sense of guilt" (p. 158). In a later paper (1915a), however, Freud returned to the idea of primary masochism. Although he still maintained that masochism was a transformation of sadism, he now thought that the original sadistic behavior of childhood was unrelated to awareness or concern with inflicting pain destructively. In adults, however, the pleasure in sadistic behavior was based on an identification with the injured person and became a projection of masochistic pleasure. Reversing his original position, he viewed sadistic pleasure as rooted in masochism. At the same time, the defensive use of sadism and masochism continued to hold Freud's attention: "In both cases (sadism and masochism), of course, it is not the pain itself which is enjoyed, but the accompanying sexual excitation—so that this can be done especially conveniently from the sadistic position" (1915a, p. 129). The idea that pain is not enjoyed in itself was carried over in his paper, "A Child Is Being Beaten" (1919).

This being beaten is now a conversion of the sense of guilt and sexual love. It is not only the punishment for the forbidden genital relation, but also the regressive substitute for that relation, and from this latter source it derives the libidinal excitation which is from this time found attached to it and finds its outlet in masturbatory acts. Here for the first time we find the essence of masochism. (p. 189)

AN INSTINCTUAL INTERPRETATION

This statement contains the important formulation that masochism represents the punishment for the sense of guilt associated with forbidden oedipal wishes. Freud is describing masochism as a defense, since guilt and the need for punishment are defensive mechanisms deriving from a wish to placate the oedipal object perceived as being aggressed upon. Freud also identified passivity with femininity and masochism with passivity, and elaborated the thesis that masochism in the male was a primary feminine wish:

> In their masochistic fantasies, as well as in performances, they invariably transfer themselves into the part of a woman; that is to say, their masochistic attitude coincides with a *feminine* one . . . it makes no difference if they keep up the fiction that a mischievous boy or page or apprentice is going to be punished. On the other hand, the persons who administer the chastisement are always women, both in fantasies and performance. This is confusing enough and the further question must be asked whether this feminine attitude already forms the basis of the masochistic elements in the *infantile* beating fantasy. (1919, p. 197).

Freud concluded that the mother as the beating figure was a disguise for the father, and that the beating was tolerated to win the father's love. The wish for paternal love was thought to be a feminine sexual wish; masochism mediated the gratification of the feminine wish.

After formulating the death instinct, Freud (1924a) abandoned the idea that pain was not enjoyed for itself. He postulated that there was a primary erotogenic masochism manifested in a lust for pain or pleasure in pain. Primary erotogenic masochism was conceived to be a representation of the death instinct; part of this instinct was directed to the outer world under the influence of

Eros to become "the destructive instinct, the instinct for mastery, or the will to power" (p. 163).

> A portion of this instinct is placed directly in the service of the sexual function; another portion does not share in this transformation outward; it remains inside the organism and with the help of accompanying sexual excitation becomes libidinally bound there. It is in this position that we have to recognize the original erotogenic masochism. (p. 163)

Thus, sadism and masochism became portions of the death instinct and were libidinized. Masochism emerged as primary and related to the death instinct, whereas sadism derived from masochism. Erotogenic masochism was integrated with the libido theory:

> Erotogenic masochism accompanies the libido through all its developmental phases and derives from them its changing psychical coatings. The fear of being eaten up by the totem animal (the father) originates from the primitive oral organization; the wish to be beaten by the father comes from the sadistic anal phase which follows it; castration, although it is later disavowed, enters into the content of masochistic fantasies as a precipitate of the phallic stage or organization; and from the final genital organization there arise, of course, the situations of being copulated with and of giving birth which are characteristic of femaleness. (p. 165)

Freud defined three types of masochism, all rooted in erotogenic masochism — erotogenic, feminine, and moral. Moral masochism emphasizes the wish to suffer rather than to experience actual physical pain. Superficially, moral masochism appears to be unrelated to sexuality, but according to Freud it is based on unconscious guilt related to oedipal wishes, thereby maintaining its basic sexual character.

In sum, Freud initially accepted Krafft-Ebing's views of sadism. Masochism was thought to be a transformation of sadism directed against the self. In his changing concepts of masochism, Freud developed the idea that it represented the punishment associated with guilt for oedipal wishes. After formulating the death instinct, he postulated a primary erotogenic masochism deriving from the death instinct and explained sadism as the directing outward of the death instinct under the influence of Eros. Primary erotogenic masochism became the instinctual basis for feminine masochism, which, in the male, was represented by sexual wishes for the father; moral masochism was represented by the wish to be beaten by the father in punishment for unacceptable oedipal desires.

AN ADAPTIVE INTERPRETATION

Freud had considered two alternative hypotheses, that masochism was instinctive or that it was adaptive. He chose to develop the instinctual hypothesis. Wilhelm Reich (1945) was the first author to discard the instinctual hypothesis:

> The change of the concept of masochism automatically involved a change of the etiological formula of the neurosis. Freud's original concept was that the psychic development takes place in the conflict between instincts and the outer world. Now the concept came to be that the psychic conflict was the result of a conflict between Eros (sexual

libido) and death instinct (instinct to self-destruction, primary masochism). The clinical starting point for this dubious hypothesis was the peculiar fact that certain patients seem to be unwilling to relinquish their suffering and keep seeking painful situations. This was in contradiction to the pleasure principle. There seemed to be a hidden inner intention to hold onto the suffering and to experience it again and again. The question was whether this "will to suffer" was a primary biological tendency or a secondary psychic formation. (p. 213)

Reich proposed that masochism was a defense and involved the principle of choosing the lesser injury. He described a patient who, in his third year, had been punished by his father for soiling himself.

The boy immediately turned on his stomach and waited for the beating with great curiosity mixed with anxiety. The blows were heavy but the boy had a feeling of relief. They were harmless compared to the anticipated injury to the genitals and thus relieved him of a good deal of anxiety. . . . The masochistic beating fantasy thus anticipates in a milder form an expected heavy punishment. . . . It represents a specific mode of defense against punishment and anxiety. (p. 221)

Further, masochism was conceptualized as an adaptive maneuver oriented toward punishing those who had disappointed the patient in his love needs during childhood.

His complaints have the following layers of meaning corresponding to the genesis of his masochism. "Look how miserable I am—please love me. You don't love me enough and you treat me badly . . . you must love me. I shall force you to or else I am going to annoy you." (p. 225)

Reich postulated that the masochist had an excessive
need for love which was based on fear of being left alone,
a fear intensely experienced in early childhood. He also
observed that the masochist was fearful of being outstanding. Freud (1916) had noted a fear of success (p. 316), but
he had not linked it to masochism as had Reich:

> Masochistic characters cannot stand praise and have a
> strong tendency toward self-depreciation. Despite a great
> ambition our patient could not stand being near the top of
> his class. "If I remained a good student I would feel as if I
> was standing in front of a crowd showing my erect penis."
> (p. 232)

The fear of receiving recognition was presumed to be the
basis for fears about genital exhibitionism stemming from
parental suppression of genital exposure. Reich's contribution to the understanding of masochism was important
in that he stressed its defensive and adaptive use. Reich
was the first to question explicitly an instinctual basis for
masochism; he concluded that it was a defense.

MASOCHISM AS EXCESSIVE SUFFERING

Karen Horney provided the next major clarification.
Krafft-Ebing had pointed out that not all cruelty was
sadistic; now Horney declared that not all suffering was
masochistic but was frequently an unintended by-product
of neurotic conflict. She considered as masochistic only
that type of neurotic suffering which resulted from "a tendency to suffer." According to Horney (1937):

> Suffering may have a direct defense value for the neurotic
> and may often in fact be the only way to protect himself

against imminent danger. By self-recrimination he avoids being accused and accusing others, by appearing ill or ignorant he avoids reproaches, by belittling himself he avoids the danger of competition—but the suffering he thereby brings on himself is at the same time a defense. (p. 262)

Horney emphasized the use of masochistic suffering as an adaptive maneuver seen in domination, exploitation, evasion of demands, and provocation of guilt in others; however, she believed that the masochist suffered more than was necessary to achieve neurotic goals: "There still remains the question of why such suffering can yield satisfaction as it obviously does in masochistic perversions and fantasies and as we suspect it does in the general neurotic tendency toward suffering" (p. 264). To explain her idea of excessive suffering she proposed "an inclination or tendency toward weakness" and "a satisfaction in losing the self in something greater by dissolving the individualistic, by getting rid of the self with its doubts, conflicts, pains, limitations and isolations" (p. 270), which she identified with the "Dionysian tendency" of Nietzsche. The conceptual similarity to Freud's theory of a death instinct may be noted in her view that there is a universal tendency to relinquish the self: "When masochistic strivings are thus integrated into the general phenomenon of a striving to relinquish the individual self, the satisfaction that is sought or obtained by weakness loses its strangeness" (p. 275). Horney's formulation of satisfaction in suffering and in weakness is an elaboration of the pleasure-in-pain hypothesis. Her addition is nevertheless based on instinct theory, despite omission of the sexual component. Horney had at first advanced the idea that masochism was a defense; however, this explanation was apparently as incomplete for her as it was for Freud.

Theodor Reik (1941) contributed a critical evaluation of Freud's theory of primary masochism and feminine masochism, rejecting the formulation of a primary masochism on the ground that it could not be demonstrated in early childhood. "An early psychologically comprehensible proof of primary masochism is nowhere to be found" (p. 188). He questioned whether the masochist *originally* sought pain for pleasure. "I am of the opinion," he wrote, "that there is no original pleasure from discomfort as is commonly attributed to masochism. Is it originally lust in pain? Or is it lust in spite of pain?" (p. 191). "The punishment has to be executed so that one can attain the forbidden pleasure. The main thing is not the punishment, but the achievement of the instinctual aim" (p. 208). Though he regarded the pain in punishment as the means toward the end of pleasure, nevertheless Reik postulated that the means could become an end in itself; pain itself could become a pleasurable goal: "The urge for pleasure is so powerful that anxiety and the idea of punishment themselves are drawn into its sphere and they are finally established as the pleasure aim" (p. 191). In this regard, Reik's disagreement with Freud is more apparent than real.

Theodor Reik's differences with Freud about feminine masochism are twofold. First, the woman as the beating figure in male masochistic fantasies and behavior was seen as a composite of the mother and the threatening father as originally organized in the oedipus complex:

> The beating person therefore is a composite figure. She is the loving and loved woman but with the punishing gesture

of the father. She stands in the place of the first love object, the mother, whom the boy has coveted but in the father's place as well, for whose sake the object had to be abandoned. The composite figure therefore consists of two people: the person one strives to possess and the other woman one wishes to be owned by. The renounced and the new figure, the adored and the dreaded figure have been fused into one. (p. 23)

Second, Reik did not regard normal femininity as masochistic:

Other features, however, resist the assumption that the relationship of masochism to femininity is as intensive as Freud believed. This relationship is by no means explained as with the passive homosexual. Passivity may not be easily separable from feminine sexuality but the suffering of pain, being beaten or tied up, disgraces or humiliations do not belong to the sexual aims of the normal woman. When such ideas appear conspicuously on the psychical surface and become conditions of sexual gratification we should call the woman concerned a masochist. (p. 197)

INTEGRATION OF INSTINCTUAL AND ADAPTIVE VIEWS

Edmund Bergler's views on masochism (1949) integrated the instinctual and adaptational hypotheses. He differentiated perversion masochism from psychic masochism though these formulations were essentially the same as sexual and moral masochism. Of perversion masochism he wrote, "The direct bodily pain is perceived by these strange human beings as pleasurable" (p. 12).

Psychic masochism was regarded as neurotically displaced aggression:

> Psychic masochism means unconscious pleasure derived from self-punishment. . . . It is an unconscious act of outwitting the punishing conscience. . . . Psychic masochism is not an unconscious wish but a complicated inner defense mechanism created by the unconscious ego. . . . Genetically psychic masochism is undigested aggression; that aggression is counteracted by guilt and secondarily libidinized. Clinically psychic masochists crave for a libidinous pleasure of refusal, humiliation and defeat. (p. 13)

Thus, in Bergler's constructs, the masochist perceives pain as pleasure and seeks it for its libidinal value.

Sandor Rado's contribution (1956) to theories of sadism and masochism stresses adaptational theory. In this context, the sadist and masochist become "pain dependent" as a way of functioning sexually:

> Pain dependence develops in early life in response to disciplinary stress. If restrictive upbringing defeats the child's defiant rage, his pursuit of forbidden pleasure may take the roundabout way of pain dependence. We define this mechanism as the forced and automatized pursuit of advance punishment as the only means by which the individual can attain license to gratify his forbidden desires. Here the anticipation of pleasure overrules the deterrent action of pain. . . . In the frightened or submissive form of pain dependence (masochism) the individual achieves orgasm by inviting the required painful stimulation from the mate; and in the angry or defiant form (sadism) by venting his rage upon the mate and thus hiding his own vicarious suffering, his true source of orgastic stimulation, beneath his sense of triumph. (pp. 201–202)

Thus, erotic sadistic satisfaction is achieved through vicarious identification with the suffering victim and not through pleasure in inflicting pain per se, a dynamic reminiscent of Freud's later position in which sadism was derived from masochism. To discriminate between sexual and nonsexual masochism Rado conceptualized "moral pain dependence" as the subjective suffering required for gratification in nonsexual functions: "This disorder belongs to the pathology not of the sexual function but of the conscience" (p. 55). Rado (1959) described this state as occurring in patients "caught in or regressed to the adaptive pattern of infantile dependence," in whom "the pride the patient now takes in his over-morality is a compensation for the pride he had originally taken in his over-assertiveness which he was then forced to renounce" (p. 55).

Clara Thompson emphasized the manipulative aspects of masochism in interpersonal relationships (1959, p. 33)—that masochism is a security operation in an attempt to gain the attention, love, and dependency lacking in childhood. Characterologically the masochist manifests "great apparently passive dependency" and "hostile aggression" through suffering and martyrdom, in this way provoking guilt in others who then feel compelled to assume the burdens of care and responsibility. Thus, she conceptualized masochism as a transactional device for personal gain.

SADISM AND MASOCHISM
AS RESPONSES TO THREAT

In general, there is a broader literature on the subject of masochism than of sadism. This may be because inflicting violence on others seems more comprehensible than the repetitive, compulsive seeking of self-injury, a confounding and provocative problem. On the subject of sadism, authors have, in the main, directed themselves to the sexual perversions, whereas, in masochism, more attention has been focused on the nonsexual aspects. In my view, masochism and sadism are maladaptive, pathological responses to a threat or a perception of threat in every context of experience. Sadism is a defensive, paranoid mechanism in which the victim is a personified representative of a variety of irrationally perceived threats; he must then be dominated, injured, neutralized, or destroyed. The affect is a complex of rage, anxiety, relief, vengeance, and frenetic ecstasy accompanying a sense of triumph in subjugating an irrationally perceived enemy or in extinguishing a threat. The affect complex has been confused with sexual pleasure, particularly when the affects *accompany* sexual excitation.

Destructive impulses and acts against the self intended consciously or unconsciously to be injurious can be divided into two major categories: (1) attitudes and behaviors having as a primary goal self-destruction, annihilation, and death; and (2) self-destructiveness that is defensive and directed toward preserving life, love, or other important interests. I consider only the latter category to represent masochism. Krafft-Ebing's and Freud's early writings on masochism were not concerned with suicide. However, after Freud had evolved his concept of a death instinct, he then related masochism to it, thereby obfuscating the motivational differences between self-destructive behaviors aiming at preservation and self-destructiveness aiming at death.

The following discussion is largely devoted to the phenomenology, psychodynamics, and transactional processes of masochism. But first, a short statement on self-destructiveness directed toward extinction. Suicidal drives are goal-directed. Death, not pleasure, is the aim. There may be anticipation of relief from torment and pain, but I do not equate such expectations with pleasure. Certainly, masochistic pleasure has never been associated with *relief* of pain.

Suicide is the ultimate dynamism of depression. The notion that intraverted hostility is one, if not the sole, salient determinant of depression has wide acceptance. I am not in accord with this view. In some cases of depression, hostility may indeed be an important factor; however, hostility is usually only one element in a constellation of interpersonal interactions. Furthermore, hostility is not always observable, for instance, when depression follows the discovery of a fatal illness. Three elements may be found to be consistently associated with depression: a sense of loss or threat of loss, overwhelming feelings of helplessness, and an unambiguous conviction of hopelessness. A sense of loss may apply to the individual's self-system, as in the loss of self-esteem, or physical attractiveness, or a function. It also may be related to the loss of a loved one, a job, money—in short, the loss of something highly valued. Hopelessness is a concomitant of a belief in inevitable defeat. Why some people accept defeat while others are impelled toward self-destruction is not yet completely understood. It is also a problem beyond the scope of this chapter. But one might speculate that those who cannot endure defeat have a low threshold of tolerance for frustration, whether of mastery, comfort, or pleasure. Nor can such individuals long withstand the pain of anxiety or of self-hatred. Children who tend to destroy what they cannot master, who give up easily and decompensate in helpless rage when mastery is uncertain, may well become adults who react to loss with self-annihilating impulses or behavior. For purposes of clarity, the extinction type of self-destructiveness must be differentiated from masochism.

Masochism, conscious or unconscious, aims at bringing pain or injury to the self; the injury may be self-inflicted, or encouraged, or tolerated in an attempt to prevent hostility and destructiveness by others; or injury may be sought as a way of evoking positive affects in others toward the self (see chapter 9). The masochistic act or attitude is a defense against even greater injury by another, as first pointed out by Reich. By injury, I refer to any effect sensed as detrimental to an optimal state at any moment in personal history. The perception of injury and one's concept of optimal state may be operant at any level of psychosomatic integration and one may or may not be capable of formulating them consciously. In masochism, the expectation of injury is almost always based on irrational grounds, although an automatic reliance on masochistic behavior may set off maladaptive attempts to cope with a realistic threat, as is illustrated in the case of a young child described further on. Self-injury may be appropriate only when there is a conscious choice of a lesser injury, as, for example, when a man, to preserve his life, amputates his finger bitten by a poisonous snake. Such an act cannot be considered masochistic since it is effective, adaptive behavior.

Masochism was originally observed and described in connection with sexuality. It integrates with sexual activity as a defensive mechanism to localize and identify the source of anticipated injury and to circumscribe the extent of threat. Two systems are integrated in masochistic sexuality—the sexual system and an interpersonal power system involving submission-domination. Masochism is a component of the power system. In a classical example of male masochism, the patient fantasies or acts out the role of victim in abject submission to a powerful female who beats him on the buttocks, thus enabling him to experience orgasm. In the sexual constellation, a woman and a man are engaged in sexual activity—the behavioral theme is heterosexual, but sexual inhibition is apparent in the exclusion of each partner's genitals from the role play. Substituting buttocks (and anus) for genitals is a *defensive* substitution resulting from the man's fear of genital contact in the heterosexual act; but it is not part of a *masochistic* defense, since injury to self is not intended.

Anal participation may occur in male homo- or heterosexual activity without concomitant masochism. In my construct, the punishment acted out in the beating *integrates* with the sexual system and is the sole aspect connected with masochism. The punishment is tolerated because of fear of injury for the sexual act. The expectation of injury derives from sexual prohibitions and anxieties stemming from a reciprocally hostile, competitive relationship with the ipsosexual parent. In the power system, the female is assigned power and dominance, whereas the male assumes a weak, helpless, submissive stance. By investing the woman with magical power, the masochist feels protected against other fearsome threats, particularly the feared, aggressive, male rival. The masochist strives to contain all expectations of injury within the powerful female, thereby delimiting the extent of injury, because, first, he does not expect her to inflict overweening injury; and second, he is aware that he can terminate the psychological farce if necessary and physically overcome the woman. By localizing the source and extent of the feared injury, the masochist is able to function sexually.

That the masochist *desires* injury is only a partial explanation. He *requires* it to perform sexually. To paraphrase Rado, the masochist is sexually injury-dependent. Further, by inflating feminine power, it is hoped that the woman will be strong enough to overcome sexual inhibitions — an inverse rape fantasy. Apart from its value as punishment, the beating serves to confirm the female's power. The delusional image of her strength is achieved through mechanisms of self-minimizing, self-degradation, and self-humiliation, mechanisms that contribute substantially to masochistic self-injury.

The sexual and power systems are also integrated in sexual sadism and, as with masochism, sadism articulates with the power system. The sadist assumes delusional power for himself, as may be observed in grandiose paranoid states. Having invested himself with power, the sadist may now dominate, neutralize, or destroy his victim, who personifies either of two symbolic condensations — agents or forces restricting his sexuality (as represented by parents, more especially by the same-sex parent), or impulses and attitudes felt to be unacceptable, such as sexuality, hostility, submission, and masochism. In the latter circumstance, the victim is punished for arousing threatening sexual impulses or for exposing to view characteristics believed to be contemptible, such as submission and masochism, which the sadist fears he may express.

The sexual masochist usually has a single, idiosyncratic erotic stimulus. For one individual, it may involve being beaten on the buttocks; for another, it may involve being stepped on with a woman's leather heel, and so forth. The stimuli are not interchangeable; the substitution of one painful stimulus for another does not elicit sexual arousal. The fetishist who desires to be stepped on with a leather heel does not wish to be whipped or pricked with pins. Moreover, there is apparently a widespread assumption that the sexual masochist experiences pain since the activities involved would produce pain in nonsexual situations; whether he actually experiences pain has not been investigated, though anecdotal evidence strongly suggests a relative absence of pain during intense sexual excitation. During rage and sexual excitement, the threshold for awareness of pain is sharply heightened, so much so that should pain be felt during sexual activity, the excitation would most probably terminate. The masochist seems to experience pain on that part of his body where he was beaten after the sexual act has been completed, but such pain does not appear to be desired; rather, it must be tolerated as the inevitable consequence of the masochistic perversion (see p. 195).

Several authors, including Krafft-Ebing and Freud, have sought a physiological explanation for the capacity to respond to painful stimuli in such a way that they initiate or enhance sexual excitation. Krafft-Ebing postulated that pain and sexual excitement were intense sensual experiences, and the very intensity of pain reinforced the intensity of the sexual experience. Freud suggested a similar idea in his economic theory, that is, when any tension reached a sufficiently high level it could overflow into sexual channels. I suggest that anxiety itself can set off and reinforce sexual excitation. Physiologically, anxiety and sexual arousal are excitatory reactions. Masochism is always accompanied by anxiety since all masochistic behavior, sexual and nonsexual, is directed toward injury to self. The masochistic perversion permits a circumvention of inhibition that would characterize the sexual act if the masochistic defense were absent, but the perversion does not permit an escape from anxiety. Thus, the masochist must choose, on the one hand, between impotence without masochism and, on the other, orgasm accompanied by the anxiety linked to masochism. The anxiety's reinforcement helps override inhibition, but it also accounts for premature orgasm, which generally accompanies masochistic sexuality.

Although sexual masochism is relatively uncommon, nonsexual masochism may be demonstrated in most psychiatric patients, as well as in many who are not patients. Masochistic defenses appearing in nonsexual behaviors are particularly evident in attitudes and acts felt to be competitive. Fears, whether real or fancied, of antagonizing competitors by successful performance and fears of evoking competitive or hostile feelings among rivals tend to induce self-sabotaging tactics. The scuttling of one's resources results, of course, in diminished effectiveness or failure. Masochistic mechanisms of this order may be observed among patients with severe work inhibitions. The self-sabotage is purposive, since it is defensively aimed at preventing anticipated injury from feared competitors. Masochistic techniques that preclude achievement or dissipate the fruits of success are common phenomena; these are defensive patterns mobilized against fears of success. Although the anticipation of threat and injury from a competitor is almost always based on neurotic distortions, the defensive sabotage is realistically hurtful to self.

Motivation for assertive, constructive action may evoke masochistic defenses when there is a conviction that satisfaction of a goal deprives or hurts others. This derives from nonrational systems of beliefs about competition. The rational wish to marry for love or to succeed in a creative venture may evoke guilt, followed by fears of reprisal. These fears are reinforced when competitive responses are expressed by others, thereby lending support in reality to false premises and promoting secondary sabotage. Action sensed as offensive to those in power positions may also be viewed as aggressive and may be defended against by a masochistic renunciation. When motives are destructive, as in minimizing or humiliating others, or when the effect is destructive, as in exploitation and domination, there may be flight toward masochism. The masochistic response is a common defense against erroneous expectations of injury for self-enhancing behavior, which is, in fact, personally and socially constructive.

Freud theorized, as had Krafft-Ebing, that masochism was instinctive in women and sadism was instinctive in men. This was consonant with Freud's view that women were submissive and passive while men were aggressive and active. He proceeded with these assumptions as though they were established facts based on innate human characteristics. The patients with masochistic sexual perversions described by Krafft-Ebing were mostly males, and though such symptoms are relatively uncommon, they seem to occur as frequently among females as among males. When masochistic behavior is not explicitly sexual, there appears to be no difference between the sexes in frequency, in quality, or in the psychodynamic processes that promote it. In general, masochism represents a

defensive adaptation to threat, even as submission represents a defensive, self-protective posture in either sex.
Passivity is not a feminine characteristic; it is the manifestation of chronic inhibition of effective resources and is as
pathological for females as for males. Submission is one of
the basic biosocial responses of the species to threat. In
Western culture, however, passivity, submissiveness, and
dependency are more acceptable for females; but such
cultural themes do not establish these attitudes and
behaviors as nonpathological. Rather, they indicate that
women are not yet fully emancipated.

Masochistic defense patterns may emerge in early
childhood, as was observed in a three-and-a-half-year-old
girl in whom self-injury had already been obvious for one
year. Since both parents were present when I examined
the child, I could witness the interactions among the
three. During the preceding year, whenever one parent,
especially the mother, punished the girl physically, the
child would inflict or threaten to inflict self-injury. She
would strike her hands or head on solid objects with sufficient force to produce hematomata; or she would burn
her hand on a radiator, or over an open gas flame if she
could get to it. By these maneuvers she was largely successful in preventing physical punishment. The mother
was noticeably hostile, overcontrolling, and resentful
about her child's seeming victory in their power struggle;
corporeal punishment was not entirely renounced, despite
the disturbing consequences. The child learned to extend
her defensive tactics. When a physician inadvertently
gagged her with a tongue depressor during pharyngeal
examination, the child tore at her buccal mucosa, drawing blood and successfully discouraging further examination. On another occasion during aural examination,

the physician apparently hurt her. She tore at the skin of her external auditory canal, this time also drawing blood. During my interview with the child, she became playfully and affectionately related to me; the mother's irritation and displeasure were overt. In this case a masochistic technique was discovered that partially controlled attack, particularly from the mother. It demonstrates a basic principle of masochism: self-inflicted injury wards off threats believed to be even more dangerous. The child's masochism was her defense against external threat. For the masochistic pattern to become established, it must have had adaptive value at some time, even though it is essentially maladaptive.

When masochistic patterns are salient in personality organization, case study generally reveals its syntonia with either or both parents who, by direct or anfractuous means, have induced such patterns of response. Thus, masochistic behavior may terminate or control parental hostility; sometimes even positive affects may be evoked. Two major types of parental psychopathology foster filial masochism: hostility and ambivalence toward a child, and the acting out of masochism through a child. In the latter instance, parental expectations of injury, including the fear of having a valued child, may be projected to that child, who becomes the focus for obsessive concern and overanxious, restrictive, overprotective behavior. The parent may identify with a child and hope to fulfill his own frustrated ambitions through the success of his offspring, only to become as anxious about the child's achievement as he was of his own. It is not my purpose here to describe the multiplicity of parental psychopathological transactions that foster masochism, but it must be emphasized that masochism emerges and develops as a patterned response because it has actually had adaptive value in coping with cardinal figures in a life history.

Freud postulated that sadism could be introverted to produce secondary masochism; Bergler held that introversion of aggression was at the core of masochism. The enraged child who bites himself instead of biting the restricting, punishing adult is familiar. According to the formulation emphasized, the child's self-inflicted injury is a milder, more controlled attack than he may expect from his stronger opponent. I have differentiated between two categories of action defended against by the masochistic maneuver; the first, in which the motivation of action is constructive and directed toward constructive goals though the motives themselves may be irrationally believed to be aggressive, as in the wish to succeed in a creative venture; and the second, in which action is intended to be destructive, as in hostility and contempt. It is only in the latter category that introversion of aggression can occur, since *the wish itself* contains destructive intent. But even in such instances the psychodynamics must be demonstrated by the data. Should masochism be interpreted to the patient as the introversion of aggression when, in fact, the masochism is a defense against fear of consummating a constructive act, the therapist only confirms the patient's neurotic fear that goal satisfaction is aggressive and hurtful to others. Such a course only reinforces irrational guilt feelings, inhibition, and depression. The interpretation that masochism is introverted aggression requires caution and support by reliable evidence.

As has been emphasized, masochism is by definition self-injurious and always precipitates anxiety. Now anxiety is not "neurotic." When there is perceptual distortion, the sense of danger that sets off an anxiety response may be a false alarm, but the anxiety itself is an automatic bio-physiological reaction to a perception of injury whether the injury is threatened by the self or others. The intensity of the anxiety is commensurate with the extent of anticipated self-destructiveness. The turbulent affect seen in agitated depressions stems in part from masochistic acting out or from impulses to act out profoundly self-destructive acts. Guilt feelings and self-recrimination usually associated with sadistic or hostile acts also follow self-injury, as in the acting out of destructiveness toward others. Guilt emerging in the wake of self-destructiveness is all the more painful and depressing since, on a conscious level, the masochist realizes the futility and waste involved in self-injury although he cannot account for the reasons. Further, guilt is intensified by an awareness of the injury done to others caught in the web of self-generated failures. The masochist often tends to pull others down with him, for example, narcotic addicts and alcoholics in whom masochism is pronounced.

The psychopathology of everyday masochism is defended against by a variety of behavioral controls. Fear of masochistically forgetting an important appointment may be defended against by fortifying one's self with various reminders; or where the home is a symbol of security and fulfillment, fear of masochistically destroying it may set off an obsessive need to check the gas jets; or fear of acting out self-injury may involve one in health and body-building fads, or in carrying unrealistically large and burdensome health and accident insurance policies.

Masochism and submission are often indistinguishable but are not identical as adaptational techniques. Each constellation, however, aims at forestalling reprisals from an external object, or preventing or extinguishing in others negative affect toward self, or evoking in the feared object positive affect. Though self-injury is intrinsic to masochism, submission may occur without self-directed injury, as in capitulation to a stronger opponent and submitting to terms of surrender without masochistic concomitants.

TREATMENT SUGGESTIONS

As the behavioral manifestations of defensive mechanisms, sadism and masochism are, in a sense, symptom complexes. One cannot, therefore, properly speak of the treatment of sadism and masochism. Psychoanalysis is no longer oriented to the treatment of symptoms per se; as in other medical specialties, treatment is directed to the underlying psychopathology, which consists of irrationally held beliefs and belief systems associated with erroneous expectations of injury. The therapeutic process is concerned primarily with the delineation of nonrational convictions; with developing the patient's insight into false premises, their history, current meaning, and elaborations; and, in specific sequences where sadism or masochism may be involved, with reinforcing realistically adaptive behavior by demonstrating the ineffectiveness of masochistic and sadistic defenses. A fundamental change in defensive patterns does not occur until the patient becomes convinced that he will not be hurt for acts that he had connected with punishment and injury to himself. Beliefs associated with anticipations of injury are not easily altered. The person who is afraid to fly is convinced that whatever plane he takes will crash.

Nor are defenses easily relinquished. The organization of a pattern of defensive reactions to the expectation of a multiplicity of potential interpersonal hurts becomes a habitual life style. Masochistic self-destructive maneuvers are attempts to defend against many kinds of anticipated hurts from others—aggression, competition, rejection, and so forth. For this reason, patients having a masochistic life style are difficult to treat successfully. Successful outcome requires a long course of therapy, along with patience and persistence to withstand the discouragement that follows repetitive, compulsive, self-defeating behavior. The compulsive loser, after years of treatment and clearing his debts, may still act out by once again losing large sums of money and getting himself into serious debt. Another patient may be able to establish a love relationship but is fearful of marriage. Even after treatment has been proceeding satisfactorily, he may break up a good potential marriage. Masochistic persons often express self-destructiveness in their marriage. Although they desire a happy union free of conflict, fears about having a successful marriage and a happy life impel such patients to provoke discord just when gratification is possible. Provocative maneuvers are frequently subtle, and the therapist must be alert to the actual state of affairs. Couples come to know each other's vulnerable spot, the Achilles' heel. Sensitivities are abraded toward masochistic ends and aggressive reactions are provoked in the mate, who is made to appear cruel and unfeeling. If the therapist fails to understand these manipulations, he may be taken in by the deception and his patient comes to be seen as victim rather than as aggressor. The evaluative task is complicated when a patient is married to a sadistic person whose sadism articulates with the patient's masochism; or, when both married partners are masochists, it becomes difficult to judge which of the two is initiating discord and which is responding and retaliating. Patients who spend session after session complaining about injustices inflicted upon them by the spouse are acting out masochistically in the therapeutic situation. Such obsessive, repetitive complaints are unproductive and preclude constructive work. The continued recounting of defeats and feelings of inadequacy is also a masochistic sabotage of treatment. The primary therapeutic task is to delineate unrealistic beliefs associated with irrational premises concerning expectations of being hurt. One must avoid losing one's self in the patient's complex, defensive maneuvers and, instead, focus on developing his insight into the connection between his masochism and his anticipation of injury against which he is trying to defend himself. When the patient begins to accept the idea that punishment and injury are not currently associated with gratification, sexual and other, it becomes possible for him to think more critically about self-destructive defenses. He may thus come to recognize that, even in the face of injury, real or imagined, masochism is a maladaptive, meaningless defense.

The same theoretical constructs and methods apply to problems involving sadism. The sadistic patient must also be brought to an awareness of his primary fears and come to understand his defensive motives and paranoid projections to his victim.

Chapter 11

Phenomenology and Psychodynamics of Sadism and Masochism

Krafft-Ebing (1892c) explained sadism in two ways; the first applied to both sexes.

At the moment of most intense lust, very excitable individuals who are otherwise normal, commit such acts as biting and scratching which are usually due to anger. It must further be remembered that love and anger are not only the most intense emotion but also they are the only two forms of robust emotion.

The idea that sex and anger are the only two forms of "robust emotion" is original and prophetic; it is a forerunner of Freud's (1920) theory that there are two basic instincts, sex and aggression. The concept that one excitatory organization—sexuality—can lock into and use behavioral components of another excitatory organization—anger and rage—gains support from the observations of ethologists who demonstrated that components of the attack constellation of behavior are incorporated into the sexual organization (Thorpe and Zangwill 1961).

Krafft-Ebing's second explanation centered around the concept of power, specifically, masculine power.

> In the intercourse of the sexes, the active or aggressive role belongs to the man; woman remains passive-defensive. It affords a man great pleasure to win a woman, to conquer her; and in the art of love making the modesty of a woman who keeps herself on the defensive until the moment of surrender, is an element of great psychological significance and importance. Under normal conditions, man meets obstacles which it is his part to overcome, and for which his nature has given him an aggressive character. This aggressive character, however, under pathological conditions may likewise be excessively developed, and express itself in an impulse to subdue absolutely the object of desire, either to destroy it or kill it.

Power was the central idea in Krafft-Ebing's view of sadism and masochism. It was conceived to be a biological component of sexuality. In sadism, power was biologically rooted and masculine; its function was to overcome feminine resistance in the service of propagation. Masochism was conceptualized as feminine, since the masochist was acted upon and submitted to the power of the other; the male masochist was thought to have feminine traits. Krafft-Ebing's explanation of sadism reappeared in Freud's (1905b) discussion of it:

> As regards active algolagnia, sadism, the roots are easy to detect in the normal. The sexuality of most male human beings contains an element of *aggressiveness* — a desire to subjugate; the biological significance of it seems to lie in the needs for overcoming the resistance of the sexual object by means other than the process of wooing. Thus, sadism would correspond to an aggressive component of the sexual instinct which has become independent and exaggerated and by displacement has usurped the leading position.

Freud equated sadism with aggression, activity, masculinity; masochism with passivity and femininity. When he expanded his concepts of sexuality to include the pregenital phases — oral and anal (genetic theory) — he assigned active and passive components to each phase. The oral active component included all activities in which the mouth acted on objects, as in eating, biting, and so forth. This active component was termed the sadistic component where he again equated action and sadism. The receptive component was conceived of as the oral passive one. In the anal phase, the rectal and perianal musculature was thought to mediate the activities of the active phase, such as in the expulsion of feces. The erotogenic anal mucosa, which was eroticized by objects, including feces acting on it, was the passive component. Note that again the active component was identified with sadism, a formulation that became the basis for theorizing an anal sadistic libidinal phase. It must be remembered that Freud's formulations on sadism and libidinal phases were highly speculative; they had no foundation in observed behavior nor any relation to the syndrome of sadism described by Krafft-Ebing.

The term "sadistic" has come to be used to describe various types of cruel and destructive behavior, particularly where the perpetrator derives pleasure from it. In a literal sense, the term should be restricted to acts of cruelty that are sexually arousing. In my view, sadism is a maladaptive response to threat; it is a paranoid constellation in which the victim is a personified representative of a variety of irrationally perceived threats. The victims may represent a parent, or an authority who threatens to punish or prohibit sexual activity; or the person who arouses dangerous sexual feelings; or one who personifies submission, masochism, or other unacceptable attitudes. The victim must then be dominated, injured, neutralized, or destroyed. The affect operant in sadistic sexual behavior is a complex of rage, anxiety, relief, vengeance, and frenetic ecstasy accompanying a sense of triumph in subjugating an enemy or otherwise extinguishing a threat. The sexual sadist confuses this affect complex with sexual arousal, most particularly because sexual excitation is actually a component part of the complex.

Cases of sexual sadism are rarely encountered in psychiatric practice today. The actual frequency of such behavior is not known. Most of the reported case material has been anecdotal and derived largely from prostitutes. An index listing under sadism for either men or women is absent even from Kinsey's studies (1948, 1953).

MASOCHISM

Krafft-Ebing introduced the term "masochism" to define a syndrome described in the writings of Sacher-Masoch, a nineteenth-century novelist who was himself a masochist. Krafft-Ebing defined masochism as the opposite of sadism:

> While the latter is the desire to cause pain and use force, the former is the wish to suffer pain and to be subjected to force. By masochism, I understand a peculiar perversion of the psychical sexual life in which the individual affected in sexual feeling and thought is controlled by the idea of being completely and unconditionally subject to the will of a person of the opposite sex; of being treated by this person as by a master, humiliated and abused. This idea is colored by lustful feelings . . . from the psychopathological point of view, the essential and common element in all these cases *is the fact that* the sexual instinct is directed to ideas of *subjugation and abuse by the opposite sex.*

In defining and describing masochism, Krafft-Ebing repeatedly stressed power rather than the pain motif. The emphasis was on subjugation and abuse, not on being physically pained, whereas in sadism he stressed both the subjugation of the victim and the infliction of pain and injury. In some instances, the masochistic activity was a prerequisite for coitus; in others, it replaced coitus and resulted in orgasm without intercourse. Krafft-Ebing's case material still has heuristic value and remains didactically useful as the following cases illustrate:

Case 1. A twenty-nine-year-old male from the age of five became sexually aroused by whipping himself or fantasying other boys being whipped. He masturbated with fantasies of whipping. On the first occasion that he visited a prostitute, he was flagellated by a pretty girl but this did not produce arousal. The second time, he fantasied the idea of subjection to the woman's will and he became sexually aroused. He would also derive pleasure from the fantasy that he was a page to a beautiful girl. The patient was also fetishistic and was aroused by women wearing high heels and short jackets.

Case 2. A twenty-six-year-old male whose masochistic pattern first surfaced at the age of seven when he took part in a fight between the pupils of his school. "[Afterwards] the victors rode on the backs of the vanquished. He thought the position of the prostrate boys a pleasant one, wanted to put himself in their place, imagining how by repeated efforts he could move the boy on his back near his face so that he might inhale the odor of the boy's genitals."[1] When he reached puberty, he began to fantasy being straddled by young women who would urinate on his face and in his mouth. He never activated his masochistic fantasies and remained totally impotent and abstinent.

Case 3. A male aged twenty-eight who at the age of six had dreams of being whipped on the buttocks by women. When he became sexually active, coitus was possible only if his partner told him how she had flagellated other impotent men and threatened to give him the same treatment. At times, it was necessary for him to either fantasy himself bound or to be, in fact, bound. "The only thing in women that interested him were the hands. Powerful women with big fists were his preference."

Case 4. A thirty-four-year-old male had strong homosexual impulses but never acted them out. "Occasionally he would obtain a prostitute, undress himself completely

---

1. In this sequence, a power figure, the victor, is eroticized—a dynamic commonly observed among male homosexuals. The emphasis on odor also illustrates the mediating role of olfaction in sexuality (Bieber 1959).

(while she did not), and have her tread upon, whip and beat him. He was filled with the greatest pleasure while this was being done, and would lick the woman's foot which was the only thing that could increase his passion and he then achieved ejaculation."

Case 5. A twenty-eight-year-old male who visited a brothel once a month, "would always announce his coming with a note reading thus: 'Dear Peggy, I shall be with you tomorrow evening between eight and nine o'clock — Whip and Knout! Kindest regards.' He always arrived at the appointed hour carrying a whip, a knout and a leather strap. After undressing, he had himself bound hand and foot and was then flogged by the girl on the soles of his feet, calves and buttocks until ejaculation ensued."

Case 6. This case of a thirty-five-year-old man most clearly illuminates the psychodynamics of masochism. "Even in my early childhood I loved to revel in the ideas about the absolute mastery of one man over others. The thought of slavery had something exciting in it for me, alike whether from the standpoint of master or servant. That one man could possess, sell, or whip another caused in me intense excitement and in reading *Uncle Tom's Cabin* which I read about the beginning of puberty, I had erections. Particularly exciting for me was the thought of a man being hitched to a wagon in which another man sat with a whip driving and whipping him." After the age of twenty-one, the fantasy of a powerful figure became exclusively that of a woman. "From this time I was always in my fantasies the subject; the mistress was a rough woman who made use of me in every way, also sexually, who harnessed me to a carriage and made me take her for a drive, whom I must follow like a dog, at whose feet I must lie naked and be punished, that is, be whipped, by her."

Krafft-Ebing's emphasis on a feeling of being subjugated as the primary motif in masochism, rather than the experience of pain, is well illustrated in the above case. The power interplay initially took place between males. It was only after the patient reached the age of twenty-one that a woman who seemed powerful became a stand-in for the feared and admired powerful man. The substitutive role of the woman is further substantiated by the patient's remarks, "I remember that when I was a boy it affected me intensely when an older boy addressed me in the second person (*du*) while I spoke to him in the third (*sie*). I would keep up a conversation with him and have this change of address (*du* and *sie*) take place as often as possible. Later, when I became more mature sexually, such things affected me only when they occurred in a woman, and one relatively older than myself."

In all, Krafft-Ebing described thirty-three cases of masochism in men. Among them were those whose initial masochistic pattern could be traced to an actual spanking on the buttocks administered more often than not by a woman, though in some instances by a man. Several of the cases were examples of what was termed "ideal" masochism, by which the author meant that fantasies of masochism were indulged in but never acted out.

These cases of ideal masochism plainly demonstrate that the persons afflicted with this anomaly do not aim at actually suffering pain. The term *algolagnia,* therefore, as applied by Schrenk-Notzing and by v. Eulenburg to this anomaly, does not signify the essence, that is, the psychical nucleus of the element of masochistic sentiment and imagination. This essence consists rather of the lustfully colored consciousness of being subject to the power of another person. The ideal of even actual enactment of violence on the part of the controlling person is only the means to the end, that is, the realization of the feeling.

Clearly, the power motif was put forward as the primary theme in both sadism and masochism.

In another group of cases, fantasies about masochistic behavior were associated with foot and shoe fetishism. In some individuals, smelling and licking sweaty or dirty feet or soiled shoes were the central fetishistic elements; in others, sexual excitement occurred when a woman urinated or defecated on the subjects' bodies.

Krafft-Ebing described only three cases of sexual masochism in women: the first became sexually excited by the fantasy of being beaten on the buttocks with a rattan cane by a man. The origin of the fantasy was traced to an experience at the age of five when a friend of her father's "took her for fun across his knee pretending to whip her." The second fantasied being whipped by another woman, the fantasy accompanied by feelings of delight. The third involved a woman who would attend medical clinics so that a gynecologist would examine her against pretended resistance.

Krafft-Ebing's statements on masochism in women are especially noteworthy when compared to Freud's concepts which were identical in all major details. Krafft-Ebing stated:

> In woman, voluntary subjection to the opposite sex is a physiological phenomenon. Owing to her passive role in procreation and long existent social conditions, ideas of subjection are, in woman, normally connected with the ideas of sexual relations. They form, so to speak, the harmonics which determine the tone quality of feminine feeling . . . thus, it is easy to regard masochism in general

as a pathological growth of specific feminine elements —
as an abnormal intensification of certain features of the
psychosexual character of woman — and to seek its primary
origin in this sex. It may, however, be held to be established, that, in woman an inclination to subordination to
man (which may be regarded as an acquired, purposeful
arrangement, a phenomenon of adaptation to social requirements) is to a certain extent a normal manifestation.

In Freud's formulations, femininity was equated with
passivity, and the notion of submission as a normal concomitant of feminine sexuality on biological and social
grounds reappeared.

Krafft-Ebing offered two theoretical explanations to
account for sadism and masochism. First, he conceptualized sadism as a pathological intensification of the
masculine sexual character; masochism was seen as "a
pathological degeneration of the distinctive psychical
peculiarities of woman." Second, he thought that sexual
stimuli emanating from the love object, including all that
are ordinarily painful, such as being bitten, are perceived
as excitatory and reinforcing. He further hypothesized
that masochism resulted from an unusually intense
dependence on the love object, which he termed "sexual
bondage."[2] He accounted for excessive sexual dependence
as a combination of strong love and weak character in
individuals whose fear of loss of the love object drove
them to submission. Yet, he did not consider sexual bondage to be pathological, despite the fact that masochism
had its roots in it.

2. Somerset Maugham described a classic situation of sexual bondage in his novel, *Of Human Bondage*. It is likely that he drew inspira-
tion from Krafft-Ebing's work which may have supplemented his own
personal experience.

Krafft-Ebing did not provide an adequate explanation for the masochist's fear of power or for his subjection and self-injury, although he pointed out that during flagellation the masochist did not experience pain as such.

> The person in a state of masochistic ecstasy feels no pain, either because, by reason of his emotional state (like that of a soldier in battle) the physical effect on the cutaneous nerves is not apperceived or because (as with religious martyrs and enthusiasts) in the preoccupation or consciousness with lustful emotions, the idea of maltreatment remains merely a symbol without the quality of pain.

Kinsey (1948) described the same phenomenon:

> Specific observation and experimental data indicate that the whole body of the individual who is sexually aroused becomes increasingly insensitive to tactile stimulation and even to sharp blows and severe injury. . . . Toward the peak of sexual arousal there may be considerable slapping and heavier blows, biting and scratching and other activities which the recipient never remembers and which appear to have a minimal, if any, effect upon him at the time they occur. Not only does the sense of touch diminish but the sense of pain is largely lost. If the blows begin mildly and do not become severe until there is a definite erotic response, the recipient in flagellation or other types of sadomasochistic behavior may receive extreme punishment without being aware that he is being subjected to more than mild tactile stimulation.

My own observations accord with those of Krafft-Ebing and Kinsey. The threshold for pain during sexual excitation rises markedly and masochists have reported to me that they do not experience pain. I have noted that should pain actually be experienced, sexual excitation rapidly terminates, as does the masochistic behavior.

In my view, a theory of sexual masochism should be consistent with the following items of behavior: (a) the sexual masochist is either impotent or is unable to attain satisfactory arousal without masochistic maneuvers and techniques; (b) the masochist does not experience actual pain during sexual excitation; (c) the individual inflicting the bondage, flagellation, or humiliation is perceived as one having much greater power than the masochist himself, or he pretends that this is so. His impotence or other sexual inadequacy indicates that he is sexually inhibited.

Sexual inhibition is based upon an expectation of injury for sexual behavior, especially with a valued love object. The masochistic constellation is a defense against an expectation of injury; it permits a circumvention of sexual inhibition and allows sexual arousal to develop. Flagellation or equated behaviors are substitutes for more severe, anticipated injury. But masochism is not only a lesser punishment than feared; it locates the punishment and establishes that it has already taken place; therefore, no further punishment need be feared for the time being. The punishing individual is the stand-in for the powerful figure from whom the subject actually expects injury. In the charades of masochistic men, this power figure is usually the father or father surrogate. The "powerful" woman is a substitute for the feared father. Many elements in masochistic play-acting represent attempts at establishing a picture of the woman's power; however, the masochist does not actually fear her; he knows that the farce can be terminated at any point in the sexual encounter.

Several of Krafft-Ebing's cases demonstrate that the original figure involved in childhood masochistic experiences and fantasies is a male and that the transformation to a female occurs after puberty. The powerful female may also represent a mother figure who rejected and punished male sexuality. In many masochistic fantasies, such a woman is beautiful, powerful, and she compels the man to have sex — a type of male rape fantasy. In such instances, instead of rejecting and punishing the sexual behavior, the woman commands and demands it. A son's actual experience in childhood where his mother spanks him on the buttocks is a situation in which the mother's hand is brought into contact with the boy's perigenital area. The proximity to his genitals may be perceived as erotic and can condition sexual masochism. An erotic situation is concealed under the presumably nonsexual act of spanking. It may be compared to the childhood game of playing doctor, where the sexual behavior is concealed in the make-believe practice of medicine.

Sexual masochism may, in fact, include two different types of behavioral constellations, which share in common problems about power. In one type, the basic goal is sexual gratification. This type of masochist fears he will be punished for sexual gratification by power figures, such as parents; he incorporates the punishment by the threatening parent into the masochistic sexual constellation. By this maneuver, he locates the threatening figure and takes the punishment together with the pleasure in an inextricable combination. The second type consists of masochists who cope with a feared power figure by eroticizing that individual. In this instance, the goal of the behavior is to neutralize threatening power through sexual channels. Krafft-Ebing stated that masochism is established as a perversion when the witnessing or experiencing of tyranny becomes an erotic stimulus. Some masochists are so responsive to power that they become stimulated simply by witnessing the exercise of authority. They eroticize power which they fear or wish to use in their own behalf (Bieber 1972). Among male homosexuals, power themes are readily delineated. The core of their fear is aggressive, masculine power and this they eroticize, a dynamic that constitutes a basic element in a homosexual adaptation. Sexual masochism occurs frequently among male homosexuals.

Individuals of both sexes who are pathologically dependent may eroticize power. Their aim is not primarily to achieve sexual gratification; it is, rather, to use or acquire power. Nonetheless, eroticizing power does produce sexual arousal and, if pursued, results in sexual gratification. Differentiation between these two types of sexual masochists may require the determination of the motivation for any specific sexual experience. In general, if an individual's sexual functioning is almost entirely dependent on masochistic techniques, he is likely to belong to the type whose goal is sexual gratification. Those who eroticize power are usually capable of sexual activity without masochistic techniques. This differentiation is not an absolute one, since some of the first type may go through periods of sexual activity free of masochism; or, sometimes, they may be able to have sexual activity with individuals who have little value to them, such as prostitutes, without the need for masochistic defenses.

Nonsexual Masochism

Krafft-Ebing defined a type of masochism, which he termed "moral masochism," that presumably was not associated with sexual arousal, although he thought there was some gratification in the suffering. Freud adopted the term, but stated that this type, too, was sexual; it was only on cursory examination that moral masochism appeared to have no connection with sex. He hypothesized that the superego was established through the desexualization of the oedipal figure. Through this defusion, morality was desexualized. He speculated that in moral masochism there was a regression to the sexualized phase of the superego and to a sexualization of morality. He concluded that moral masochism was rooted in sexuality.

Occurring much more frequently than sexual masochism is a category of behavior in which the individual self inflicts or invites injury, the goal being the extinction of threat, or the evocation of positive feelings in others. I mean by the term "injury" any condition or situation deemed inimical to one's integrity or safety. This may include physical injury, or such other items as humiliation, rejection, neglect, and so forth. Masochistic patterns can be identified in almost everyone, but individuals in whom they are salient are referred to as masochistic characters.

Masochistic Goals

A major goal of masochistic behavior is the prevention or extinction of hostile aggression in others, in particular, powerful others. Elsewhere, I have defined power as the capability to influence, direct, or control matters of value in another's life (Bieber 1972). If this capability extends to matters of life and death, then the power is supreme. The wielder of power and the target may be an individual, group, institution, or government.

Psychoanalysis has made much of the fear of one's own aggressive impulses and acts. The fear of aggression of others has been very much underemphasized; in general, people are far more afraid of the aggression of others than of their own. When masochism is directed toward controlling the aggression of others, the behavior is a masochistic defense.

A child's first experience with power occurs within the family. The parents are all-powerful, and perceived parental power is proportional to the child's helplessness. First exposure to aggression is from parents and siblings; masochistic defenses develop and become prominent when protection is needed against their hostile aggression. I observed well-established masochistic defense patterns in a three-and-a-half-year-old girl, in whom self-injury had already been obvious for one year (see chapter 10). In this case, a masochistic technique was discovered that partially controlled attack, particularly from the mother. It demonstrates a basic principle of masochism: self-inflicted injury wards off threats believed to be even more dangerous. The child's masochism was her defense against external threat. For the masochistic pattern to become established, it must have had adaptive value at some time, even though it is essentially maladaptive.

Physical aggression is the most primitive and obvious manifestation of the abuse of parental power. Parents may also aggress in less obvious ways. They may exploit their children in pursuit of their own needs and desires; they may compete with them; they may constrict and extinguish those areas of functioning and development that are felt to be strange, dissonant, or threatening. Such areas may include sexuality, creativeness, and other behavior reflecting successful enterprise. Parental aggression in such instances may be characterized by explicit negative responses or failure to relate appropriately and enthusiastically to their child's achievements.

When children are given nonambivalent parental affection only when ill, injured, or failing in some respect, it would appear quite certain that the parents are hostile and destructive, and that the victim will likely evolve masochistic coping behavior. Although the psychopathology of masochism is in most cases traceable to destructive family influences, nonetheless, the family is usually felt as a haven from the cruelties of strangers and the outside world. The family, nuclear and extended, among its many other institutionalized functions, is a human unit from which the individual draws strength for coping with life's vicissitudes, including aggression from others. Fear that the envy of others has the potential of destructive, aggressive predation, has been expressed in the culturally rooted and paranoid idea of the evil eye, a myth defended against by masochistic techniques. Valued possessions may be concealed, denied, and minimized; riches may be hidden behind a façade of poverty. In Oriental cultures, children, possessions, and self are often minimized, presumably out of humility and good manners, but actually out of an institutionalized expression of masochism.

Minority groups continue to be targets for aggression, but these days they usually fight back. In the past, however, masochistic stereotypes were common. Stepin Fetchit, a movie actor of a by-gone era, was a stereotypic black masochist. He looked defective, was slow-moving, and always submissively addressed his white master as "Yassuh, boss." In the period before the Black Power movement, especially in the South, black parents inculcated submissive patterns, particularly in their sons, as life-saving devices. To what extent masochistic behavior is explicitly taught or acquired through identification with masochistic parents has yet to be determined. Among the upwardly mobile, particularly among minorities, maso-chistic behavior may be quite prominent. More often than not, they are a target for attack by an established power hierarchy although members of their own group may attack out of competitive resentment or fear of losing one of their number to the majority. The function of the masochistic adaptation is to permit the achievement of desired goals, sexual and other, while neutralizing or extinguishing anticipated aggression for the achievement of these goals.

Masochism and Love

In pursuit of love, acceptance, affection, a kind look, or because of a fear or reluctance to hurt the feelings of others, some individuals may injure themselves or their best interests. If one believes he is better looking, more accomplished, more successful, or more desirable than the individual whose acceptance is sought and who there-fore will turn away in envy or become aggressive, then those resources thought to incite envy will be sabotaged. When one sabotages efforts, constricts maximum poten-tial, or renounces constructive goals, on the assumption that fulfillment and gratification will alienate sought-for positive feelings in another, the motivation may be love-preserving but the behavior is masochistic and maladaptive. As noted previously, such patterns develop as a consequence of parental aggression. In these cases, one or both parents were jealous of their child, or were made anxious by his achievements. Such parents subtly communicate their displeasure, or show a lack of interest or enthusiasm. Children soon discern the parents' meaning and submissively renounce gratifications. Older siblings who are jealous and competitive may also promote masochistic behavior, especially if they are admired and respected. Peermates and significant others outside the family may set off masochistically inspired inhibitions in academic work or in occupational interests, out of fear of group rejection. Gifted students sometimes relinquish high-level performance, because peermates disparage it by such epithets as bookworm, egghead, sissy, and so forth. In adult life, beliefs about the prerequisites for love, affection, and acceptance may be derived, on the one hand, from beliefs about what others desire or demand, and on the other, from the projections of personal responses to those situations that either evoke or inhibit positive affects in oneself. An individual may feel threatened by another who is believed to be superior in some way and whose acceptance is valued and desired. Because of fear of superseding that individual, the tendency will be to sabotage those personal attributes believed to be a threat to the power figure who then might withhold goods, services, or wished-for affection; or, worse, turn into an attacking, fearsome rival.

Masochistic techniques to evoke positive affects in others or as responses to affection by valued others constitute a psychological trap. Masochistic characters become very fearful of acceptance, much as they may wish to have it, for they hate their own masochism which they cannot control, yet fear they may act it out and lose the personal assets they wish to retain. Hence, such people fear affection and avoid closeness to others lest they become enslaved. In treatment, these patients lose such fears when

they develop confidence in their ability to control masochistic, submissive behavior in situations where affection
is being given or withheld.

Those who react masochistically in situations perceived
as a choice between hurting themselves or others have a
somewhat different problem. They choose a masochistic
route even when they do not care about or desire the
affection and acceptance of the individual(s) being
"saved." This type of masochist cannot bear to inflict discomfort or suffering on others. The background of some
such patients often reveals a childhood saddened by a parent who had undergone considerable physical or psychological suffering. Others may have had parents who used
real or simulated suffering as a way of provoking guilt and
as a technique of control. If the parents' suffering is
perceived by the child to be the consequence of his own
activities, he may then attempt to ease their distress by
masochistic renunciation of his own normal wishes. The
inability to tolerate the suffering of another is therefore
not necessarily a reaction formation to one's own sadistic
instincts, as classical theory proposes. The repression of
sadistic desires is but one parameter, and one which I
have been able to delineate rather infrequently.

In treating patients who respond masochistically to the
hurt feelings of others, they should be led to the realization that hurt feelings are hardly fatal. The point to be
emphasized is that if intent and behavior are constructive,
the patient is not then responsible for possible neurotic
reactions in another. A good criterion for readiness for
discharge from treatment is an immunity to masochistic
responses when hurt feelings are manifested by others.

Masochistic Phenomena

Masochistic maneuvers are as varied as man's inventiveness. Injury may be solicited or self-inflicted; it may be directed to one's person, to a function, to a valued possession—be it object or person. If one were to select any single type of dynamic constellation to exemplify the psychopathology of everyday life, masochism would be a good choice. Few, if any, are totally free of masochistic behavior. Accident-proneness, in and out of automobiles, is often masochistic. Car accidents, even of a trivial sort, are a way of acting out anxiety about achievement, since among its many uses, automobiles serve as symbols of achievement and luxury.

The fear of success, whether in work, romance, or other important spheres of life, may be defended against by a masochistically inspired disability. The realization of a meaningful aspiration or the start of an enterprise that promises success may be followed by an accident or illness. Certain behaviors are overtly masochistic and may directly promote accidents or illness, such as in the excessive use of alcohol, tobacco, drugs, and activities that result in getting the insufficient rest and sleep that promote exhaustion syndromes. Fending off a normal level of health and vigor compatible with the energy needed to sustain one's efforts indicates a masochistic drive to sabotage potential success. All drug abuse, be it with alcohol, marijuana, or heroin, has a masochistic motive—physical self-injury through the toxic effect; social damage through the opprobrium and degradation associated with the life of the addict.

Food abuse through overeating is similarly a masochistic syndrome. In most such cases, the masochistic orientation is toward impairing physical attractiveness, health, and vitality. There are, of course, motivational components other than masochism in drug abuse and obesity, as, for example, where the effects of intake are sought to alleviate intense anxiety and agitation.

Most patients who have developed a well-defined line of masochistic behaviors have also convinced themselves that they can control at will and reverse damaging consequences. They tend to discount the irreversible effects of long-term smoking, drinking, drug or food abuse, and they cling to the illusion that they will somehow be forgiven the injuries and destructiveness their masochistic activities cause others.

Major insults to one's security and prestige may be courted with illegal involvements where apprehension would lead to financial disaster and social disgrace. Risk-taking and brinkmanship are inspired by a masochistic orientation toward self and may include one's family.

Sometimes a child becomes the symbol of masochism, and the parents become excessively preoccupied with the masochistic focus he personifies. In such a family, the youngster's every illness, injury, or other vicissitude, no matter how minor, becomes a source of great travail. The parents believe and create the impression that were it not for their child's difficulties, life would be an idyll. The victim almost always pursues the assigned masochistic role, in part as patterned behavior, in part as a way of obtaining and preserving parental interest and love.

The dissipation of financial resources is commonly acted out in a masochistic gambit. Despite an excellent income, debts may be accumulated, in some cases as a result of compulsive gambling. One such patient was excellent at cards, but when in masochistic gear, he would pile up huge losses. Like others in this category, he had fears of success, and was driven to lose, rather than gather up the evidence of successful play. It was quite predictable that he would lose large sums just when he had almost paid up his debts, or when he had accomplished something notable in his work. Among patients whose fortunes are in alternate phases of waxing and waning, rich one period and poor the next, I have always been able to observe self-sabotage.

A mechanism similar to the need to lose money is the masochistic loss or destruction of objects of value. In the repertoire of such lost objects, some are more frequently represented because of their symbolic value—wallets, handbags, briefcases containing important papers, and so forth. The lost and found departments are the repositories for acted-out masochism. During the great depression of the 1930s, I treated a patient whose masochism reflected the stringent times. One evening, when returning from work, the patient discovered she had left her handbag on a subway train. She could ill afford to lose the twenty-dollar bill her purse contained. As she undressed later that night, she found the money in one of her shoes but had no memory of having put it there. She had a masochistic need to lose a symbol of value represented by her purse, yet she was too practical to lose her money as well.

Forgetfulness may be viewed as a variant of masochistic losing behavior. Blocking on the name of someone well-known to one, particularly when performing a social introduction, forgetting information needed to pass an important examination, or forgetting theater and travel tickets—each may represent an item of forgetfulness in the psychopathology of everyday masochism. Some individuals "forget" what time it has gotten to be and manage to come late to an event they had looked forward to; sometimes, an event may be overlooked entirely, or attended a day or a week too late.

Some individuals are made anxious when they perceive that they are presenting themselves in a good light to others; they are then compelled to minimize themselves in some way. Such compulsive acts may include inappropriate remarks, socially unacceptable behavior, such as nose-picking, awkward manners at table, and so forth. A good clinical test for discerning a masochistic character is his response to a compliment; usually, a self-minimizing remark or act will follow.

Masochism and Humor

Humor, especially masochistic humor, is an effective technique for coping with aggression. If one can manage to be a target for laughter, one is not likely to be a target for hostility. Laughter extinguishes anger, hostility, and allied affects, at least for the period during which the laughter continues. Many comedians use masochistic techniques to evoke laughter, particularly when an audience is being unresponsive. Arieti (1950) has clearly described masochistic wit in the following passage:

> Granted that Jewish jokes originating by non-Jews are more offensive than those originating with Jews, the fact remains that even the latter may be offensive. Jews know that even mild jokes dealing with dirtiness and thriftiness may be used by anti-Semites as a disparaging weapon. I have the feeling that this habit of the Jews is paradoxically an unconscious defense against anti-Semitism. Aware as they have been in the course of centuries of the great hostility by which they were surrounded, the Jews have tried

to make the Gentiles discharge their hostility by means of these not too harmful jokes. It is better to be accused of stinginess and dirtiness than of ritual murder. It is better to be laughed at than to be massacred.

Masochism and Suicide

By definition, the techniques of masochism involve self-injury as this term has been defined; however, the goals of masochism are the *preservation* of life and the attainment of maximum integrity compatible with the threat against which the masochistic defense is being used. In suicide, the goal is the *extinction* of one's life. Suicide and masochism have in common self-destructiveness, but here the similarity ends. Freud associated masochism with femininity, with passivity, with a desire to experience pain. He interpreted masochism, not as a defense against aggression, but as a manifestation of the aggressive instinct turned in against the self. Starting with this assumption, it was logical for him to conceptualize suicide as the ultimate point on a masochistic continuum. Yet clinical observations reveal that a central motif in suicide is to relieve intolerable pain and to escape irrevocably from a hopeless entrapment in suffering. According to Freud's concept of masochism, there is pleasure in experiencing pain; certainly not pleasure in the *relief* of pain. The confusion of suicide with masochism has resulted in theoretical and therapeutic errors. To be sure, some masochists may commit suicide because life has become too weighed down by psychopathology and too painful to tolerate. They do not commit suicide, however, to experience the ultimate in masochistic pleasure!

A dynamic known as "riddance" is closely related to masochism. A phylogenetic analogy to riddance may be seen in the capability of some reptiles to shed a limb or tail that has been trapped or injured. Humans may also attempt to eliminate a structure or function that has become a source of pain and distress. Transsexuals seek to have themselves castrated in order to eliminate a structure to which they attribute their profound suffering and whose malfunction seems beyond repair. Riddance phenomena may be observed in other types of obsessive, masochistic patients who also seek out surgical intervention. A woman in her early thirties whom I treated some years ago was tormented by a conflict arising from an ardent desire to have a second child, yet she was prevented from becoming pregnant because of her overweening fears about it. While I was away on vacation, she located an obliging gynecologist who removed her uterus. In sum, riddance is concerned with destroying a part of oneself in order to preserve one's life, while the goal in suicide is to eliminate life itself.

MASOCHISM AND
PSYCHIATRIC SYNDROMES

Since masochism threatens to produce or produces self-injury, it activates basic security operations, both biological and psychological. Anxiety and inhibition are the most prominent biological defenses.

The term "anxiety" connotes a constellation of perceived physiological reactions that represent a hypermobilization of somatic resources preparatory to meeting a threat. Masochistic impulses and acts almost always evoke anxiety. The compulsive gambler referred to previously was an excellent poker player, but when in a masochistic mood he would gamble recklessly and for excessively high stakes. He would, at these times, experience severe anxiety, an affective state he had long interpreted as excitement or enthusiasm, expectation, pleasure, and so forth. Anxiety is often mistaken for these types of excitement. One patient who experienced extreme anxiety during sexual activity, in a slip of the tongue coined the word "anxirement," a composite of anxiety, desire, and excitement. When masochists play a game of brinkmanship with dangerous situations, anxiety is triggered, although it may be experienced as excitement.

Inhibition is an automatic "braking" to prevent action perceived as potentially injurious. Undoubtedly, many masochistic impulses are inhibited, yet many masochistic situations are mediated through inhibition. Those who seek achievement but become inhibited because of their neurotic fears of success may masochistically have their opportunities destroyed through inhibition. This may occur among actors who forget lines when given an important role, speakers who develop stage fright, athletes who lose concentration during the crucial period of an important event, and so forth; avoidance behavior is a defense mechanism transitional between inhibition and a range of psychological defenses. Avoidance may be as automatic and unconscious as inhibition; it, too, is a way of preventing or avoiding actions or situations that threaten to be injurious. Avoidance linked to masochism manifests itself in essentially three types of situations. In the first, the individual is tempted to act out a masochistic impulse and, fearing he may arrange to humiliate or otherwise injure himself, he bypasses the situation; in the second, the individual finds himself in conflict over a wish to win, with its attendant anxieties, and a masochistic impulse to lose, also a frightening prospect. Either

alternative is defended against by an avoidance maneuver. The third type of masochistic avoidance, and the
most destructive, may be observed among individuals
who are bent upon acting out a self-destructive impulse;
they will avoid anyone who they suspect might interfere
with their masochistic acting out. It must be kept in mind
that masochism is a defense mechanism; it is a way of
avoiding a greater injury by inviting or sustaining a lesser
one. Individuals who are on a compulsively masochistic
course are actually trying to prevent a greater catastrophe
from befalling them; hence, they avoid anyone who might
prevent their masochistic behavior, however irrational it
might appear. The avoidance of constructive figures not
infrequently includes the analyst; it is during a masochistic period that patients tend to skip sessions or fail to
discuss ongoing problems and decisions.

Masochism and Obsessive Symptoms

Masochism is often a core element of obsessive reactions. For example, a man may become obsessed with
turning off gas jets and faucets, impelling him to turn
back after leaving his home just to check out his obsessive
doubts. Such doubts arise because of an unconscious
masochistic impulse to burn down his home or flood it.
His masochistic defense is motivated by anxiety about
possessing an object of great value to him. Individuals
who masochistically run themselves down physically, may
become obsessively concerned about matters of health.
Obsessive dread of accidents, illness, contagious diseases,
and dying, may represent fears about masochistic self-
injury. Such fears are sometimes projected to a loved one
who becomes the focus of an overanxious parent, child, or

spouse. Pregnant women may become obsessed with fear that there will be something seriously wrong with their newborn. In my clinical experience with such patients, most were expressing fears about their own masochistic impulse to injure their child in order to protect themselves from being attacked for having a wished-for baby. Homosexual obsessions may surface when an individual who fears success in work or in a relationship with a woman sabotages his efforts and brings on a masochistically inspired defeat. Psychologically, the defeat is a submission to a feared competitor (father or brother figure) who will then spare the vanquished. Whenever homosexual obsessions appear in heterosexuals, one can always identify a significant masochistic component. To reemphasize the essential point: masochistic mechanisms are often identifiable in the dynamics of obsessions. The therapeutic gain in teasing out these mechanisms is obvious.

Phobias are closely similar to obsessions, so much so that where obsessiveness is a salient characteristic, phobias may be identified in childhood history and current functioning. As with all psychological defenses, there is no single explanation for a phobic defense; however, in acrophobia and the fear of falling, there appears to be a direct dynamic connection with masochism. Patients who are definitely not suicidal may, in a masochistic period, develop fears of walking through a window during sleep, or become panicky about falling from a height. One patient who feared he would walk to his death during sleep, tied his foot to the bed to prevent himself from leaving it.

Masochism and Depression

Some of the consequences of masochistic acting out are self-anger, self-hatred, loss of self-esteem and confidence, and a reactive depression. The depression may be consciously felt or repressed out of awareness; it may be visible or masked, evanescent or chronic. The psychodynamics of masochism may be identified in almost all depressive states. Where such dynamics are central and the patient is compulsively bent on destroying something of value to himself, the depression will be of an agitated type. The conflict between impulses toward destructive action and attempts to conserve valued objects and functions, despite fears about holding on, is often the crucial conflict in an agitated depression. When in a state of depression, patients may destroy their business or profession that took years to build; they may dissipate fortunes, break up a marriage with a beloved spouse, ruin valued friendships, and so forth. When masochism is acted out with such destructive consequences, the patient may become potentially or actually suicidal. Losses resulting from masochistic behavior are extremely painful, if only because they are self-inflicted and thus accompanied by enormous self-hatred and contempt.

Masochism and Paranoid Mechanisms

Paranoia as a description of behavior basically refers to an irrational expectation of injury from others. A discussion in depth on paranoid mechanisms is not germane to this chapter, but since its relation to masochism has a significant bearing on our subject, three types will be briefly described. The first involves victimization; mistrust, suspicion, and hostility are experientially derived and then irrationally transferred to others who may even be constructively related. This type may be termed the "transferential paranoia." The second involves being taught paranoid ideation by paranoid parents or surrogates. One who emerges from such influences might be termed the "indoctrinated paranoid." The third is the psychiatrically familiar and classical type in which the paranoia involves the projection onto others of unacceptable feelings and impulses—"projectional paranoia." In this type, sexual and aggressive wishes are usually recognized psychiatrically; however, the projection of masochistic impulses is generally overlooked or insufficiently emphasized, yet such projections are common features. The individual who masochistically loses in gambling may suspect others of cheating; a masochist who somehow destroys an opportunity for advancement may accuse his employer of keeping him down or unfairly preferring someone else. Individuals who sabotage their appearance through obesity or a bizarre style of dressing or makeup may believe that others are laughing at them, showing them contempt, deriding them, and so forth.

Masochism and Pathological Dependency

In general, masochism is a psychodynamic component in pathological dependency. Where an individual is pathologically dependent upon another, he must be prepared to please and placate the object of his dependency. This may require submissiveness, or self-demeaning, minimizing, and noncompetitive behavior. Masochistic attitudes and behavior are almost always present in individuals whose adaptation is a significantly dependent one. A common dynamic in dependency is the inflation of the image of the person depended on. This enlargement effect is achieved through minimizing the self. The deflation of self is a masochistic process, since it involves damaging one's self-image and inhibiting one's own resourcefulness, in order to magically obtain hoped-for advantages from the enlarged other. These psychodynamics appear in exaggerated forms among psychotics. Their paranoid fears may derive, in part, from their irrational concept of inflated power which they ascribe to individuals seen as likely ones to be dependent upon. Because of the anxiety associated with the masochistic components inherent in pathological dependency, defensive maneuvers against becoming dependent on another may consist in avoiding those individuals with whom one would be tempted to form such a relationship, or responding to them with hostility—attempts to minimize or degrade them, or otherwise make them inaccessible for such a role.

Treatment of Masochism

Masochistic behavior may be conceptualized as an aggregation of adaptational mechanisms. Based upon this formulation, therapy may be oriented toward working out the adaptational significance of every masochistic mechanism whenever it occurs. If, for example, it is oriented toward extinguishing another's aggression, the patient is made aware that inflicting self-injury in order to prevent injury from others is maladaptive. He must learn that fear of reprisal from others for fulfilling his wishes is, in general, unfounded, but that even where actual aggression may eventuate, the injury anticipated is almost always grossly distorted. Where real aggression is a possibility, the patient must learn to recognize and reality-test effective techniques for coping with another's aggression, and that coping behavior does not include masochistic, maladaptive defenses. Where a patient is masochistic in order to evoke love or conserve it, he has to become convinced that those who demand masochistic behavior in exchange for affection are exacting an exorbitant price, hardly worth it.

As a general principle of therapeutic technique, I do not analyze defenses until the fears that have established and maintained them are understood. Thus, if a patient fears displacement by a preferred sibling, I engage this problem before approaching his competitiveness toward the sibling. After the patient has become familiar with his underlying fears, the next phase may include the analysis of his desire to surpass or even annihilate the sibling or his transferential representatives. Exceptions to this rule concern (a) the analysis of defenses that produce analytic resistances which may interfere with treatment or threaten its continuity, and (b) the analysis of masochistic defenses. When a patient prepares to act out a masochistic impulse, the therapist should endeavor to prevent it, especially if it threatens to be significantly harmful. Insight should be given into the meaning of the masochism and its injurious consequences; even directive techniques, if they can be effective, should be employed. Despite the traditional pessimism about successfully treating masochistic characters, I have found that the maladaptive processes inherent in masochism can be significantly altered in most cases, and actually extinguished in some.

Chapter 12

The Meaning of
Suffering in Therapy

Suffering may be broadly referred to as a function of pain in total adaptation, affecting mood, behavior, and attitudes to self and others. Suffering—physical and psychic—may include all types of pained feelings which differ in quality and intensity. The pain of anxiety differs from the oppressive discomfort of boredom or the pained despair of depression. Moreover, the same individual responds differently to a range of painful stimuli and responds differently to the same painful stimulus at different times. It may be useful to think of suffering as an equation between the intensity of psychic or physical pain over a period of time and the individual's tolerance for it.

Although conscious awareness usually accompanies suffering, it may occur independently of awareness. I have seen individuals visibly suffer from tension states or physical pain who were unaware of it and denied it. One such patient, who had an abdominal tumor, showed the *facies* of pain and the easy fatigability and irritability of suffering, yet was quite unaware of any suffering until the neoplasm was surgically removed. As a result of the marked contrast in physical comfort following her surgery, her previous suffering came into awareness. The same individual, on the other hand, was keenly aware of and articulate about the slightest emotional distress to such an extent that it had become the focus of her life and was carried over to her analysis. The meaning of her suffering in analysis was the same as its more generalized meaning within the pattern of all her distress responses.

As with pain denial on a physical level, patients may be unaware of psychologic distress indicated by manifestations such as excessive sweating, overalertness, and tense postures reflecting rigidity and guardedness. Particularly at the beginning stages of treatment, such patients frequently deny psychic distress and rationalize around some external situation. Anxiety, tension, defensive reactions, maladaptive behavior with its resulting frustrations, diminished self-esteem, and guilt feelings are among the painful affects seen in therapy.

SOME THERAPEUTIC CONCEPTS AND TECHNIQUES

Patients enter psychoanalysis because they suffer, whether or not they are aware of it. It is the expectation of relief from suffering that brings them to treatment and motivates their continuing it. Suffering does not disappear, however, simply because the patient has come into treatment. The frequently observed early "lift" and subsequent "letdown" can serve to introduce the patient to the idea that the suffering is and has been connected with his or her psychopathology, not with the analysis itself; that suffering can be substantially relieved only when its determinants are understood and worked through. The willingness to work in the direction of resolving pain-producing conflicts must replace the wish for magical relief. At the same time, the therapist must be related to and aware of the patient's suffering throughout the course of the analysis, and the extent to which this suffering can be tolerated. Each patient has a threshold of tolerance for suffering and this threshold varies from patient to patient. The analyst must know the limit of tolerance for each and, as much as possible, steer the patient away from approaching his tolerance limits.

There is a notion that prevails among some analysts that relief of pain and suffering militates against thera-peutic change. They will thus justify provoking anxiety and be wary about undue relief of a patient's suffering. I consider such attitudes and practices unreasonable. Granting the rationale that in some cases pain and suffer-ing may motivate a patient to change, it would then log-ically follow that the patient's psychopathology and even his recollection of past suffering supply sufficient pain and suffering to motivate change without iatrogenic assis-tance. Although pain or suffering may mobilize a patient to act in a constructive direction, it is, nonetheless, a double-edged sword, since it may also promote inhibition and resistance. When a patient links his suffering to the analysis, serious resistances tend to arise that threaten continuance of the analysis. As is well-known, the fear that treatment will increase suffering often discourages people who need treatment from seeking it. The emphasis on the alleviation of emotional suffering in analysis does not imply that meaningless reassurances be offered or that the analyst refrain from giving appropriate and necessary interpretations that may elicit pain or anxiety reactions. If, however, the analyst relates to his patient as to an individual in stress and if suffering *in itself* is viewed as undesirable and to be avoided where possible, then even those interpretations that stimulate pained feelings will be given in such a manner as to evoke minimum pain.

The technique of minimizing patients' suffering during analysis involves a basic principle: defenses or character traits representing reasonably stabilized defensive systems must not be analytically approached before working out the irrational concepts underlying the fears on which the defenses rest. The management of neurotic dependency is offered as an illustration.

Pathologic dependency is an adaptation to a neurotic inhibition of personality resources. If dependency traits are analyzed before analyzing the irrational beliefs maintaining the neurotic inhibitions, the patient is left with a feeling analogous to that of a crippled person using a crutch he feels not entitled to have. We may convince the patient that he is infantile and exploitative for using the dependency "crutch." We may even convince him to give up the "crutch" by shaming him out of it, yet all we have succeeded in doing is to get him going with the same "broken leg" with which he entered analysis, while depriving him of his compensatory aid. The precipitous attack of a defense such as pathologic dependency only serves to increase the patient's sense of helplessness, hopelessness, and suffering. Similarly, a patient may be made aware of hostile feelings and acts. Yet, unless the insight is accompanied by the recognition that irrational hostility is a defensive reaction to an unrealistic perception of threat and unless the irrational beliefs connected with the threat are delineated, the patient will be left with diminished self-esteem and feelings of unacceptability for harboring antisocial feelings. However, where the analyst delineates hostility as a response to an irrationally felt threat and works out with the patient the specificity of the perceived threat itself, self-esteem is not injured nor are meaningless guilt feelings stimulated. Drives to power, neurotic ambition, drives toward domination, the need to be the center of attention, and so forth, are other defensive constellations which, in the course of treatment, first require the analysis of its underpinnings before dealing with the superstructures. My own technique, therefore, is oriented first, toward delineating the irrational convictions behind the fears supporting defensive integrations. Second, the defenses *are* analyzed, as they must be, but only after the primary analytic work has been accomplished. When the analysis of defenses is undertaken, it is always integrated with the analysis of the patient's underlying fears on which his defenses are based.

Two other iatrogenically triggered wellsprings of suffering are related to the problem of communication with the patient and to the analysis of transference. First, most patients enter therapy with the belief, by and large well-founded, that people do not understand them. The genesis of this complaint usually can be traced to parents who, for one reason or another, did not care, or were unable, to understand the patient. As symptomatic of their psychopathology as adults, the communications of such patients are often esoteric and idiosyncratic. If, however, the analyst is related to what the patient is talking about and if he can divorce himself from theoretical preconceptions, he will, in general, be able to understand the meaning of even obscure productions. Understanding the patient—and this understanding is inevitably communicated—usually relieves suffering. Failure to understand—and this is also communicated—usually increases suffering. A good technical guide for the analyst is to be aware that in each session the patient is likely to discuss one or two major themes. If the patient is not interrupted for the first ten or fifteen minutes, the theme of the session, in most instances, can be determined. By directing ensuing remarks to this theme, the analyst demonstrates that he or she is in communication with the patient. If this technique is followed routinely, the patient develops a feeling of empathy and of communication with the analyst. Conversely, it is a source of anxiety and pain when a patient does not believe that the analyst understands.

Second, subsumed under the general importance of understanding the patient is the analyst's understanding of the transference situation at all stages of treatment. Two types of transference reactions are particularly painful to the patient: (1) hostile reactions to the analyst which threaten the relationship by disrupting the feeling of contact and by fears of retaliation via counter-hostility and rejection; and (2) positive feelings to the analyst for reasons which differ in male and female patients. Suffering related to transference responses is frequently manifested in resistances which increase the patient's suffering. When transference anxiety is worked through and resistances diminish, suffering accompanying this phase is relieved.

In summary, the analyst's point of view regarding the extent and intensity of suffering as a condition for improvement is an important determinant of how much any particular patient will suffer. The more convinced an analyst is that suffering is a deterrent and not an aid, the less painful the analysis will be. I, for one, am convinced that it can be carried out in a reasonably painless way, that the therapeutic alleviation of emotional suffering in no way reduces the potency of the experience, and that a more successful outcome is predictable when the analyst considers suffering to be a hazard rather than experientially necessary in the life situation or in treatment.

PART II

Clinical

Perspectives

The chapters that follow illustrate the application of cognitive psychoanalysis in treatment, and describe psychopathologic conditions and dynamics from a viewpoint not usually considered in traditional psychoanalysis.

Parental preference is a major source of psychopathology in children that follows them into adult life. It is a theme that needs to be emphasized much more than it has in the past. Chapter 13, "Pathogenicity of Parental Preference," delineates the dynamics and describes the cognitive derivates in patients whose problems have been shaped in large part by parental preference and nonpreference.

Cognitive responses to the threat of fatal illness are discussed in chapter 14. "Depressive and Paranoid Reactions" describes changes in belief systems when ideas associated with the preservation of health and physical integrity are assaulted.

In "Psychological Adaptation to Serious Illness and Organ Ablation," major principles are defined for understanding, predicting, preventing, and treating psychopathologic responses to organ ablation. These principles are based on an investigation of how the patients' beliefs affected their self-esteem, expectations of personal acceptance by others, and the ability to function. Depending upon the beliefs held about a specific organ, its ablation elicited a wide range of responses in different patients.

Chapter 16, "Dreams of Heroin Addicts," documents the value of dreams in delineating the irrational beliefs associated with expectations of injury. Freud referred to the dream as the royal road to the unconscious. In cognitive psychoanalysis, the metaphor is paraphrased—the dream is the royal road to irrational beliefs. An outstanding characteristic of the addicts' dreams is the vivid, lurid symbolism.

My paper on the "Treatment of the 'Borderline' Patient," chapter 17, was originally presented at a symposium of the Society of Medical Psychoanalysts in 1956 under the title "Schizophrenia in Office Practice." The patients about whom I wrote were diagnosed as ambulatory schizophrenic, latent schizophrenic, or "borderline," terms which at that time were used interchangeably. Today, the diagnosis for most of these patients would be "borderline syndrome." Whether they fall within the spectrum of schizophrenia is a matter of diagnostic semantics. I do not agree with those who demand, before making this diagnosis, signs of advanced schizophrenia as outlined by the Schneiderian criteria. A doctor need not insist that a patient have all the signs and symptoms of cardiac failure before making a diagnosis of cardiac pathology.

Borderline patients tend to have similar personality features as described in a recent study of eighteen patients by Perry and Klerman (1980). Most of the patients were between the ages 20–40 and of the eighteen, only three were married and only one-fourth were employed. Most did not maintain long-term social relationships. The group were frequently inappropriately angry, had high levels of anxiety, chronic feelings of emptiness, suffered from episodes of depersonalization and derealization, and they had had an average of three psychiatric hospitalizations.

Patients who fall into the category of borderline syndrome comprise two groups: those who are clearly schizophrenic and those who are not. I would consider most patients in the Perry and Klerman sample at risk for schizophrenic decompensation, particularly if not adequately treated. In my experience in treating borderline patients, I note that most have been women—as in the sample of eighteen, three-fourths of whom were women. I find that borderline patients respond rapidly with anxiety to a multitude of stimuli and situations and become quickly and bitterly angry at anyone whom they hold responsible for evoking their anxiety. Their flash angers and intense anxiety demand sensitivity and perceptiveness in the analytic situation. Patients whose capacity for productive work is relatively unimpaired have a good prognosis if they have competent psychiatric treatment. I have followed three such patients for more than thirty years and they have led productive, comfortable lives.

Chapter 13

Pathogenicity of Parental Preference

Few psychologic constellations are more prevalent or consistently pathogenic in their effects than preference by a parent of one child over another. This phenomenon is the major theme of this chapter, although preference for a child over a spouse will also be considered.

Parents express favoritism in various overt acts and attitudes of partiality shown by affection, intimacy, admiration, and interest. Preferred and nonpreferred children soon learn which one of them has greater value to the parents, and each child suffers by it. I am not suggesting that parents respond to their children with unvarying sameness. Every human being has an individuality. In normal circumstances, parents relate differently but appropriately to the uniqueness of each of their children without assigning greater value to one over another.

In a context of favoritism, specific personality characteristics tend to develop. Preferred children usually become grandiose on the one hand, and subject to easily triggered guilt feelings on the other. I have found it useful to conceptualize grandiosity as of two types: primary and secondary. In primary grandiosity the individual has a basic belief that he is truly superior to his peers, as seen among royalty who are brought up to think that way of themselves—a belief continuously confirmed and reinforced by the surrounding society. Secondary grandiosity is compensatory. It is an outgrowth of reparative maneuvers in a defense against feelings of inferiority. Preferred children have a primary grandiosity not unlike royalty with all their prerogatives; but while the royal child need not delineate for himself why he holds an exalted position—his birthright is sufficient—the preferred child needs to rationalize why he has been chosen. Generally, the reasons center on ability—intellectual, artistic, musical, dramatic, and so forth—or physical attributes—strength and beauty—or personal charm. Knowing the source of his power helps the favored child retain it by efforts to excel in those areas believed to be the key to superior status in the family.

The specific attributes and skills that seem to assure parental preference become the areas of competition not only with siblings, but with playmates and peer groups. If, in accord with a family's value system, intellectual superiority is stressed, a child may strive to be intellectually superior. If physical attributes are emphasized, a child may try to be the most beautiful or handsome, strongest and athletic. Parental preference creates the belief that the world beyond the family also is organized along lines of personal preference—the "in's" and the "out's." This notion, established early in life, later fits in with the economic ideology of a competitive society such as ours, which serves to reinforce the "I'm in, you're out" paradigm.

As to the guilt feelings among favored children, the guilt is based essentially on the belief that because he or she exists, siblings are deprived of their fair share of parental affection, respect, and support. A corollary is the belief that had the preferred child never been in the picture, the other siblings would have been given their rightful share of parental love. The guilt may also incorporate concepts of fairness and justice, depending on the depth of affectional feelings toward other siblings and the wish not to deprive them. Guilt dynamics may block the development and expression of the very attributes believed to have claimed parental preference or if potential personal resources are not inhibited, achievement may be accompanied by anxiety.

Although there is a general tendency to quantify psychopathology, as in such descriptions as "patient A is as neurotic or more neurotic than patient B," quantifying a syndrome has, at best, limited application. Yet, one can safely say that preferred children are profoundly disturbed by parental preference and that they fare no better than nonpreferred siblings in the extensiveness of subsequent psychopathology.

The following is a case of a favorite son that illustrates some of these points.

Sam is a very "correct" twenty-six-year-old man, now completing graduate work as a top student. He entered analysis upon the encouragement of a friend who himself was helped by treatment. Sam's initial attitude was one of veiled skepticism and distrust along with depression, obsessiveness about finding a high-status position after completing his studies, and anxiety about his romantic life. I use the term "romantic" rather than "sexual" since he is free of any functional disorder. He attracts young women, but has difficulty finding someone who interests him.

He is the eldest of four sons and the favorite of both parents, each successful in their respective fields, especially the father. Sam very much resembles his father and there is a close identification between them; yet, despite an interest in his father's profession, Sam avoided it. The mother has been the more driving, ambitious parent, following her son's every venture with avid, intrusive interest. Except when away at college, he lived, until recently, at the home of his parents and was the "good son" who carefully avoided displeasing them.

The next son, fourteen months younger, had a disturbed adolescence including bad trips on drugs which, on one occasion, required a brief hospitalization; however, he was able to overcome many of these difficulties, complete college, enter a profession after a somewhat lengthy hiatus, and marry. There was always a distance between the two brothers that precluded any exchange of confidences. In fact, Sam hardly talked to any of his brothers. Of the other two, one interested himself in rather esoteric subjects while the youngest spent most of his time between pursuing a superficial interest in computers and watching television. Sam's aloofness covered an underlying disdain, a sense of superiority, and a rivalrous hostility, topped by a reaction formation of sharing his parents' concern and solicitude about their other sons' problems.

Sam is intensely competitive with peers and distrust is easily evoked, though easily dispelled. Anxiety about success is manifested in compulsive ambition retarded by work sabotage in various time wasters that only increase his anxiety. His problems with work are traceable, in part, to guilt that his achievements will keep his brothers in their deprived place and fear that if he is successful the mother will absorb him, leaving the father abandoned — an oedipal dynamic. Though the parents love their children, they have assigned the role of crown prince to the first-born, thus separating him from siblings and to some extent, from peers.

In contrast to the favorite, the nonpreferred child tends to develop basic feelings of inferiority, hostility to the preferred child, hostility to the parent who shows partiality, and an overweening desire for acceptance. The nonpreferred one, like his favored sibling, also needs to delineate those qualities that seemingly win preference. If it is intellectual ability that apparently garners a star role, then there may be strong motivation to excel over the achievements of the preferred child with the hope that success will dislodge the rival and at long last win full parental recognition and love. In the competitive striving to displace the rival, the nonpreferred child also experiences guilt because displacement means taking responsibility for inflicting upon another the pain of being a second-class child. Yet, despite the rivalry and hostility, the nonpreferred individual usually admires the favorite. Running a close second to the yearning for a full share of love and recognition from the parent, there is a persistent wish to win the acceptance and affection of the preferred child.

In families characterized by preference patterns, a child may be the favorite of one parent and nonpreferred by the other. In these instances, personality characteristics of both preferred and nonpreferred children may then emerge. If an individual is the mother's favorite, grandiosity and guilt will likely be associated with the traits and skills perceived to be valued by her, but there will be feelings of inferiority associated with attributes valued by the father who prefers another sibling. If it is an athletic brother, then the father's nonpreferred son may develop feelings of physical inferiority. Among the various types of preferential patterns, another is that of the parent who has a greater affectional intimacy with one child but more admires another who does not share the intimacy. Although the admiration may mitigate feelings of inferiority, particularly for the characteristics that elicit the admiration, nonetheless there are negative effects for both such children; in the former, a sense of inferiority about ability; in the latter, untoward sensitivity about being excluded in interpersonal relationships and social activities, and uncertainty about being valued in a love relationship.

When parental preference is determined by the gender of the cross-sex child — that is, a mother prefers her son, and the father, his daughter — there usually is significant pathology in gender identification and sexual functioning. A son rejected by a father who strongly prefers a sister may develop the wish to be a woman as part of an envious, competitive reaction to the sister for the father's love and attention. Conversely, a woman whose brother the mother prefers may develop the wish to be a boy. It is this psychological dynamic that, at least in part, accounts for the continuation of so-called penis envy into adult life.

Individuals who were preferred over their same-sex parent are in a population at risk for severe postpartum reactions, particularly if the newborn is of the same sex. Such persons harbor the fear that a same-sex child will displace them in the affections of the spouse as they believe they themselves did with their own parent. Illustrative is the case of a thirty-seven-year-old woman who entered treatment shortly after the birth of her fourth child. She had suffered a severe postpartum depression following her second and third deliveries and she had explained it to herself as a reaction of disappointment to having had only sons. Her fourth baby was a daughter and she suffered the worst depression of all. She then entered analysis.

The patient was the youngest of three and the only daughter. She was her daddy's darling and also had a close intellectual relationship with him which excluded the mother, a simple ignorant woman. The patient was unequivocally preferred by her father and the mother just as clearly preferred the older of the two sons. The patient felt deeply rejected by her mother, profoundly envied her brother and was extremely competitive with him. Once she brought a dream that there was a contest in which the prize was the mother's breasts. The brother was so confident of the mother's love that he disdained even to enter the contest. One of the ways the patient attempted to defeat him was to marry a man who was in a similar profession, but much more successful. At the same time, she would try in all sorts of ways to win her brother's approval and affection.

Children respond to parental preference as though it were rational and realistic when in fact it is irrational and unrealistic. As I have observed it through the years, parental preference is always an expression of neurosis. It is a transference reaction which may encompass admixtures of transferences referable to significant persons in the family of origin and to aspects of self. One patient had a twin brother whom the mother openly preferred and whom she had named after her own favorite older brother. Maternal preference was clearly based on this transference. The preferred son was the youngest of three sons and twin to his only sister. From early childhood, it was apparent to the patient and to the other siblings that the twin brother was the star. The mother lived into her nineties and as she became senile her favoritism became more and more vivid. When her children visited her, this son was the only one to whom she reacted with clear recognition and continued animation. Some few years later, the preferred son died. At the funeral and thereafter she would refer to him as her husband.

The patient had had intensely ambivalent feelings toward her twin brother. She was close to him, affectionate, loyal, and genuinely concerned with his welfare; yet, she was very competitive. Her strivings to outdo him were the salient dynamics underlying her work problems, and in the course of her analysis we were able to track her severe work inhibitions to her envy. Successful work performance would usually be followed by dreams depicting her brother as either severely ill or already dead. In an outstanding dream she had had at about the age of eight, she threw the book of knowledge at him. It hit him in the head and killed him. An intelligent, intellectual woman, she was unable to complete college and had dropped out midway. When she worked through her competitive attitudes, she was able to face her work inhibitions, return to college, complete it, and subsequently become involved in a meaningful career.

In another family, whom I knew personally, there were seven children: four women and three men. The oldest, a son, was a man of unusual endowment—handsome, charismatic, a brilliant engineer and well-known and respected by his colleagues. Although the mother loved him—as indeed she did her other children, but more especially her sons—her favorite was the middle son, who bore a marked physical resemblance to her only brother whom she adored. This son could do no wrong. In contrast to the older son, this one was work inhibited and, though very charming and likeable, was essentially a loser. He would flit from job to job and habitually sleep until noon when unemployed, a frequent situation. The mother was consistently indulgent and excused him by asserting that he needed lots of sleep. The older son, despite his clearly superior qualities, was competitive and envious of this brother, but not of his younger brother.

In many instances, parents exploit the favored child to fulfill some need of their own. If ambitions have been frustrated, usually by their own work inhibitions, a child may be selected who is perceived as a likely candidate to fulfill lost dreams and fantasies. The stage mother is a well-recognized example. A woman who is sexually insecure may select an attractive daughter to act out wishes to be a sexpot or the belle of the ball. A father who is uncertain about his capabilities and effectiveness may try to develop, usually in a son, strivings for power and position. A child may be picked as a favorite who can fulfill significant interpersonal needs. Parents who mistrust others of the same sex and have difficulty establishing good social relationships with them may select a same-sex child to fill this gap. A mother may choose a daughter to be her companion and develop a close, possessive relationship with her, a relationship that may interfere with the daughter's social, sexual, and creative development. A parent whose sexual anxieties keep him or her from choosing a spouse who could satisfy romantic needs, or a parent who is unable to maintain a good relationship after marriage and children, may try to redeem lost romance with a child. This type of background is especially common among homosexuals, though it occurs frequently enough in families where the sons do not become homosexual. In general, the son who becomes a romantic target is a transference object either from the mother's father or other significant male figure—an uncle, brother, even a grandfather. The child who is preferred over the cross-sex parent more often than not develops serious problems and difficulties. Invariably, sexuality is affected adversely. In adult life, the father may seem inadequate or weak, but in childhood the father is perceived as a towering figure. A son who is preferred by a mother to her husband develops a primary grandiosity more severe than when there is preference over a sibling. The guilt at having displaced the father in the affections of the mother is also more severe. In this type of pattern, the preference articulates with the son's oedipal wishes and thus with fears of retaliation and castration anxieties referable to the father.

Preference over a parent also leads the child to overestimate those attributes he believes established the preference. The feeling of being responsible for disrupting the interparental relationship provokes guilt and intense, if unconscious, fears of retaliation. Valued attributes and skills generally undergo inhibition and become the focus of masochistic renunciation. A girl who believes her father prefers her because she is prettier than her mother, or a son who thinks his mother prefers him because he is better looking than his father, may become afraid of appearing attractive and masochistically sabotage good looks by overeating and becoming obese, by drinking or dressing unbecomingly, or otherwise engaging in physically self-destructive activities. When homosexuality evolves as a solution for overcoming guilt and fear of the avenging father, the preferring female is renounced as a love object. The notion that homosexuals are afraid of women has validity only insofar as such a man fears that the heterosexual relationship involves the woman's choice of him over another man and that this situation will set off dangerous hostility in male rivals. Thus, for safety's sake, and as a submissive gesture to feared opponents, the woman is renounced.

In the therapeutic treatment of adults whose psychopathology is associated with preferential parents, I find it necessary to bring the patient to recognize the irrationality of playing favorites and the irrational beliefs favoritism engenders. As mentioned earlier, when a preferred child has a primary grandiosity, he becomes convinced that he is superior to his siblings, often to his parents, too. If he comes to recognize that the preference is not based on his superiority but is the expression of parental transference, he is able to make headway in correcting false beliefs about his effect on others—beliefs that in such cases are very often associated with underlying masochistic and inhibitory tendencies. Superior endowment and effectiveness can then be accepted as hurting no one and as resources to be enjoyed.

When parents of patients are still living and available for examination, I try to see them in consultation, if at all possible. The data thus obtained are useful in establishing the source of parental transference and in reconstructing the reality situation for the patient. As I have also dilated upon earlier, the nonpreferred child believes in his inferiority as firmly as the preferred one believes in his superiority. These patients must become convinced that their lower status in the family represents a defect not in them, but in the parents. When patients are able to develop the conviction that parental preference is an irrationality, therapeutic resolution of the psychopathology associated with preference is greatly advanced.

Chapter 14

Depressive and
Paranoid Reactions

The Section of Research Psychiatry at Sloan-Kettering Institute and the Neuropsychiatric service at Memorial Hospital have conducted studies of patients who have undergone abdominoperineal resection (Sutherland et al. 1952), radical mastectomy (Bard 1955), total gastrectomy, or hysterectomy (Drellich, Bieber, and Sutherland 1956), to identify the psychological problems associated with cancer and specific surgical procedures. The major purposes of these investigations were to determine the measures which could be employed (1) to reduce the incidence and severity of postoperative hypochondriasis with

In collaboration with Charles E. Orbach, Ph.D.

associated curtailment of activity, and (2) to provide a rationale for the establishment of a rehabilitation program for patients with cancer.

During the course of research with the above objectives the development of major psychiatric disorders other than hypochondriacal reactions has been observed. Depressive and paranoid reactions have been observed where there was no evidence of prior occurrence in such form. (This does not imply, however, that potential psychopathology was not present, or even manifest, in certain patterns of thinking and feeling.) These reactions frequently appeared simultaneously or occurred during different phases of treatment in the same patients. There has also been an opportunity to confirm these observations in our contact with patients referred for specific management problems or for psychiatric evaluation. Many of the latter patients have been as intensively studied as those included in the controlled investigations.

Composition of the Study Group

The entire group, which will be discussed in this report, except for a few cases, were clinic patients at Memorial Center. Although such a group contains many persons of a higher socioeconomic level than would be found in a clinic population in other major New York hospitals, the average occupational and educational level is lower than that of a private patient population. The largest ethnic and religious group in the total sample is composed of first-generation Eastern European Jews. The exact composition of the samples in the colostomy and mastectomy investigations, which were utilized in this study also, is reported in detail in previous publications

(Bard 1955, Sutherland et al. 1952). The other important characteristic of the sample is that it is not drawn from a psychiatric population. The entire range of human adaptation, from extremely well-integrated persons to non-institutionalized psychotics, is represented. In fact, a high proportion of patients available for psychological study can be regarded as "normal" by ordinary community standards.

Theoretical Orientation

Research in a hospital which treats serious somatic disease provides an opportunity for observing the integrative thinking and behavioral processes by which people attempt to cope with threats to their survival, integrity, and acceptability to other people. In addition, the disruptive effects of these threats upon the patient's adaptive techniques promote the direct communication of many basic beliefs and expectancies underlying behavior.

Cognitive processes are attributed such an important role in our conceptualization of adaptation to illness and its treatment that some further elaboration of the nature and function of beliefs and assumptions is necessary. Beliefs and assumptions are the distillates of antecedent experience, the organization of past experience, both personal and collective, into cognitive guides for future action. They may be nonreportable or unformulated, though our experience at Memorial Center has indicated that many are formulated and fully reportable, since they are the products of childhood indoctrination in familial and community conceptions about disease, health, and medical treatment. Cantril and associates (1952) have discussed the same concepts in terms with which we are in considerable agreement except for their heavy emphasis upon the nonreportable and noncognitive aspects of man's assumptive world:

> Man builds up his assumptive or form world largely in an unconscious nonintellectual way, in the process of adjustment and development as he goes about the business of life; that is, as he tries to act effectively to achieve his purposes. . . . Because man inevitably builds up for himself an assumptive world in carrying out his purposive activities, the world he is related to, the world he sees, the world he is operating on and the world that is operating on him is the result of a transactional process in which man himself plays an active role. Man carries out his activities in the midst of concrete events which themselves delimit the significances he must deal with.

> In the process man is himself changed in greater or lesser degree by having his own assumptive world changed-through confirmation or denial as a result of action.

Action based upon beliefs and assumptions is dependent upon their prognostic reliability, that is, whether they function adequately as guides to action. When they are fundamentally challenged by events, so that confidence in their prognostic reliability can no longer be maintained, the constellation of action patterns derived from them becomes disturbed. This disruption of techniques of mastery results in a variety of reactions, such as the depressive and paranoid ones which will be discussed.

A hospital engaged in active cancer treatment, therefore, offers a "laboratory" type of situation for the investigation of complex processes involved in the elaboration of psychiatric disorders. Psychologic reactions can be intensively studied as patients attempt to integrate a sequence of serious threats involved in diagnosis and treatment. At the time of diagnosis the patient is exposed to the possibility of knowing that he has cancer, a disease often regarded by the community as repellent, ravaging, and invariably fatal. Data reported by Abrams and Finesinger (1953) support this interpretation of the significance of cancer to patients, particularly the repellent connotations. They found that the most significant and characteristic concept held by a group of sixty patients was that cancer was a disease of unclean origin and repellent to other people.

Although all diseases threatening life are capable of producing disruptive reactions in patients, the specific connotations of cancer tend to increase their appearance quantitatively and probably contribute unique qualitative aspects to the reactions. The threat to survival is undoubtedly an extremely important factor in the emotional reactions of patients with cancer throughout treatment and, in some instances, during their entire lives. However, previous studies at Memorial Hospital indicate that other factors are very significant in the psychologic reactions of the cancer patient. Two factors have been identified as having an important role in the production of depressive, paranoid, and hypochondriacal reactions: (1) the threat posed by disease to the patient's long-term psychologic techniques for preserving health and integrity, and (2) the disruption of his techniques for maintaining interpersonal relationships. It is with the elaboration of these factors that our present report is essentially concerned.

CLINICAL MATERIAL

Techniques for Achieving Acceptability

All humans have the biosocial need to be acceptable to other humans. The term "acceptability" as used in this paper implies one individual coming into a positive relation with another. The relationship described as positive is characterized by the presence of one or more of the following attributes: (1) affectionate, affective responses; (2) utilization of the resources of the accepting person for the constructive development and expansion of the other; and (3) utilization of the resources of the accepting person for help in those situations where help is needed and for protection against noxious forces. In most humans the desire to be acceptable to all others can be demonstrated, even though the desire to be accepted by people especially meaningful to them may be greater than the desire to be accepted by those of less significance in their lives.

In all, the need to be acceptable to at least one other person can be shown. Acceptance by others is necessary for survival, since, to varying degrees, it guarantees the availability of the resources of others or of the society as a whole to the individual. Ostracism from a tightly knit, homogeneous society has frequently been equivalent to a death sentence for the excluded person. Techniques for guaranteeing acceptance by others are developed from early life, and the earliest techniques are developed in relation to parents or their surrogates. The techniques and the value systems associated with them are conditioned by the approving, affectionate, and rewarding responses, or their opposite, of parents and surrogates. Important concepts concerning acceptable behavior are derived from cultural patterns and values. These are interpreted for and transmitted to the individual by his family and community. Certain concepts of acceptability, however, may be highly individual, reflecting the idiosyncratic aspects of pathological personality organization.

The need for acceptance by others, though constantly present, fluctuates quantitatively in a dynamic relationship with the strength of the feeling of need for others at any particular moment in a person's life history. The greater the need for others at any moment, the greater will be the need for acceptance and the more active and varied the techniques for acceptability. Helplessness in coping with the reality threat of a potentially fatal disease, such as cancer, places the person in a position where increased dependence on others is realistically necessary. Situations or states connected with increased needs for dependency on others increase the needs for acceptability. This promotes the exaggerated use of usual techniques, such as excessive cleanliness and conformity, the reinstatement of earlier techniques presumably renounced in the process of development (frequently called regressions), or the invention of new ones. In these situations the dependent attitudes are especially oriented to those persons perceived as powerful enough to cope with the specific threats and their resulting anxieties. Our observations indicate that these persons are generally the physicians and surgeons concerned with treatment. Devaluated self-esteem, associated with irrational concepts of personal culpability—for example, sinfulness and badness—in the causation of their disease increases the feelings of unacceptability. Unfortunately, feelings of unworthiness may lead the patient to doubt his acceptability to medical personnel and, according to the findings of Abrams and Finesinger, to misinterpret aspects of their behavior as evidence of rejection.

Confusion about dependency concepts exists in the psychiatric literature because of a failure to distinguish (1) normal dependent needs expressed in interdependent interaction with others; (2) heightened dependent needs mobilized by a crisis situation or threat; and (3) a pathological adaptation in which control or possession of another's resources is believed to be the primary way of achieving personally significant goals and preventing injury or disease. Although it is not the purpose of this paper to provide this much-needed clarification, our experience indicates that in situations of crisis it is difficult, without careful investigation of the past history, to differentiate a chronically pathological dependent adaptation from heightened dependent needs arising from reality helplessness.

There is a group of people who, because parental or cultural demands for acceptance were such as to preclude normal development or fulfillment of individual needs and experience, became pathologically independent characters. Mistrust of others, especially when help may be needed, is characteristic of this group. In the face of a reality situation demanding it, members of this group fail to seek help or, in seeking it, face profound anxiety with paranoid decompensatory reactions.

As we have already indicated, situations of helplessness precipitated by the pressure of serious disease often promote an exaggerated need for acceptance and an increased fear of and sensitivity to rejection, with a consequent caricaturing of usual techniques of acceptability. In the patients we have observed, the techniques prominently involved were cleanliness, goodness, devotion to duty, industriousness and achievement, self-sacrifice, and submissiveness. When, in face of the increased helplessness and the increased need for acceptability, either the disease itself or the attendant necessary surgery produces a situation which precludes the use of one or more important techniques for acceptability, catastrophic threats to personality organization and functioning results. Patients with abdominoperineal resections for rectal carcinoma, in whom cleanliness was an important prerequisite for acceptability preoperatively, clearly demonstrate such mechanisms in their grossly excessive irrigation, massive withdrawal from social participation, and multiple compulsive practices. The following formulations and case material further illustrate the dynamics of such mechanisms.

Reactions to the disruption of techniques of acceptability. The disruption of techniques of acceptability usually results in self-hatred and depression.

1. A mastectomy or hysterectomy may result in thinking, "I am ugly and unattractive, particularly to men."

> I feel terrible just even looking at that cut. There's nothing left in life for me. I was a woman and felt like any other woman. We're all born for love and affection. I wasn't any different. I wanted the same thing that other women wanted. How can I look at the scar on my body? I feel so disgusted when I look at the scar that I walk around without a shower for so long that potatoes are growing out of my feet. This cut disgusts me so much that I am afraid even to look at it. I curse myself. I used to think my body was beautiful. I would never go near a man now. I am frightened and would think that I did something bad. When a girl walks on the street she dresses to attract men.

That's the way the whole life is. You want to look nice, but now I don't care. All of my ambition is gone with this operation.

2. A colostomy may result in thinking, "I'm dirty and smelly now and not fit for human companionship."

My whole personality has changed since this happened to me. I got to be a sourpuss and am not the same person. I can't smile and be with people when I'm afraid that I'm oozing. The other night I felt this way and when I got home I was unclean. I'm afraid to be with people because I feel I might be dirty and smell. All I want is to be free to go among people and not imagine that they're sniffing and smelling me. I don't want to go to a hospital again even if I need to. I just don't like to be handled or touched because I am dirty and filthy and they have to wash and clean you. Whenever I spilled in the house I would have dreams that I was among people and it was coming out of me and they were running away from me.

Techniques for Preserving Health and Integrity (or Controlling the Occurrence of Disease and Injury)

Identifiable in many of our patients were beliefs that by fulfilling their criteria for acceptability they were simultaneously guaranteeing themselves against the occurrence of either serious illness or injury. The dynamics of such beliefs contained the premise that powerful people or their supernatural extensions would protect them from harm if they were good. One corollary of these beliefs is that illness results from antisocial acts or transgressions against the wishes of authoritative figures. Such a concept of the causation of cancer was also verbalized by a number of patients in studies reported by Abrams and Finesinger (1953) and Bard and Dyk (1955). These patients attributed their illness to occurrences such as contracting venereal disease and a variety of misdeeds, real or imagined. Another set of techniques for preserving health derives essentially from parental indoctrination and reflects parental and cultural convictions about health and disease. These techniques include such ideas as getting proper nourishment or enough sleep, keeping the bowels regulated, avoiding overindulgences, etc. Violation of these health codes was seen as the cause or a contributory factor by many patients.

When a serious illness like cancer occurs, previous beliefs about maintenance of health and integrity are profoundly challenged. The challenge to such basic conceptions provokes the appearance of anxiety reactions and depressive and paranoid responses. The pattern of the reaction is in large part determined by whether the original beliefs are maintained, significantly altered, or renounced. The retention of the original beliefs, in the face of so profound a reality threat as cancer and the attendant surgery usually necessary, requires the utilization of a variety of psychological defenses.

Reactions in which the original beliefs are maintained. "If I am good, nothing harmful will happen to me."

A. "I brought this on myself."

1. "I was bad and deserve punishment." This belief results in feelings of unworthiness and depression.

> I believed God was punishing me for something I did wrong. We were always taught that if God sends you something it's for something you have done. I didn't

question what sins I may have committed. I just felt I had to take it; it was my cross to bear. I could always take punishment when I deserved it. If we're punished, we're punished and that's all there is to it. When I deserved it, I knew I was bad.

2. "I didn't take care of myself." This belief results in self-condemnation, feelings of unworthiness, and depression, since its corollary is, "I could have prevented this from happening if only I had been more careful."

In my own family we were not rich but they cared for the children, and the children were well fed, had good food, good milk, fresh, clean vegetables. We had bread, not riches, but we were healthy. I only bought the best of food for my children, which was one of the first things I spent money for. Only one of my children had a serious sickness. The good food they had prevented other sicknesses. I could never understand how I got sick. I always ate good food. You know Jewish people only eat the finest and cleanest foods; so how could it come to me? I was ashamed because maybe my getting sick meant that I didn't eat good food.

3. "I did this to myself" is transformed into the belief, "He did this to me." The original depressive reaction, in turn, is changed to a paranoid one, or the two reactions fluctuate if the first belief is not banished.

Everybody makes her own bed and then has to lay in it. I say to myself, "Why didn't I plan a different life for myself instead of going for an operation?" If I was a fool enough to go under this operation, I should have died under the knife. They frighten women and tell them that tumors will turn into cancers. I'd never get cancer even if I had 500 tumors. They put the fear of cancer into people's minds, and even if they are not sick to begin with, they get sick by worrying and thinking they get cancer after the doctor tells them that they have tumors. They develop cancer from fright.

B. "I have been good, but the world has been neglectful or unjust." This belief preserves a sense of worth by blaming others. It results in depression with paranoid features, however, because of the failure of the technique of goodness to guarantee safety.

I never squawked about anything and was always a good person. I never asked for anything or bothered anyone. I didn't want to burden anyone with my problems. I did everything for myself and was so clean. I'm sorry that I had the operation, and why didn't I call my sister, because she would have taken me out of the hospital. Instead I called on the wrong people for help. I called on my brother Jack, who says that he told me lots of things. I told him and his wife recently that I didn't want them to go to my funeral because they didn't stop me from going under the knife. They should have broken my feet to prevent me from going.

C. The transformation of a catastrophe into a privilege. "God chastises those whom He loves best." This belief is sometimes accompanied by feelings of exaltation and mania, constituting a manic equivalent. Even in the absence of exaltation, self-esteem is heightened because of thinking that the injury is a sign of special status and value.

Sometimes I and my husband ask each other what we did to be punished so in having our son get leukemia. I don't feel that we have done anything wrong but, instead, have been good to our families and others. One of my friends said, "God chooses his favorites to make them suffer," and I feel that this may be right. In any case, God gave me my son to begin with, and I can do nothing if He wants to take him back.

Reactions in which the original beliefs are altered or renounced. The renunciation of beliefs may result in thinking, "I have no way of controlling illness now; I'm vulnerable." This, in turn, results in an inhibitory depression with anxiety.

I did a lot of charitable work and when my cousin said it was God's will that people got sick I said it was nonsense and shouldn't happen to good people. Why don't people who cause war and destruction get sick and have operations like me? Why did it have to happen to me? I never did anyone any harm and was so good to everybody. My husband was in the fruit business and sent food anywhere I felt it was badly needed. I no longer believe in God if He would do that to me when I have been so good. People who murder and kill and do awful things to others are well, and I have done no harm to anyone.

Reactions in which current reality is altered or rejected to avoid any challenge to the original beliefs. The mechanism of denial sustained by a paranoid reaction: "I had no disease. They just butchered me for their own advantage." This type of thinking results in depression over an undeserved fate and paranoid rage directed at the designated injurer.

"I was a healthy and strong girl. I could have lived to 500 years if people lived to 500 years. I was so strong until

I came to this hospital that I would have lived not to 100, but at least to 150. Now all I ask is a quick death, and I have never wanted to die. A lot of doctors don't know what they're doing. They just like to practice on you. I just hate doctors. I can't explain to you what butchers they are. They ruined my life. I had everything to live for before this operation.

Techniques of Mastery and Concepts of Bodily Integrity

In the last analysis, no technique of mastery or concept of one's physical integrity can be divorced from the larger context of relatedness to other people. Nevertheless, a group of depressive and paranoid responses can be related to beliefs such as "I have lost functions so important to my living that life is no longer worthwhile"; "I have been so mutilated that what is structurally left of me is not adequate for human living"; and "I have not been made inferior by what has happened to me but am better than I was before."

A. The disruption of or interference with techniques of mastery.

1. A hysterectomy can result in believing that total functioning has been compromised, that the keystone organ has been removed.

I used to feel much better with it. A woman feels so much better when she menstruates. The mind works so much better with it. Everything feels so much different. Before, I felt like a little girl, and now I feel like an old lady. When a girl has her period she feels that if something goes wrong today, that tomorrow will be a good day. I swear that with my period I felt so much cooler and my brain worked so much better. They took away a woman's period, the most beautiful thing in life. You don't realize how important it is until you lose it.

2. The amputation of a limb can result in thinking that the limitation of motility eliminates or reduces the possibility of gratification or enjoyment in life from previously valued activities.

> I was a pretty active guy in work and sports. As much as a guy can cram into thirty-five years of enjoyment, I did. I had a full life, Doc. I did everything I wanted to. Everything I did I enjoyed—every bit of it. My only regret is that I can't do everything I did before; work, and play, everything. I feel that I've had it and will never be able to do what I enjoy, that is to the full extent of enjoying it. I have never dreamt of being a double amputee. All of my dreams have been just as if my life before I got sick was continuing without change. I work in the shop doing my ordinary duties, walking around and talking. I have spent several weekends fishing and hunting as I used to. The thing that's killing me, Doc, is hanging around the house. An old man couldn't stand that, and I'm only forty-one years old. I would rather live only two years, if I could go out in any kind of weather and be on the move, than to hang around the house for ten years. What am I going to do, watch TV and see other people do what I used to do? That I can't take at all.

3. A loss of potency associated with urinary-tract difficulties and the disruption of confidence and adequacy associated with invalidism following abdominoperineal resection can result in the initial thought, "I am no longer a man and life is over," which is then transformed into, "I am superior to other men."

The fact is that after the operation I didn't care to live. Particularly when I knew I was, what do you call the word, impotent. After the operation it was impossible to come any more with my wife because there was no erection, and if there would occur such a thing then the complete seed has disappeared. It wasn't a good feeling. Life was insignificant to me for a long, long time. I don't know why this operation should be connected with that. Another man who had the same operation told me that he is still able to have intercourse with his wife, which made me feel worse. Before my operation I was a designer on ladies' knit goods. My branch was to make the patterns and to get out the styles. You could call it being a designer on ladies' dresses and suits. I took charge in a plant of about twenty to twenty-five people. After this, and until the operation, I was in a little business of my own. I made up samples and submitted them to jobbers. If the jobber liked them, he would give an order for 100 dresses and those he rejected, he rejected. After the operation I didn't work for three or four years. I didn't have any confidence. I sold a new car and didn't think I would be able to come back at all. During this time I took in work at home and did it for artists. They gave me a picture, and I made them a suit of clothes; and since I'm a good craftsman, they were glad to make the exchange. One time Dr. B. examined me and said, "Why don't you go back to work?" And since he said that he put a new thing in my life; he gave me courage. I didn't go back as a designer but as an operator on ladies' clothes because sitting was easier than walking around all day long.

Since the operation something else developed, Doctor. I think I have a kind of persecution complex — is that what they call it? Since after the operation the development comes, and it goes on. I feel that I'm disliked in my shop. I'm disliked among people. Either they feel that I'm superior to them, or they feel that I can work better than they do. In my own case maybe I'm a little bit too proud of myself. My foreman hates me, and I wouldn't like to leave because in the other place it might be the same development.

B. Reactions to the violations of body integrity by surgery. "My integrity has been so badly violated that what is left of me is not worthwhile living with." This belief results in profound depression and, in addition to involving feelings of inacceptability to others, focuses upon a tragic sense of incompleteness.

Why did I go and have this done? Two-thirds of your body they took away. I don't even think they had to do it. Look what they did. It didn't bother me. My sister said, "You wore falsies before; why worry now?" But it isn't that. I should thank God I'm living. To go through such an operation is no little thing. I feel self-conscious of it. Not only for men; it's for women too. I feel that way. When a woman puts on a dress, it's the most important part of her. I'm even ashamed to go home. The relatives come to see me, but in the neighborhood I feel worse. That's why I stayed away so long. I feel that everyone is looking at me. My whole system is different than before. My whole face is even changed. I even have blotches all over my face. Before I always used to be smiling; and it's terrible to be around a person who cries and broods, and I know it. They tell me you better get out of it, but I can't help it.

Comment

A thesis is proposed and supported by illustrative clinical observations that malignant disease and its treatment by radical surgery are a fundamental threat to many patients, not only because of the reality danger to survival and bodily integrity but also because of their impact upon adaptational patterns. The threat associated with malignant disease and surgery disrupts important adaptive techniques and profoundly challenges the beliefs and assumptions underlying these techniques. With the disruption of adaptive techniques, whose objective was the prevention of illness or injury, or the promotion of acceptability and self-respect, a crisis situation is created. The thinking associated with these techniques must be either affirmed or renounced; the significance of the event altered or its reality denied. Ordinarily the validity of these beliefs and assumptions is not subjected to critical testing except under special circumstances of life, such as serious disease. At such times evidence that might contradict their validity may be considered. Affirmations, renunciations, alterations of significance, and denial of reality are often accompanied by intense, overt affective reactions of depression, rage, and elation. In the following outline there have been summarized, under the headings of (1) depression, (2) paranoid reactions, and (3) elation, the nature of the adaptive techniques disrupted, the thinking processes basic to the affective reactions, and, wherever applicable, whether the conviction underlying the techniques has been affirmed or renounced.

I. Depression
   A. Related to techniques for control of illness and injury.
      1. "I brought this on myself."

      (*a*) "I was bad and deserve punishment." (technique preserved)

      (*b*) "I didn't take care of myself properly." (technique preserved)

  2. "I have been good, but the world has been neglectful and unjust." (technique preserved)

  3. "I have no way of controlling illness. I am vulnerable." (Inhibitory depression with anxiety) (technique renounced)

B. Related to disruption of the techniques of mastery and techniques for maintaining acceptability consequent to disease and radical surgery

  1. Disruption of techniques of mastery

      (*a*) Loss of limb: "I can't walk, dance, or participate in athletics, etc."

      (*b*) Hysterectomy: "I can't have a baby," or the irrational belief, "I can no longer participate fully in sexual intercourse."

  2. Disruption of techniques of acceptability

      (*a*) Colostomy: "I am dirty, smelly and no longer fit for human companionship."

      (*b*) Mastectomy or hysterectomy: "I am ugly and unattractive, particularly to men."

C. Related to violation of bodily integrity

  1. "What is left of me is not worth living with."

  2. "The functioning of my body has been compromised because important aspects of its structure have been destroyed."

II. Paranoid reactions

A. Related to techniques for control of illness and injury

  1. "I haven't been bad. It's not my fault. Someone else did this to me." (technique preserved)

  2. Idea of neglect and poor care: "The world has neglected me and hasn't recognized my worth and goodness." (technique preserved)

B. Distortion of the fact of illness
   1. Derivative of the mechanism of denial: "I am not sick. The surgeon operated on me to experiment."
   2. Derivative of the mechanism of denial and attribution of illness to the malevolence of another person: "The surgeon made me sick so he could practice on me."
C. Inteference with techniques of mastery
   1. Despair is transformed into a belief about one's superiority to others, accompanied by irrational expectations of injury: "I am no longer a man," is changed to "I am superior to other men who resent me because of this."

III. Elation
   A. The significance of illness is altered
      1. A catastrophe is transformed into a privilege: "God chooses his favorites to make them suffer."

One of the important observations which emerge from inspection of this outline is that the assignment of blame is a critical factor in both depressive and paranoid reactions related to the disruption of techniques for maintaining control over illness and injury. The decision-making process in assigning the direction of blame determines which of the two reactions results. Where blame is attributed to the self, feelings of unworthiness and badness are prominent; guilt is experienced, and depression occurs. Where blame is assigned to others, feelings of worthiness and goodness are prominent; anger is experienced over unjustified injury, and paranoid reactions occur. The factors determining assignment of blame are complex and beyond the scope of this study. The paranoid reaction, however, whether it is intended to or not, protects the patient against the depressive reaction resulting from self-blame. The occurrence of self-referred guilt frequently is associated with an attempt to preserve techniques of control over illness and injury. In effect, what is implied is the assumption that what has occurred is due not to the invalidity of the beliefs and adaptive techniques but, rather, to the patient's failure to follow them. Guilt in this context has two important functions. The first is to preserve interpersonal relations through the declaration, "I have been bad; I want to repent and be forgiven." The relationship may be with actual or symbolized figures of authority or with their supernatural extensions. The second function of guilt, as already indicated, is to preserve the techniques utilized for illusory control over illness and injury, and the associated beliefs, which constitute an important conception of reality.

Schmideberg (1956), in a discussion which also points out the multiple functions that can be served by guilt, emphasizes that under certain circumstances the assumption of responsibility is preferable to a sense of helplessness.

> Guilt implies responsibility; and however painful guilt is, it may be preferable to helplessness. Medieval man believed that the plague was a punishment for his sins; by castigating himself, he hoped to atone to God and for every evil. He had no other alternative in his helplessness.

What is implied in this formulation, as well as in our own, is that the irrational assumption of personal responsibility goes hand in hand with an insistence upon omnipotent control, which is preferred to the acceptance of actual helplessness in certain situations. This leads to an unrealistic conception of personal responsibility where responsibility does not exist and control is not possible. With atonement or expiation for past misdeeds which are attributed a causative role in disease, and a resolution to be good or righteous in the future, the sense of helplessness is dissipated and an illusory control over illness and injury regained.

The assignment of blame following the occurrence of injury or illness, irrespective of the direction of the blame, presupposes the assumption that control is still possible. In self-blame the implication is: "I failed to do what is effective or to behave in such a way that I could induce others to prevent the occurrence of injury and illness." The belief which accompanies the assignment of blame to others or judgment of failure on their part is one of being entitled to what has not been accomplished in one's behalf or of others intentionally producing the harm for their own selfish purposes. When the injury is attributed to another's malevolence or exploitativeness, there is frequently a history of perceiving significant people in the environment prior to the current experience as hostile or manipulative.

Sullivan (1956) has also emphasized the importance of blaming others in the development of paranoid reactions. He has formulated, moreover, that "the essence of the paranoid dynamism is the transference of blame" (p. 147), a formulation with which we are not in agreement, since in our data the development of paranoid reactions has been observed also in relation to irrational expectations of injury where blame played no role. Sullivan made an important contribution to an understanding of the processes involved in paranoia, however, by pointing out that transference of blame, when it does occur, is protected against challenge or critical testing by others through the invention of rationale for the imputed hostility or persecution. For patients with malignant disease the rationale for explanation of injury by others (e.g., producing cancer or performing unnecessary surgery) is frequently (1) the need for practice in order to improve surgical skill, or (2) pecuniary gain.

The mechanism of denial is implicitly basic to both depressive and paranoid reactions which occur in response to the disruption of magical techniques for the control of illness and injury. What is denied is the fact that such omnipotent control is impossible or that a state of helplessness exists in the face of a grave threat to survival. In certain of the paranoid reactions this reaches the point where any knowledge about the occurrence of the disease or its seriousness is denied and the disease and its treatment are attributed to the malevolence of another person. This maneuver is a form of indirect insistence upon the possibility of control over disease and injury. The person to whom the malevolent causation of disease or its unnecessary treatment is attributed is irrationally delegated the power to bring about a dread illness or to flout professional ethics and community morals without fear of retaliation.

Some of the reactions involving either self-blame or blame of others are not necessarily irrational. There are situations in which patients, because of their fears of learning about threatening realities, have caused unnecessary delay in diagnosis and treatment. In view of the widely disseminated information about the necessity for early diagnosis and prompt treatment, patients who blame themselves for unnecessary delay in diagnosis and treatment have some reality basis for their depression. Similarly, patients who have not benefited from advanced medical knowledge because of professional deficiencies in care have some reason for resentment and blame.

Where disease and its treatment have either limited or destroyed continued participation in activities which are prized sources of gratification, the ensuing psychologic reactions, such as depression, are not necessarily evidence of psychopathology. For instance, in the case of an athlete or a dancer who has had a leg amputation for a sarcoma, a reality adaptation has been disrupted by the curtailment of motility. The crisis provoked does not require the reconciliation of illusion and reality, but, instead, necessitates adapting to the loss of prized sources of gratification and fulfillment. The task which has to be accomplished, therefore, is the utilization of alternative techniques for the attainment of the same objectives or a reorientation in which substitute sources of gratification acquire value. Neither will be attempted if the patient does not believe that the objectives are possible to attain or if he is committed to the conviction that what has been lost is primarily what made life worthwhile.

Chapter 15

Psychological Adaptation to Serious Illness and Organ Ablation

The psychological effects of awareness or suspicion of malignant disease and the psychological reactions to ablation of the affected organs have been studied at Memorial Center since 1950. The research included studies of patients who had undergone colectomy, with establishment of an abdominal colostomy, for malignancy of the large bowel, gastrectomy for malignancy of the stomach, mastectomy for malignancy of the breast, and hysterectomy for both malignant and nonmalignant conditions of the uterus and adnexae. Patients were also studied who had undergone oophorectomy, adrenalectomy, and

In collaboration with Marvin G. Drellich, M.D.

hypophysectomy for control of metastatic lesions arising from certain types of breast cancer.

The psychological reactions can be divided into two major categories: (1) reactions related to awareness of a life-threatening illness, and (2) reactions involving concern about how the illness and necessary surgery would affect the patient's ordinary life.

REACTIONS TO LIFE-THREATENING ILLNESS

The immediate response to the discovery of malignancy is generally severe anxiety involving various degrees of agitation and depression. Such reactions are soon complicated by concern over the surgery which is frequently undertaken soon after the diagnosis of cancer has been made. Since much of the apprehension about surgery is related to survival, this factor reinforces the anxiety about death. Effective psychological defenses usually do not develop until the surgical phase of the treatment is over. In the preoperative period of psychological crisis many patients attempt to explain why they became ill. The content of patients' etiologic formulations offer us insight into their highly personalized concepts of the processes determining health and disease.

In chapter 14 (see also Bard and Dyk 1955), some of the explanations offered by patients to account for their illness were described in detail. One patient stated: "I believe God was punishing me for something I did wrong. We were always taught that if God sends you something, it's for something you have done. I didn't question what sins I may have committed. I just felt I had to take it. It was my cross to bear." This patient held the belief, which had not been previously conceptualized, that if she were a worthy person and did not commit sins, her health would be preserved; thus, illness represented punishment for sins that she had committed. Another patient was committed to the proposition that cleanliness was next to godliness; to that end, she would bathe twice daily. From time to time, however, reality demands would interfere with her ritual. She ascribed her illness to these lapses and ascribed them to laziness and carelessness.

Still another patient was convinced that eating only the purest and best food would protect her and her family against serious illness, and she had therefore always been careful about selecting the finest and most wholesome products. When she found out that she had a malignancy, she nonetheless continued to believe in the protective value of food she considered healthful, and she decided she must have been eating improperly. This patient manifested a belief system, rather commonly held by many individuals but often not consciously formulated, that adequate nutrition and the intake of proper foods maintain health and prevent illness. Although nutrition obviously is realistically related to good health, these individuals create mystical and magical systems of beliefs and control focused on concepts of nutrition. This magical relating of food to illness is common among civilized as well as primitive peoples. Even among physicians, reasons for illness are often ascribed to improper nutrition or excessive indulgence in rich foods and alcoholic beverages despite the fact that such etiologic factors may play little or no part. A common diagnosis made by French physicians in particular is *crise de foie*. In our country there is also an undue preoccupation with gastrointestinal function. We are deluged with advertisements for proprietory drugs which appeal to consumer anxieties centering around health and vigor; the preparations presume to correct or prevent assumed disturbances, such as improper elimination, inadequate nutrition, and faulty liver function.

In the face of grave illness many patients tend to attribute exaggerated powers to their physicians and to hospitals. Some patients explicitly refer to their doctors as "Gods." This behavior is generally accompanied by an intensification of dependent attitudes. If events proceed favorably, these patients tend to be excessively grateful and reverential. Physicians should be wary of idolatrous patients, however, since these very individuals may become paranoid under adverse circumstances. Paranoid reactions, not uncommon in serious illness, are seen both in patients and in their immediate families. The paranoia is often directed against the physician, the hospital, or both. An example of a paranoid response is that of a patient whose malignancy was discovered during the course of a routine gynecological examination. She became convinced that everything would have been all right if only she had not been examined. She became suspicious that the surgeons who were making such diagnoses did so in order to have subjects to practice on. Another patient thought that the doctors brought about a cancerous condition in their patients by frightening them about tumors.

From these and many similar statements by patients we concluded that many individuals need to believe that they possess potent techniques for warding off illness and injury. These techniques may include behavior such as: being good, being God-fearing, being clean, taking proper nourishment, avoiding the provocation of hostility, and so forth. Although some of these techniques may at times have some validity, in many patients they form part of magical systems of control which are presumed to maintain health and prevent disease. These belief systems are in general not consciously formulated nor expressed until serious illness occurs. When such a patient becomes aware of a life-threatening illness, beliefs about maintaining health, as well as associated techniques for assuring good health, are challenged. Response to such challenges determines the further course of the patient's attitudes and symptoms. If the original magical belief systems are maintained, the patient is compelled to continue to distort his sense of reality. If he continues to believe that being good, for example, guarantees health, he must accept the idea that he has sinned as an explanation for his catastrophic illness. Such an explanation, in turn, provides additional content for distortion, resulting in depressive reactions.

An occasional patient will renounce magical beliefs. One such person had been a devout woman who, in the face of her life-threatening illness, gave up her belief in God. She had been brought up in a small, midwestern community, the daughter of very religious parents whose social life was integrated with church affairs. When the patient moved to the East after her marriage, she again organized her social life around church and charitable work. Before her illness, she had been an active, seemingly well-adjusted woman—a model wife and mother. Her husband described her as an attractive, strong-minded person concerned with fairness and justice. She regarded her illness as "unfair" in view of her exemplary life, and she renounced her belief in God rather than give up the belief in her own goodness.

Few individuals can face life-threatening illness without some unrealistic defenses, such as magical techniques of mastery or denial of reality. Mark Twain commented on the use of magical techniques in the face of illness, comparing the situation of an ailing person who had no vices to give up to a sinking ship that had no ballast to throw overboard.

It is important that the physician recognize the psychological defenses operative in the patient's attempt to cope with serious illness. This will help him understand the patient's reactions and guide his handling of the situation. It is unwise to challenge or to attempt to undermine a patient's defenses when he is in crisis. If, for example, a patient clearly indicates a reluctance to know the gravity of his situation, he is best left with the defense of denial unless it decisively interferes with necessary therapeutic procedures. Similarly, a patient who entertains magical beliefs about control of disease is not likely to face serious illness without resorting to such techniques, despite the increase in reality distortion it inevitably brings about.

In most instances, acute reactions to the fear of dying disappear when survival from the operative procedure terminates the threat of immediate death. Psychological defense mechanisms, notably denial, become operative in relation to the continuing threat to survival implicit in malignant disease. One would expect patients who have or believe they have cancer to be predominantly preoccupied with death, since cancer has become synonomous with death in the minds of many people. Curiously enough, this is not the case with many of the patients seen at Memorial Center. Despite evidence to the contrary, they frequently believe that in their particular case the cancer either will be cured or has already been cured by the surgery or drug therapy. Without minimizing the number of patients who, in fact, are cured of cancer, it must be pointed out that many patients with advanced disease will deny the certain fatal outcome of their illness.

RESPONSE TO ORGAN ABLATION AND BODILY DISFIGUREMENT

When an organ is ablated, the patient's statements reveal his idiosyncratic concepts of the anatomy and physiology of the organ. These concepts are in general based on a combination of realistic beliefs and a series of misconceptions resulting from inadequate or distorted information and individualistically derived erroneous conclusions. A patient, for example, may know that her uterus is involved in childbearing and menstruation but may also believe that the uterus is necessary for the maintenance of physical strength and good health. Such a woman invariably will respond to hysterectomy with feelings of debilitation and invalidism. The mode of reaction to organ ablation will in large part depend on the concept of organ function. It will also depend on the part that the conceptualized functions play in the patient's life, or, phrased in psychological terms, the part these functions play in the total psychological economy or adaptation of the individual.

Psychiatric reactions to organ ablation supervene under the following circumstances: (1) when there is significant diminution of self-esteem as a result of the ablation; (2) when there is interference in the individual's relatedness to other people; and (3) when organ ablation either diminishes or eliminates a function which is important for the individual's gratification or defensive adaptation.

Organ Ablation Associated with Diminution in Self-Esteem

All women in the study who underwent mastectomy suffered injury to self-esteem. Psychological injury was greater in those women who believed that their attractiveness to men was based largely on physical attributes. Such a belief was held particularly by so-called narcissistic women whose personal histories had already indicated a disturbed relationship with men. Those women who were in a close, loving relationship with their husband and were capable of experiencing sexual gratification did not believe that they had lost their attractiveness to men. Thus, the degree of injury to self-esteem consequent to mastectomy is a function of total personality. One can predict that a woman who is reasonably free of major neurotic difficulties will weather the stress of a mastectomy. If we know the nature of her self-image and how she has related to others before her illness, we can predict, with a fair degree of accuracy, the type and extent of psychiatric disability that will follow a mastectomy. Prognostic predictability offers important prophylactic possibilities. Women who are to undergo mastectomy should always receive some psychological preparation. Since the salient fear in women undergoing mastectomy is that she may become sexually undesirable, free discussion and reassurance by a male physician is helpful. In those instances in which there is reason to expect more severe psychiatric sequaelae, the patient should receive more intense psychotherapy pre- and postoperatively.

Organ Ablation Associated with Disturbances in Interpersonal Relationships

Although organ ablations of the type we are considering usually result in some disturbance in interpersonal relationships, ablation of certain organs, particularly the large bowel, produces dramatic psychiatric symptoms. Since colectomy with abdominal colostomy involves removal of the anal sphincter and terminates the patient's sphincteric control over the elimination of feces and flatus, many patients consider it to be a serious threat to social acceptability. The fear that they might expel feces or pass flatus when in the presence of other people creates in many patients an unwillingness to continue social relationships. Feelings of unacceptability are often so strong that they feel themselves to be pariahs, not worthy of tolerance by others. As in mastectomy cases, the degree of injury to social adaptation varies in each colostomy patient. The more entrenched the belief that cleanliness is a necessary prerequisite for acceptance by other people, the more distressing is the idea of spilling feces or passing flatus. Consequently, those individuals who have been meticulously and compulsively clean as part of their total social adaptation suffer severe disruption of interpersonal relationships following colectomy.

A number of patients studied became deeply depressed, since they were convinced that they could no longer pursue their previous associations with people. They refused to mix with others and some even refused to leave their homes. On the other hand, there was a group of patients who adapted remarkably well and did not disrupt their social relationships. These patients learned to substitute control through irrigations, and after a time could train themselves to have reasonably good control over elimination of both feces and flatus. If the patient was married, the spouse's reaction to the colostomy played a determining role in the patient's rehabilitation. Patients with good marital relationships in the main adapted well to colostomy. This was particularly evident where sexual relations were mutually satisfactory. As with the mastectomy group, a review of the patient's personality and the nature of his social adaptation is a reliable guide for predicting postoperative psychiatric reaction.

Organ Ablation Associated with Interference or Abrogation of Important Functions

The study of hysterectomy patients offered the opportunity to observe specific types of psychiatric disturbances consequent to interference with important functions, particularly childbearing. It must be emphasized that the categories under which these data are being presented are not mutually exclusive. The hysterectomy study offered the opportunity to study (1) the psychodynamics of self-esteem in women and (2) the reactions to a stress situation involving interference with feminine functions.

The biological functions terminated by hysterectomy are childbearing and menstruation, but many women assign other functions to the uterus, such as the preservation of sexual desire, the capacity for sexual enjoyment, and the preservation of sexual attractiveness and of youthfulness and physical vigor. These projections and assignments of function are part of idiosyncratic, unrealistic belief systems. Premenopausal women who underwent hysterectomy manifested feelings of loss and regret regarding the termination of the childbearing potential, even patients who, for whatever reason, had consciously decided against further pregnancy. Some patients denied apprehension over the loss of their reproductive organs and some consciously seemed to welcome the operation, but this was often a denial of intolerable feelings about the impending loss.

Denial of feelings regarding loss of uterus. A thirty-five-year-old, unmarried woman was originally admitted to the hospital with a diagnosis of fibroid of the uterus and was informed that she was to have a hysterectomy. She evidenced no conscious regret over the loss of the uterus and indicated that she was interested only in having her disease cured. It was discovered at operation that a myomectomy rather than a hysterectomy was needed, and she was informed postoperatively that her uterus was intact. She responded with feelings of elation and indicated that she had been trying to conceal her deep regret over her expected sterilization.

The ability to have children and the bearing and raising of children serves a variety of differing and adaptive functions. For some women child-bearing and rearing are consciously valued as a source of pleasure and fulfillment. For others, it is verbalized as a necessary concession to men, an act of giving which satisfies the husband's paternal need, his masculine pride. In others, even though children are not desired, the knowledge that they have the physiologic capacity to bear children gives them a feeling of completeness and of femininity, while the loss of the childbearing function is viewed as rendering them less complete as females. Thus, the part child-bearing plays in the total psychological economy of a woman will determine her reaction to the termination of the child-bearing potential. Here again, as in the instance of mastectomy and colectomy, there are prognostic guides. The physician may ask himself: "What does child-bearing mean to this particular woman? What does it mean to her in relation to her sense of femininity and her feeling of self-esteem? What does it mean to her in terms of her relatedness to her husband and other significant people in her life situation? And how much is the gratification of being pregnant, of having a child and of rearing a child necessary to her psychological feeling of well-being?" The answer to these questions will alert the physician to the possibility of anxiety or depressive reactions following hysterectomy.

Another instance of loss of a central function secondary to removal of an organ is evidenced in the following case of a man who suffered the loss of both lower extremities.

Significance of loss of function in a double amputee. Mobility is a function whose loss or serious impairment is a source of distress to anyone so afflicted. There are certain individuals, however, who become chronically and irreparably depressed by the loss of mobility. A patient who had become a double amputee (see p. 260) became chronically depressed as a result of this loss. His need for mobility had been at the core of many of the activities that held his interest and that he enjoyed. Though he was an active participant in several sports and in such outdoor activities as hunting and fishing, he did not enjoy being an observer of sports events. After the loss of his legs it became intolerable for him to watch others do what he was no longer able to. Apart from the pleasure in physical activity, mobility is an important component in the defense of flight; it is also a significant mechanism for the release of tension. Individuals who, for whatever reason, have not developed the capacity to sustain attention and interest in intellectual pursuits, are particularly vulnerable to the loss of mobility. Those who have developed intellectual or social interests react more favorably when mobility is lost. There are many examples of people who have suffered crippling illness or injury but were able to lead productive and satisfying lives, notably Franklin D. Roosevelt, who had been an ardent sailing enthusiast and golfer before he was struck down by polio. Reactions to the loss of function depend upon its previous value in the individual's psychologic economy as well as upon adaptive flexibility, a flexibility that itself depends upon the availability and viability of other functions.

Another instance in which the loss of function played an important role in adaptation was seen in a series of women in whom bilateral adrenalectomy was performed for palliative treatment of breast malignancy. All of the women in the adrenalectomy study reported decided loss of sexual desire and sexual responsivity, and the psychiatric sequelae of this depended on the importance of sexual responsivity to the patient's feelings of self-esteem and femininity, to her feelings of acceptability to men, as well as to the extent to which sexual pleasure was a source of gratification. Those women who customarily experienced orgasm in intercourse became depressed in the face of this unexpected loss of sexual desire and responsivity. Depression was even more profound in those women who felt little or no affection for their spouses despite a previously active sexual life. Since most patients were not aware of the existence nor of the function of the adrenals, in these instances distorted concepts about the anatomy and physiology of this organ played no part in the psychological response to adrenalectomy.

SUMMARY AND CONCLUSIONS

The psychiatric study of patients with malignancy who suffered the ablation of significant organs resulted in establishing several principles which we believe are applicable in situations involving other types of life-threatening illnesses and resecting surgical procedures. These principles are:

1. Individuals react to life-threatening illnesses with anxiety or depression. The way in which an individual reacts to the threat of death reflects his entire personality and life history.

2. The disruption of the patient's techniques for controlling health and disease by the advent of illness is a determinant of emotional reactions to serious illness.

3. Highly personalized and idiosyncratic concepts of anatomy and physiology determine psychological responses to disease or surgery of particular organs and organ systems.

4. The nature and degree of emotional disturbance subsequent to organ ablation will depend on (a) the extent of disruption of functions attributed realistically or unrealistically to the organ and (b) the importance placed on the lost functions in the psychological economy of the individual.

5. The reactions to bodily disfigurement resulting from surgery will depend on the extent to which the individual relies on physical attributes for self-esteem and acceptability to others.

Chapter 16

Dreams of Heroin Addicts: a Psychodynamic Appraisal

Psychoanalysis is, in general, inaccessible to the large majority of narcotic addicts, and they, in turn, tend not to be amenable to such treatment. Few psychoanalysts have had the opportunity to treat or observe significant numbers of addicts since, by and large, such patients go to hospitals for treatment rather than to private practitioners. For these reasons, there has been a paucity of psychoanalytic studies of addiction.

Our experience with addicts at Metropolitan Hospital has been extensive. During Kishner's five-year association with the addiction program, he examined psychiatrically

In collaboration with Martin Kishner, M.D.

hundreds of addicts. In the course of four years, Bieber examined about one hundred addicts. Outstanding in the psychopathology of the drug dependent was the unremitting severity of work and sexual inhibitions. Despite at least normal intelligence and a resourcefulness often noted through their ingenuity in stealing techniques, the patients were unable to sustain a reasonable level of effectiveness in socially acceptable work. They sabotaged successful performance and were unable to move upward occupationally, academically, or socially, due to profound fears of success. Potency difficulties were common, and most did not enter into or sustain a love relationship in or out of marriage.

We hypothesized that their dream life would reflect the problems and disturbances of their real life and would reveal the thematic contexts in which references to heroin occurred. Thus, we undertook this exploratory, descriptive dream study designed to tap psychodynamic processes among drug dependents.

SETTING AND METHOD

The male ward at Metropolitan Hospital devoted to the treatment of drug addiction was part of the Department of Psychiatry of the New York Medical College. Most patients were heroin addicts; all were detoxified during their hospital stay. Each subject of this study was addicted to heroin. Each newly admitted patient was asked to report his dreams and to recall any before entering the hospital. In all, eighty consecutive newly admitted patients were interviewed, of whom thirty were unable to recall dreams; thus, fifty heroin addicts comprised the sample. The data were collected by Dr. Kishner who made daily rounds gathering the patients' dreams of the previous night's sleep.

Manifest content was studied to delineate salient themes and contexts in which these themes appeared. We assumed that problems and areas of conflict would be depicted in the manifest dream content. While free associations may track explanatory historical data and illuminate the latent content, they do not alter the significance of the dream theme itself. We decided to restrict our inferences to the open data of manifest content since attempts to interpret latent meanings would involve inference-making shaped by theoretical orientation and thus introduce unnecessary bias.

Each patient was examined psychiatrically and followed during his hospital stay. We were therefore able to get information that supported our inferences about manifest content. Thus, if a patient described a dream in which he was taking a "fix" with a woman and we inferred that a sexual theme was being depicted, support was added if the patient, in fact, was in a sexual relationship with the woman in the dream.

The sample. There were eighteen blacks, seventeen Puerto Ricans, and fifteen whites. Among them were twenty-nine Catholics, twenty-two Protestants and seven Jews. Only one Protestant was white. Of the total hospital population, 7% were white Protestants, suggesting an underrepresentation of white Protestants among the addicts at Metropolitan Hospital, whose addiction wards served the entire city.

The educational mean was at the eleventh grade. Educational achievement ranged from the fifth grade to college graduation. The educational mean was somewhat lower for the Puerto Ricans than for the other two groups.

In the lower fifty percentile were twelve Puerto Ricans (71% of the Puerto Rican group), nine blacks (50% of the black group), and four whites (12.7% of the white group). The median age at starting drugs among the blacks was seventeen, the ages ranging from twelve to twenty-eight; the Puerto Ricans also started drugs at median age seventeen, with an age range of thirteen to twenty-six. The whites were somewhat older. Their median age at starting drugs was twenty, the ages ranging from fifteen to thirty-three. The median number of years on drugs was eleven for blacks, eleven for Puerto Ricans and seven for whites.

Marital status. Of the fifty patients in the sample, only seven were currently married: five blacks, one Puerto Rican and one white. Single addicts numbered twenty-one; sixteen had separated; five were divorced; one was widowed. Of the total sample, 65% had had repetitive homosexual experiences in adult life, although only 4% were exclusively homosexual.

Results. Of the dreams contributed, twenty patients gave only one dream; nine gave two; ten gave three; eleven gave more than three. Four salient themes appeared in manifest dream content: combat, sexuality, the use of heroin, and death. The themes are not mutually exclusive but tend rather to be interrelated: that is, dreams of combat may center around sexual activity and be concerned with death or the use of heroin.

CLINICAL MATERIAL

Dreams of Combat

In dreams of combat the patient would be attacked or attack others. In 32 cases patients dreamed of being attacked by other men; in 4 cases attack came from animals or monsters. In 13 cases the patients dreamed of attacking other men. In 15 cases attacks by other men were associated with the use of heroin.

A fifty-year-old white male on drugs for twenty-two years dreamed that an older man attacked him with a knife. The older man threw him out of a window and the patient landed on a spiked fence. Then the man cut the patient's head off. In another dream this patient was in bed with a fifteen-year-old female and just as he was about to have intercourse, two frog men (one an older man) entered. The older man snatched the girl and jumped into the water. The patient followed and cut his head off. (Parenthetically, we consistently attempted to determine the age status of figures in a dream. This gave us some notion of the patient's image of himself in relation to others; it gave us some leads about oedipal conflicts; it enriched the detail of the manifest content.)

A thirty-year-old Puerto Rican, on drugs for seventeen years, dreamed that an older black was attacking him with a razor at a dance when he, the patient, was "taking off," that is, taking a "fix."

A twenty-eight-year-old black on drugs for thirteen years dreamed that a pusher stabbed him as he was about to "take off."

A twenty-three-year-old white on drugs for four years dreamed he was attacked by three bears. He rammed butter down their mouths and saved his father and mother who were sleeping in an adjacent room. In another dream the same patient was in church with his aunt (his father's pretty, younger sister) and her husband. Someone came in and swallowed the uncle's head.

A thirty-one-year-old black on drugs for three years dreamed that he killed hundreds of people, all men. He found himself chasing an older woman but she escaped in a series of vertical slots where he could not follow her.

Robbery occurred in seven dreams. Each depicted men and heroin. Despite the fact that the addicts rob mostly women, since they are easier prey, no dreams were reported in which women were robbed. The above patient also dreamed that he and a friend were robbing a drug store for narcotics when the police gave chase. Every building the patient ran into blew up and he awakened with acute anxiety. In 12 cases police were the attacking figures. In half these cases police were explicitly depicted as older men; in one-third the police were killed by the patient or his allies.

Dreams of attack upon women or by women were infrequent. In only 2 cases the dreams depicted the patient attacking a woman—the patient already described who dreamed he killed hundreds of men and chased a woman who escaped; and a twenty-year-old white, six years on drugs, who dreamed he attacked two older school teachers with a knife. In 4 cases a woman was depicted as being attacked by someone who also attacked the patient, as in a dream showing Communists attacking the patient and an attractive young girlfriend. In only 2 cases women appeared as the attacker of men, but in both cases the attacker was not hostile to the patient. The first was a thirty-three-year-old black, nine years on drugs, who dreamed an attractive girl was attacking an older man and a young man held the patient responsible for the attack upon her; the second was a twenty-six-year-old black, eleven years on drugs, who dreamed he was in a long corridor and smelled an animal odor (see Bieber

1959). The scene then changed and he saw an attractive older female. He reached out for her. They lay down on the ground and when they began to have intercourse she changed into a female ape. He tried to push her away but she drew him closer. He awoke frightened, feeling she had bitten him.

In 13 cases content was highly bizarre; all such dreams depicted combat. Of these weird dreams eight occurred in white patients, three in blacks, and two in Puerto Ricans. The more frequent occurrence of weird dreams among whites was significant at the .02 level.

The following weird dream was reported by a twenty-six-year-old black, eleven years on drugs. A female with a large head and feet, but without a body, was reading poetry. She was attacked by an animal with a body of a horse and two heads of men. The animal was holding a razor and a meat cleaver. It chopped off the female's head and then attacked the patient as he fell into a valley, terrified. The patient awakened, very frightened.

In dreams of attack with a cutting weapon such as a knife or razor, no differences in choice of weapons was noted among the three groups.

Sexual Dreams

In 35 cases dream themes were explicitly heterosexual. In 27 of these cases, the sexual activity depicted was mainly intercourse. Explicit homosexual content appeared in the dreams of only four patients, of whom two were exclusively homosexual. Dreams with incestuous content were strongly suggested in 7 cases; such content was explicitly stated in 8 cases.

A thirty-three-year-old Puerto Rican, on drugs for fifteen years, dreamed he was "banging" an older sister all over with a yellow baseball bat. She was dressed in a flimsy red negligee. The patient had slept in the same bed with his sister until he was eleven years old. The same patient also dreamed he married a younger woman and then her face changed to that of his mother.

A forty-seven-year-old black, on drugs for twenty-five years, dreamed he was with his mother and his best friend in his mother's apartment. The friend gave the patient a bottle of champagne and then took the mother into the bedroom.

A dream with a suggested incest theme occurred in a twenty-nine-year-old black, eleven years on drugs. The patient was in a bar drinking with an older female. He was kissing and fondling her and wanted to have intercourse with her. He suggested they go to a hotel. She agreed but said, "Let's wait until Mother's Day." The patient retorted, "Are you crazy? Making it at a hotel on Mother's Day?"

In 24 cases dreams depicted a sexual triangle:

A twenty-five-year-old Puerto Rican, five years on drugs, repetitively dreamed he was having intercourse with an older woman. An older man entered, thus preventing climax. This dream always occurred when the patient was at his mother's apartment.

A twenty-nine-year-old black, twelve years on drugs, dreamed that he met one of the ward nurses, an older woman, with her husband on the street. The nurse promised to meet the patient in a few days. The scene shifted to the patient's mother's home, where a male friend warned him that the husband was a tough guy.

A twenty-three-year-old black, married, ten years on drugs, dreamed he entered his home and saw his wife dressed in a negligee, lying on a couch with a man. He was in his underwear and his head was in the wife's lap.

In the sexual dreams of 15 cases, attack or threat of attack by another male was depicted. Each dream involved a triangular situation, as the following dream illustrates. The patient was watching his older brother having intercourse with his wife. The patient stepped in and punched him. In another dream this patient was in bed with his friend's sister and was about to have intercourse with her when the girl's brother walked in and tried to stop them. Another friend of the patient, an older man, walked in and cut the brother's throat. The patient awakened with anxiety, feeling that he, too, was to have been killed.

Orality in narcotic addiction is heavily emphasized in the literature; hence, we were particularly oriented to oral symbolism. We could discern oral symbolism in only 8 cases:

A twenty-year-old black, three years on drugs and exclusively homosexual, dreamed he was having fellatio performed upon him by another man.

A thirty-one-year-old black dreamed he was at a party with his family and a homosexual friend. They were all eating chicken. The patient became upset when an older brother and a friend were given big portions, while he himself got only the small end of a wing with two bones in it.

A twenty-six-year-old black, eleven years on drugs, dreamed that during intercourse the woman "popped a titty in my mouth." (This was the patient who dreamed that a female turned into an ape and bit him.)

A thirty-six-year-old black, nineteen years on drugs, dreamed he was having an orgy which involved "69" with a woman, anal intercourse, and vaginal intercourse.

A twenty-five-year-old Puerto Rican, five years on drugs, dreamed he told a pig he would eat him when he wanted pork chops.

A thirty-year-old Puerto Rican, eleven years on drugs, dreamed of having "69" with a woman, followed by intercourse.

A twenty-three-year-old white, four years on drugs, dreamed of ramming butter in the mouth of three bears and someone swallowing his uncle's head, as previously cited. This patient also dreamed of cunnilingus and fellatio.

A forty-year-old white, twelve years on drugs, dreamed of fellatio, cunnilingus, and intercourse.

Seven of the above eight patients reported repetitive homosexual experiences in adulthood.

Because pathologic dependency is generally associated with orality, all references to dependency were recorded. Such evidences were noted in the dreams of eight patients. The manifest content involved seeking money or assistance from others in obtaining drugs or seeking protection by females from attacking males. None of these 8 cases had dreams with symbols of orality, and only three patients in this group reported homosexual experiences as adults.

Dreams with anal symbolism were reported by six patients. In 3 cases this concerned sodomy—in 1 case homosexual, and in 2 cases heterosexual sodomy. A fourth patient, a thirty-year-old Puerto Rican, seventeen years on drugs, dreamed that a black was grabbing him around the buttocks. A fifth patient, a twenty-four-year-old white, four years on drugs, dreamed he was moving his bowels into a barrel while his mother watched him from behind a tree. A sixth patient, a twenty-seven-year-old white, six years on drugs, dreamed that an older and a younger man were fighting in his mother's bedroom near her bed. The older man stabbed the younger one in the chest, abdomen, and anus with a pair of scissors and twisted the scissors in the anus. The patient awaked feeling as if there was a rat in his rectum. Each of these six patients reported homosexual experiences as adults.

Dreams Concerning Heroin

Reference was made to the use of narcotics in the dreams of twenty-seven patients. The thematic context in which heroin appeared and the order of frequency follows: dreams of attack — 14 cases, including the 7 cases in which robbery occurred; sexual dreams — 11 cases (10 with heterosexual content and 1 with homosexual content); dreams of pathologic dependency — 7 cases; dreams of death from overdose — 4 cases; dreams about leaving the hospital and getting a fix — 4 cases; dreams of being chased by police while taking a fix — 4 cases; dreams that the mother was dead — 3 cases; frustration dreams — 3 cases.

Dreams concerned with the use of heroin that depicted scenes of attack and robbery have already been described. Sexual themes tended to be explicit in heroin dreams. Where a patient dreams he is "taking off" with a woman, either he has actually had intercourse with her, or intercourse occurs or is considered in the dream. One patient dreamed he got into a car with an older man and a younger woman "to cop a fix." Actually the patient had impregnated this woman. In another dream he was involved in a strange neighborhood looking for "the works." He met an older woman and they "took off" together. The woman wanted intercourse, but the patient refused because she looked like his sister. Another patient dreamed he was "taking off" with a group of girls. He felt sexy and scratched the crotches of several of the girls. He went into the street and met a girl who offered to have intercourse with him if he gave her a fix. They "took off" together and had intercourse. The patient awakened at the point of orgasm. When off drugs, he had had premature ejaculations for the past five years.

Several patients described conscious reactions and fantasies when taking heroin. One stated he experienced erection whenever he "took off." Another fantasied pretty girls. A third fantasied pretty girls and "daisy chains." A fourth fantasied anal intercourse with women and men. A fifth said he felt like having intercourse all the time when on drugs. One overt homosexual experienced an increased desire for homosexual activity and consistently fantasied a short, good-looking man performing fellatio on him.

In heroin dreams with a dependency theme, most figures depended upon were women. One patient dreamed his older brother refused to give him three dollars for a fix. The pusher, an older man, gave the patient a three-dollar bag.

A pusher's wife gave the dreamer a fix, and he "took off" in her bedroom.

The patient got a fix from an older female, a cousin.

The patient and his wife were arrested for possession of drugs. He told the judge that the cop had planted it on them. The wife pleaded guilty and took the rap for both of them. The patient then attacked the judge and the cop.

Dreams of Death

Themes concerning death occurred in eleven patients — two blacks, three whites, and six Puerto Ricans. In 2 cases the theme concerned death through overdose. In one such dream the patient was approached by a friend, an older male, who suggested they "cop a fix." The friend smiled, and they never "took off." The scene then changed, and the friend was dead of an overdose. In another dream the patient was going to his mother's house to borrow money for a fix. She was dead, and he never got there. The second patient dreamed he gave his mother drugs and she died of an overdose.

Dreams of death as a result of aggressive attack appeared in 2 cases. In the first, an eight-year-old girl was killed by a black car while he, the patient, was walking with a sexy female. In the second, the patient dreamed he was lying dead on a slab in the morgue with a tag on his big toe. A group of people were standing around, including a younger woman and an older man. The older man performed the autopsy. The group became noisy, and the older man quieted them down. He then removed the patient's brain and sewed him up. The patient awoke in a cold sweat. In 2 other cases, dead relatives populated the dreams. One patient's dream seemed to relate sexuality to death. He was about to have intercourse with one of the ward nurses when she asked him to call a certain number. They got out of bed and she told him to dial DI. Then he awakened.

DISCUSSION

Explanatory psychoanalytic concepts of core pathology in narcotic addiction rest upon two major constructs—

orality and infantile dependency. Most writers emphasize the pathological relationship between the addict and his mother. The postulated infantile character of the addict has been linked to an intolerance of pain, assumed to be similar in its dynamics to such intolerance in the incompletely organized, developing infant.

Savitt (1963), in a report on four cases, concluded:

> The common denominator of the addictive process is impulsivity, that is, the inability to tolerate delay in gratification. In terms of personality organization the opiate addict is comparable to the immature psychic structure of the newborn infant and young child, who is unable to tolerate delay in feeding and must be gratified almost immediately.
>
> The predisposition to addiction is basically due to the failure in early mother-child relationships. In the four cases . . . the mother-child relationship was abruptly interrupted in the early months of infancy, either because the mother returned to work or because of her illness. Later in life, through the use of drugs, the addict repeatedly seeks to symbolically restore the original union with the mother. To the addict, opiate drugs have the symbolic meaning of birth, milk and food; in fact, many addicts go through a stage of milk addiction before going on the opiates.

Glover (1956) placed less emphasis on fixation in the oral phase and more emphasis on the symptom of addiction. He described it as a transition state between psychotic and psychoneurotic phases, serving the function of controlling sadism and preventing regression to a psychosis of the paranoid type. "The drug is a powerful fecal or urinary substance which can destroy dangerous sadistic substances in the body of the patient. These dangerous sadistic substances represent part of the body or the feces of an ambivalently loved object."

Rado (1926) pointed out that the addict without his drug suffers from a tense depression which is then relieved by pharmacogenic elation, characterized in two ways: "1. The elation is brought about by the ego itself at will and therefore gives the addict an omnipotent sense of control over his mood. 2. The elation has an orgastic pattern, 'the alimentary orgasm,' that is, the addict experiences a feeling of well being which is diffused throughout the entire body, as following the ingestion of a meal."

Chein and associates (1964), Ganger and Schugart (1966), and Attardo (1966) document a symbiotic mother-son relationship, where the mother exploits and controls her addicted son. The addict's mother tends to discourage any development or activity perceived as threatening separation. She overtly or covertly cooperates in maintaining his habit by supplying funds or opportunities to purchase narcotics. According to these authors, mother-son separation in early life is not a modal experience among addicts. The maternal figure is markedly similar to the modal type of mother described in the homosexuality study by Bieber et al. (1962). One important difference is that the mothers of the homosexuals were generally ambitious for their sons. This attitude tended to lead to a development of personal resources and promoted greater effectiveness as contrasted with the constricted development characteristic of the addicted patients in this sample. In discussing the families of narcotic addicts, Chein et al. (1964) reported that the fathers were either absent, detached, or hostile to their sons. Again, one sees a striking similarity to the modal father reported in the homosexuality study. Although Chein et al. point out the deleterious paternal influence on the masculine identification of the subjects in their sample, the major thrust of their study was in the direction of the symbiotic mother-son relationship. The frequency of combative themes in the present dream study strongly suggests that a seriously defective relationship with cardinal male figures, certainly with the father, has a primary and perhaps decisive bearing on addictive outcome.

Our material does not support the conclusions of those authors who emphasize the centrality of orality in addicts. It is not germaine to this report to offer a critique of Freud's concepts of pregenital orality. In another paper, Bieber (1967) has done so. Oral behavior during infancy described under the rubric of pregenital sexuality has no discernible relationship to sexuality; rather, oral sexuality is organized when the oedipus complex comes into phase and may be manifested later, partly in relation to olfactory experiences (Bieber 1959). Oral sexual behavior seen in older children and adults represents either normal components of heterosexual arousal or may be substitutive when genital function has been inhibited. Cunnilingus or fellatio is part of the human sexual repertoire, as it is in other mammalian species. When individuals, whether drug addicted or not, dream of orality as represented by cunnilingus and fellatio, sexual phenomena are indeed being depicted, but not necessarily infantile sexuality. In our view, if an addict restricts himself to oral sexuality because he is *unable* to have genital intercourse, it indicates inhibition of phallic function due to anxiety and fear.

Closely connected with the concept of orality is the concept of infantile dependency. Pathologic dependency in adults may be viewed as an adaptation *sui generis* to one's own inhibitions rather than as regression to infantile dependency or a continuation of this state. An addict's pathologic dependency upon his mother is an adaptation to severe inhibition of his own personal resources, while the mother may exploit and encourage her son's dependency in the service of her wish to keep him attached to her. Where a mother has fostered a close, binding relationship, the son often comes to believe that his mother's welfare and even her survival depends upon him. Such men tend to develop feelings of guilt when they attempt to leave, believing the mother will suffer because of their absence. Such sons cannot endure any evidence of maternal suffering. The mothers of addicts may loudly complain about their son's habit but seem to tolerate it far better than the threat of separation. The addict's awareness of this situation reinforces his guilt which, in turn, articulates with his inability to form meaningful social and romantic relationships and furthers his adhesive tie to his mother. In addition to the dependency constellation, the dream data revealed a central, sexual element in the mother-son relationship. Themes of incest were prominent.

Heroin and sexuality. Heroin usage produces varying effects upon sexual functioning. Addicts who suffer from potency problems are not infrequently free of such symptoms when under the influence of heroin, but at the same time they generally lose their capacity for orgasm. Despite this, the sense of inadequacy associated with sexual impotence is temporarily alleviated and it is replaced by a spurious feeling of hypermasculinity based on the pharmacologically induced capability of maintaining an erection for long periods during intercourse. Chein et al. (1964) noted, "Heroin may diminish anxiety associated with sexuality more than it inhibits the sexual functioning per se." Of the 550 cases described in the 1966 report by SARDA (Society for Aid and Rehabilitation of Drug Addicts), one-third used narcotics as an aphrodisiac. Long-standing habituation or the continued use of toxic quantities has, however, the opposite effect—it reduces sexual desire. Goodman and Gillman (1965) found the action of the drug reduced hunger, pain, and aggressive and sexual drives. When taking an intravenous injection of heroin, many addicts experience sensations which they identify as sexual. R. B. Chessick (1960) in a study of fifty addicts at Lexington, Kentucky, reported that after an intravenous injection of heroin, several patients experienced erection at the high point of sensation and had various other tingling feelings in the genitals. These patients had erections even when dreaming of an intravenous injection.

Wickler and Rasor (1953) wrote, "The self administration of drugs, particularly by the parenteral route, is associated with erotic functions of various sorts— masturbatory, incestuous, castrative, etc., of a highly symbolic nature. . . . Intravenous injection . . . produces a transient thrill akin to sexual orgasm, except that it is centered in the abdomen." Goodman and Gillman (1965) also described this reaction. "The rapid intravenous injection produces a warm flushing of the skin and sensations in the lower abdomen described by addicts as similar in intensity and quality to sexual orgasm and known as a 'kick' or 'thrill.'" Rado (1926) termed it "alimentary orgasm," because he believed it was similar to the reaction of well-being following a meal and perhaps also because the sensations are perceived in the lower abdomen. Chessick (1960) termed this phenomenon "the pharmacogenic orgasm," though he cautioned against being mislead by the term "orgasm." In all, the evidence leaves no doubt that some patients experience sexual sensations, and the intravenous injection itself as sexual. One patient in our series had an erection whenever he took intravenous injections of heroin. The dreams of sexual activity accompanying or following intravenous injection of heroin and dreams depicting the patient "taking a fix" with a female provide additional evidence that the administration and immediate effects of heroin injection are erotogenic to many addicts, whether on a pharmacological or psychological basis, or both.

Our data support the work of Zimmering and associates (1952) and those others who posit sexual psychopathology as a core problem in addiction. The prominence of incest themes, triangular situations, and of combat between men illuminates the addict's conflict about sexual competition. The exceedingly high frequency of homosexual behavior in our sample (64%), and the close, binding mother/detached hostile father as bacground factors, suggest a type of disordered nurturance pattern similar to the patients of the homosexual study. The addicts' perception of competition as combative and as potentially lethal has an inhibitory influence on any undertaking even dimly viewed as competitive. This becomes evident in their fear and avoidance of constructive work.

Heroin and aggression. Some authors view the need to control aggression or aggressive impulses as a central determinant of narcotic habituation. Glover (1956) asserted: "The defensive function of drug addiction is to control sadistic charges. A necessary formula appears to be that the individual's own hate impulses, together with identification with objects toward whom he is ambivalent, constitute a dangerous state." Nyswander (1956) postulated that the addict's core problem is an inability to acknowledge aggressive impulses and to express them — so that drugs are used to submerge hostility.

Concepts of aggression as they are used in psychiatry apply to two categories of behavior. One concerns hostility and combative attitudes and behavior; the other concerns self-assertiveness, by which is meant the pursuit of constructive, appropriate, self-fulfilling, and socially beneficial aims. The constricted interests and life style of the addict attest to serious inhibition of self-assertiveness. Some addicts may use drugs to facilitate expressiveness, both sexual and other, but the likelihood is that the majority attempt to narcotize themselves against expressing feared impulses. The masochistic use of drugs to the point of toxicity is, in general, oriented toward a somatic devitalization and toward cancelling out the constructive use of personal resources. Most addicts probably narcotize hostile and combative impulses, though Ganger and Shugart (1966) point out, as did Chein et al. (1964), that the addict is frequently more expressively hostile to his mother when on drugs and that the very use of drugs may represent the acting out of hostile impulses to parents. We found that combative and hostile dream content appeared more often than any other single theme, one way of responding to the pervasive frustration and inhibition characteristic of the addict's functioning and life situation.

Heroin and themes of death. Heroin addicts suffer from an underlying depression. Death from overdose is not rare.

Chronic depression always accompanies chronic, severe inhibition of effective resources. The average addict in our sample had spent at least half his adult life in prison or hospitals. The depressive trend is reflected in dreams of death, frustration, and the absence of optimistic motifs.

Apart from the weird dreams described earlier, there were no significant differences in the major themes noted in the three ethnic groups represented in our sample. This points to psychogenic similarities underlying addiction in various groups. During a Hong Kong sojourn, Kishner interviewed ten Chinese narcotic addicts ranging in age from twenty-five to forty. A Chinese social worker acted as interpreter. The addicts were patients at the Shek Kwu Chau treatment center, a 200-bed facility where methadone was used during withdrawal stages. The patients' central dream themes were: ambition, impotence, threat of being injured by another male, being chased by police, and getting ready to have intercourse when interrupted by a third person. Their dreams were essentially no different from those in our series, further strengthening our conclusion that psychogenic factors in drug addiction cross ethnic lines.

Our study is an investigation of psychological phenomena and process in a lower-class sample. The majority of addicts are to be found in lower socioeconomic and underprivileged groups. Yet, the majority of the siblings of the patients studied were brought up under similar socioeconomic conditions but did not become addicts. This suggests that intrafamily dynamics play a determining role in addictive outcome. As for cultural differences, whites who become addicts may be more profoundly disturbed. We regard weird dreams as symptomatic of pervasive and profound psychopathology and suggestive of

psychotic processes. We found a significantly greater frequency of weird dreams among the whites. Parameters of
personality marked by this study may characterize the
psychological make-up of a susceptible population. When
rooted in underprivileged, intellectually barren, unstimu-
lating environments where there is easy access to drugs,
such individuals become easy prey to narcotic addiction.

Chapter 17

Treatment of the "Borderline" Patient

In recent years there has been a greater inclination to classify as "borderline" many of the patients who were formerly diagnosed as schizophrenic. It seems apparent that analysts are treating many patients who might not have been accepted for analysis in the past. The greater plasticity of techniques, developed through the treatment of a wide range of psychiatric disorders, has led to this change. Offered here is a discussion of my analytic technique and theoretical principles as they concern the borderline syndrome, but which also has application to other psychopathologies.

What is generally called the ego, I call the sum of available adaptive organizations. Adaptive organization may be compatible with integrated functioning — the ability to relate to reality and its requirements — or it may be characterized by a dominance of defensive patterns brought about by intense anxiety, where reality is rapidly renounced in pursuit of defensive needs. A prominent feature of the schizophrenic personality organization is its extreme lability and potential for unpredictable, often instantaneous shifting from one adaptation to another. Consequent to a perception of threat, real or imagined, the borderline patient may suddenly shift from an attitude of seeming relatedness and affability, to profound withdrawal and intense hostility. The patient may shift with equal rapidity from an assertive, expressive attitude to one of submission, masochism, and inhibition. Massive anxiety and hostility may appear with lightning rapidity, precipitating psychotic decompensation that may last from minutes to months.

The potential for sudden, disintegrating anxiety, hostility, and rapid emotional change sets the therapeutic guidelines. I am committed to the principle that early in therapy and for a long time thereafter, the analysis of defenses should be avoided. This technique is especially necessary in borderline and ambulatory schizophrenic conditions. The barricades of defense need to be left in place; instead, the irrational ideas underlying the defenses should be pursued, always bearing in mind the limits of a patient's capacity to understand the determinants of the anxiety and the ability to tolerate it. When a reasonable tolerance level has been established, the analysis of defenses can be approached without serious danger of decompensation.

I have found that unnecessary *Sturm und Drang* is avoided if minor testing and defensive maneuvers are disregarded.

Occasional lateness or a skipped session receive no comment. I do not analyze the motives of gift-giving but accept it as an expression of affection, which it usually is. Sometimes it is a submissive, ingratiating, or another type of acted-out gesture, but analysis of transferential behavior on this level only precipitates feelings of depression and resistance. If defensive behavior becomes a major resistance and a threat to the treatment process, however, it must be handled.

This technique encourages a positive patient-analyst relationship, the key to successful treatment of the borderline patient. The communication of understanding, acceptance, warmth, compassion, and patience is essential. This type of individual has suffered so much psychological damage and reacts with such exquisite alertness to any perception of further injury, that a therapeutic environment free of threat and provocation is an absolute requirement. The demands of such patients, however, cannot always be met. They tend to have a multitude of wishes, often in polar opposition, that make fulfillment impossible. On one hand, endless love and attention are sought; on the other, should the analyst indicate affection, the patient is apt to become frightened. The sensitive analyst must chart a course guided by the patient's cues. Trust in the analyst is a *sine qua non* for successful reconstructive therapy. Trust provides the essential substratum that permits the borderline patient to view irrational ideation without feeling attacked and encourages the development of confidence in reality concepts. Trust strengthens the foundation for a realistic dependence on the therapist and militates toward resolving magical dependency. Many borderline and schizophrenic patients respond with rage and depression to the frustration of magical wishes.

Anxiety is one of the central problems in the psychopathology of the borderline syndrome. Why massive anxiety can be so easily and rapidly precipitated in borderline and schizophrenic patients and why it has such decompensating, disintegrating effects, are questions that still remain unanswered. Pronouncements such as "the ego is weak" are descriptive, not explanatory; why the ego is "weak" is not clarified by the various metapsychological speculations. I think that Rado's formulations of emergency control (1969) which takes into account early disturbances in the organization of basic biological defenses such as anxiety, offer the most promising road to understanding this aspect of the problem. In any event, the therapist must exercise great caution not to provoke massive anxiety responses. All interpretations and procedures must be oriented around this principle. If intense anxiety has not abated by the end of a session, the patient should be asked to remain until the reaction has subsided. This sometimes necessitates cancelling another session, or it may require the patient to return later that day when time is available.

Because anxiety has a decompensating effect on borderline patients, anxiety and tension states should be terminated as soon as possible. Telephone communication with me is available for all patients, but the borderline patient, especially, must have a sense of contact with the therapist and confidence that he or she does not resent being called. If a telephone conversation is insufficient to diminish anxiety, I arrange for a session. I have heard objections from colleagues that such a technique tends to encourage dependency. I have not found this to be so;

rather, it guards against decompensation and promotes increasing trust in the analyst. As the patient becomes more able to cope with problems and anxiety, telephone calls become less frequent. The abuse of this privilege is rare, and if it does occur, it can eventually be worked out in treatment.

When this article originally appeared (1957), the wide array of neuroleptic drugs on the market today were not available. At that time, I prescribed barbiturates and amphetamines. Now I prescribe mainly valium and meprobromate. These drugs should be used during extended periods of anxiety but the chronic use of any such drug should be strongly discouraged. A sufficient amount of deep, restful sleep is extremely helpful during periods of intense anxiety. Deep sleep tends to extinguish the anxiety reaction and this extinction, even if temporary, permits the organism to reconstitute cerebral integration. For this reason, insomnia for several consecutive nights should be short-circuited. There is a wide range of effective hypnotics, and the drug and dosage most suitable for each patient should be recommended.

A second major problem in treating borderline patients is their rapid mobilization of hostility. Extensive hostility is secondary to the severity of their psychological injuries that lead to the inordinate alertness and vulnerability to threat. In my view, hostility is not a manifestation of an aggressive instinct; rather, it serves both as a defensive and reparative response though in reality it achieves neither. As a defense, hostility puts a separating wall between the patient and the perceived injurer. As a reparative technique, the hostility functions to scare away the threatener and in this way an attempt is made to prevent a repetition of hurtful experience. The feelings of isolation, and the actual isolation brought about by chronic feelings of hostility, trigger anxiety which, in turn, sets off secondary hostility toward the object perceived as a threat for having created a disastrous situation.

Manifestations of hostility toward the analyst must be dealt with as soon as they are discerned; the misinterpretations of the situation that led to the hostility must be exposed and resolved. Needless to say, the analyst does not respond to a patient's hostility with hostility. Hostile acting out against the analyst, other than verbal hostility expressed in the confines of the office, tends to have decompensating effects on such patients. Analytic criticism of such behavior provides a point of reality reference. An indiscriminate permissiveness of hostile acting out is damaging to these patients in that it further distorts their already tenuous hold on reality.

A final point is the problem of the borderline patient's responses to reality situations. Many defenses, notably denial, are predicated on a distortion of reality. The massive anxiety referred to has a disorganizing effect on cerebral integration, providing an organic basis for disturbances in reality functioning. Such disturbances, though secondary to anxiety, can themselves produce serious anxiety such as states of depersonalization, which are very frightening. By decompensation, I mean that the dominant adaptive organization at the time of decompensation is not capable of sustaining integrated reality relatedness. Critical to the therapeutic work is maintaining and strengthening reality relatedness by the analysis of irrational ideas, avoiding as much as possible precipitation of massive anxiety, and clarifying situations that confuse the patient. The use of the couch is contraindicated for the borderline patient. To enhance the feeling of contact, the patient should sit up and face the analyst. The sight of the analyst helps confirm his or her reality existence, and at the same time protects the patient against the fear of unexpected attack from the analyst. The patient may become dependent on the analyst for a long period of time but this will not lead to pathologic dependence if the analysis of the underlying irrationalities proceeds satisfactorily.

PART III

Critiques

The first article in this section, "The Genetic Theory," considers Freud's genetic concepts from a cognitive viewpoint that stresses the biosocial roots of childhood sexuality. The second paper is a critique of the libido theory in which his energic views are examined, and third is a critique of his structural theory as developed in his concept of the superego.

Few analysts today are seriously concerned with psychic energy: it has no operational value in therapeutic transactions. Since Freud's time, the advances in methodological sophistication, physics, mathematics, biology, communication theory, and so forth, make the conceptual leap into metapsychology a metaphorical move that ends in a scientific *cul de sac.* Yet, instinctivist concepts still prevail—as in a recently presented view that an aggressive instinct can produce emotional states of anger and hostility without provocation. This could happen in a decorticate animal, but not in an intact human. As a cognitive psychoanalyst, I assert that anger and hostility are *always* reactive to cognitive processes, to beliefs that one has been hurt, or to a perception of threat of injury.

Finally, I think it fitting that this volume conclude with "Cognitive Psychoanalysis and Moral Values." It emphasizes the influence on the patient of the analyst's own concepts of reality. The evaluation of personal values are an integral part of analytic work and to the extent it is possible, the analyst's system of values should be derived from the best available scientific data. Values that derive from culture, family and ethnic background are often part of unsubstantiated folklore and, in the interests of the patient, must be differentiated from the proven distillates of human experience.

Chapter 18

The Genetic Theory

Freud first presented his genetic theory in the *Three Essays on the Theory of Sexuality* in 1905, which marked his departure from reliance on observable data — the hallmark of his monumental discoveries as they appeared in *The Interpretation of Dreams* in 1900. He chose instead to concentrate on the often mystical and speculative theories that characterize his metapsychology. It is in the *Three Essays* that he first enunciated his concept of orality as a psychosexual developmental phase, a concept that he wrote was based upon his "regarding thumb-sucking as a sexual manifestation and choosing it for our study of the essential features of infantile sexuality." The reasons Freud gave (1905b) for claiming thumb-sucking as a sexual phenomenon deserve review:

1. "Sensual sucking involves a complete absorption of the attention and leads either to sleep or even to a motor reaction in the nature of an orgasm." Thus, one way he attempted to establish sucking as sexual was to compare it with orgasm in adults. Sucking may indeed absorb a child's attention but attentiveness does not equate a behavioral sequence with sexuality. Many sorts of stimuli may command attention, such as dangling a colored object in the crib, smiling and nodding, or rocking the child— activities in no way sexual. Further, sucking does not necessarily lead to sleep, nor, incidentally, does orgasm in adults. But even if sucking invariably did lead to sleep, this would not prove sucking to be a sexual phenomenon. Eating is often followed by drowsiness or sleep; exercise, too, may promote sleep. As for infantile sucking leading to orgasm—I have never observed it, nor has any pediatrician with whom I have discussed it.

2. Freud stated that sucking "is not infrequently combined with rubbing some sensuous part of the body such as the breast or the external genitalia. Many children proceed by this path from sucking to masturbation." Sucking and grasping are associated movements in infancy and childhood, and Freud referred to this association in the *Three Essays*. In 1936, I reported a study of neonate sucking and grasping (Bieber 1937, 1940), where I emphasized this association. I hypothesized that the association of sucking and grasping represented our mammalian heritage from primates where the clinging response of infants to the mother enabled them to nurse. In 1938, Fulton and I reported our neurophysiological experiments on primates which established that grasping was part of the postural reflex system, thus supporting my earlier hypothesis. The rubbing movements which Freud

referred to are associated hand movements to the sucking, akin to associated grasping. As for the parts of the body rubbed, Freud chose the breast and genitals — sexual organs — as the involved areas. The origins of his choice of blocks in his theory building are extremely interesting. Freud obtained his material from a Dr. Lindner who did not, however, describe the breast and genitals as the usual areas rubbed. Lindner (1878) named those children who rubbed a part of their body while they sucked, "suckers with combination." Later, the word "combined" re-appeared in Freud's description, "[Sucking] is not infrequently combined with rubbing some sensuous part of the body." Lindner had stated that "all ordinary (simple) suckers can increase their pleasure of sucking by active assistance; the index fingers of one or both hands rub any sensuous spot (erogenous zone) on the head, the neck, the breast, and the abdomen, or pelvis, or thighs." As Lindner stated it, "the most sensitive points of the head are the hairy scalp, one or both sides of the nose, one nostril, one or both earlobes, and one or both lips simultaneously. The most sensuous points on the neck are the areas of the larynx. On the chest it is the nipple, on the abdomen it is the navel, and in the pelvic area, the genitals are chosen." Of the sixty-nine cases of thumb-suckers described by Lindner, only four rubbed their genitals and, of these, only two did it consistently. Freud's mention of only breast and genitals as areas that the child rubs was not exactly accurate reporting. When he attempted to support the sexual character of sucking in his conclusion that genital rubbing associated with sucking leads children from sucking to masturbation, his argument became obviously specious. First, only a small percentage of the suckers rubbed their genitals. Second, in a careful study of 500 children, Lindner found only sixty-nine, that is 13.8%, who were suckers. It seems clear that since all children masturbate, sucking is not the route that usually brings them to genital activity. The argument that sucking is a sexual phenomenon because it leads to masturbation, can, in all fairness, be dismissed.

3. Freud stated in the *Three Essays,* "in the nursery, sucking is often passed along with other kinds of sexual 'naughtiness' of children." I don't think parents or their surrogates tend to view sucking as sexual or even naughty. It seems to me sucking is viewed more as undesirable, inappropriate, infantile, and so forth, but not sexual.

4. Freud stated, "Lindner himself clearly recognized the sexual nature of this activity and emphasized it without qualification." This is inaccurate. Lindner did not regard sucking as sexual nor did he emphasize it without qualification, although there were indications that he thought there might be some connection. The *Three Essays* went through four editions: 1905, 1910, 1915 and 1920. The statement about Lindner appeared in the 1915 edition. In the 1905 and 1910 editions, Freud wrote, "No observer has felt any doubt as to the sexual nature of this activity," but Freud himself seems to have had some gnawing doubts about the sexual nature of sucking. In the 1920 edition, he included the following footnote: "In 1919 a Dr. Galant published under the title of 'Das Lutscherli' the confession of a grown-up girl who had never given up this infantile sexual activity and who represents the satisfaction to be gained from sucking as something completely analogous to sexual satisfaction particularly when this is obtained from a lover's kiss." Freud then quoted Dr. Galant as saying, "Not every kiss is equal to a

Lutscherli—no, no, not by any means! It is important to describe what a lovely feeling goes through your whole body when you suck; you are right away from this world . . .". How sure was Freud about the sexual nature of sucking during childhood if, fifteen years after he originally proposed his theory, he used this farfetched example of an adult woman to substantiate his views?

To return to Lindner, Freud's remark that he "clearly recognized the sexual nature of sucking and emphasized it without qualification," appeared in the 1915 edition. Lindner was a Hungarian pediatrician who in 1878 published a very good study on pleasure sucking or what we today refer to as nonnutritional sucking. It might well be one of the first pediatric statistical studies. Because Freud had placed so much weight on this study, I had it translated.[1] The following were the only allusions to sexuality in Lindner's paper: the terms, "excited," "exalted," and "ecstatic" were used to describe one type of sucker; for example, "the six-year-old son of a cigar store owner who sucks his right thumb, digs his nostril with his little finger of the same hand until the blood comes and runs down over his lips." Lindner then mentioned the four children who rubbed their genitals while sucking, adding, "There is no doubt about it that as the years go on the tickling of the genitals can lead to proper masturbation." In a footnote there appeared the statement that quiet suckers who need no rocking or singing to put them to sleep rub pleasure points which are the same as one finds in adults as their erotic areas. These are Lindner's only allusions to sexuality. He demonstrated statistically that thumbsucking or pleasure sucking has no connection with too

1. By Martha Schon, M.D.

much or too little breast-feeding or too much or too little exposure to pleasure pacifiers. Freud's later formulation that oral eroticism had an experiential base in too much or too little oral gratification finds no support in Lindner's study.

In elaborating secondary developments, Freud stated, "It is not every child who sucks in this way [pleasure sucking]. It may be assumed that those children do so in whom there is a constitutional intensification of the erotogenic significance of the labial region. If that significance persists, these same children when they grow up will become epicures in kissing, will be inclined to perverse kissing [probably a reference to French kissing], or, if males, will have a powerful motive for drinking and smoking. If, however, repression ensues, they will feel disgust at food and will produce hysterical vomiting." This summarizes Freud's basic assumptions underlying his hypothesis that there is normally an oral sexual phase in childhood development.

From a physiological viewpoint, the responses consequent to sucking are almost the opposite of what occurs when an adult is sexually stimulated orally. In sucking, there is a quieting of all excitation; there is a decrease in heart rate, heart rate variability, respiratory rate, and motoric phenomena. In adults, kissing and other oral erotic stimuli trigger increasing arousal with concomitant physical excitation. Sucking can also be viewed as a mechanism for tension release. Bridger and Birns (1968) have shown that if an infant is exposed to a noxious stimulus, like immersing a foot in icewater, sucking behavior is initiated even in children who have just been fed. This type of stimulation and the ensuing behavior are not sexual.

Since Freud, no one has offered any more solid data than he had in support of his hypothesis that infantile sucking and orality are sexual. This idea has been accepted as if it had been methodologically established. And it continues to be accepted and taught as proven doctrine. From time to time I have discussed this matter with colleagues who have the classical point of view. They argue, first, that my view of sexuality is too literal; that theirs is the broad view, though this broadened view has developed out of an unsupported and, I believe, erroneous assumption that infantile orality is sexual. Second, they propose that even if it were not sexual, orality still represents the dominant way in which infants symbolize their relationship with the mother, as well as other aspects of the world as they perceive it. Undoubtedly, the feeding relationship between mother and child is very important; it is, however, only one variable in the immensely complex growth process. Surely psychological development cannot be reduced to orifice-phallus psychology. The mother-child bond may be variously symbolized in terms other than oral. I have, for example, seen maternal deprivation appear in dream scenes of coldness and barrenness, which are thermal and visual symbols.

The Anal Phase

Freud based his concept of an anal phase following an oral phase on the fact that the anus could be used as a sexual organ in both homo- and heterosexual activity and that many individuals experienced erotic sensations in this area. Again, using adult sexuality as a model, he viewed the anus as a type of vagina and the fecal column as a phallic substitute. Since the feces could stimulate the receptive anal mucosa, this potential gave it great value. The child then became reluctant to part with valued feces and when he did, he sustained a sense of loss, for example, castration with the loss of feces. Traits of stubbornness, rebelliousness, and stinginess were presumably the derivatives of anxiety associated with this sense of loss. My own observations do not support Freud's schema. I have been able to delineate three psychodynamic processes associated with the bowel and anus. Two are connected with sexuality; the third is not. The first has to do with anal odors and is a component of the oedipus complex; the second has to do with the use of the anus as a genital substitute after genital functioning has been inhibited. I shall discuss both mechanisms later on. The third process concerns power relationships between parent and child. Bowel training used to be, and in many families still is, the first major area of a power struggle between mother and child. A dominating, controlling mother demands action and rapid returns; a rebellious, stubborn child refuses. Traits of stubbornness and rebelliousness, when rooted in bowel training disturbances, are the by-products of power dynamics.

Sexual Development

The earliest behavior that I have been able to identify as possibly sexual is the infantile manipulation of the genitals which begins in the male between the sixth and ninth month. As far as I know, there are no recorded observations as to when this begins in the female. Shortly before his death, Bela Mittelman told me he thought it occurred somewhat later in females, closer to the end of the first year. Recently, I obtained two observations on female infants. In both, the behavior was present at nine months. If not interfered with, such behavior continues into a masturbatory pattern during childhood, preadolescence, adolescence, and adulthood. In Freud's era, infantile manipulation and childhood masturbation were almost always interrupted as soon as detected. In the *Three Essays*, Freud (1905b) has this to say: "The masturbation of early infancy seems to disappear after a short time; but it may persist uninterruptedly until puberty, and this would constitute the first great deviation from the course of development laid down for civilized men. At some period of infancy, as a rule before the fourth year, the sexual instinct belonging to the genital zone usually revives and persists again for a time until it is once more suppressed, or it may continue without interruption."

I referred to infantile manipulation of the genitals as possibly being sexual, since the genitals are involved in the activity. Freud observed and reported that stimulation of the infant's genitals produced a quiescence. Because of this, he noted, unscrupulous nursemaids quieted children in this manner. I myself have not verified this observation but if it checked out, as I believe it would, then the physical responses to infantile genital manipulation are similar to those following sucking and the opposite of what occurs in later life when the genitals are stimulated. Whether or not an infant's manipulation of his genitals is sexual, the parents interpret it that way so that, from a sociobiological viewpoint, it can be termed sexual behavior. It is important for heuristic purposes to determine when the physical response to genital stimulation changes from quiescence to excitation. One would think that with the volumes written on infantile sexuality, we would have known this by now. We do know that by the fourth year, genital manipulation produces arousal and excitation. I observed a three-and-a-half-year-old genitally masturbating who came to orgasm and I have a patient who assures me that by the age of five, certainly, he was able to come to orgasm by masturbating. Kinsey (1953), in his volume on female sexuality, reported the case of a five-year-old girl who was observed by her mother masturbating to orgasm. Eleanor Galenson (1977) has reported that she observed erections in a male child as erotic responses to his mother when he was two years old. This may well be the earliest age at which such a response has been recorded.

The evidence is very suggestive that the arousal reaction to genital manipulation develops with the oedipus complex. Freud termed infantile masturbation "auto-erotic" because it was not initiated by other objects nor did the behavior depend upon a relationship with other objects. Object-related sexuality begins with the oedipus complex somewhere between the ages of two and five. From birth on, the child participates in ever increasingly complex social interactions with parents and others. I do not consider such interactions as sexual before the oedipus complex develops. A sexual system can be defined just as one can define a respiratory, cardiovascular, or gastrointestinal system, each with its own anatomy, physiology, and biology. The genitals are clearly part of the sexual anatomy as are the organs of reproduction — uterus, tubes, gonads, and those organs that represent secondary sexual characteristics such as breasts and so forth. Those parts of the nervous system specifically identified with sexual arousal and behavior, such as parts of the limbic lobe, are part of the sexual anatomy. Physiological aspects of sex include processes operant in arousal and release in orgasm as described by Masters and Johnson (1966) and include specific hormone function. Waxenberg, Drellich, and Sutherland (1959) have demonstrated that a minimal level of sexual steroids was essential to maintain the sexual function. In their study, women who had been deprived of all steroids, estrogens, and androgens by oophorectomy, hypophysectomy, and adrenalectomy lost all capability for sexual arousal or interest. Sexual elements disappeared even from their dreams. These women did, however, maintain a wish to be held and be shown affection by their husbands, thus clearly distinguishing between a sexual and an affectional system. The women had lost their sexuality but not their desire for an affectionate relationship.

As to the oedipus complex—this phenomenon may be divided into two components consisting of (1) the initiation of heterosexual responsivity, and (2) the rivalry with same-sex individuals. This type of division may be more persuasive for those who do not accept the oedipus complex as a constellation of observable data but see it merely as metapsychological theory. These days, analysts of varying viewpoints seem agreed that the capability of responding to the opposite sex with specific sexual interest and excitation does not begin as late as puberty. Most of us can clearly recall our own interest in the opposite sex, certainly be the age of six. I have had many patients, male and female, who remember being sexually interested by the age of four or five; in males it often included responding with erection. If we are agreed that children indeed respond heterosexually at such an early age to their peer mates, this capability must also extend to all members of the opposite sex, in particular, those in one's intimate family environment; for boys, it is the mother and sisters; for girls, it is father and brothers.

In 1959, I published a paper entitled "Olfaction in Sexual Development and Adult Sexual Organization." I advanced the hypothesis that olfaction was a primary modality in the initiation of heterosexual arousal in humans, and I offered supporting data. For clarification, an explicatory digression is indicated. A male dog of three months has an acute sense of smell but will not respond to the odor of a bitch in heat. He will respond when he is nine months old. Somewhere between the third and ninth month, a development has taken place in his central nervous system that makes possible a response to an olfactory stimulus, known among odor researchers as a pheromone. I believe that the same phenomenon occurs in humans. The capability of reacting with a specific response to olfactory stimuli from the opposite sex is established somewhere between the ages of two and five. Once the olfactory response occurs, all other sensory modalities are rapidly integrated into the sexual system — vision, touch, hearing, and so forth. In 1963, Kalogerakis reported the only case in the literature on the olfactory sexual experiences of a child during his oedipal phase, including a description of the development of a foot fetish in this boy. He initially began to enjoy smelling the feet of his young aunt who lived with his parents. He was clearly turned on by the experience. His response became generalized to other women but never to men. Then he began to look with interest at, and become excited by, the ads of women's stockings in the newspapers. A reaction which was initially olfactory thus became integrated with another sensory modality, vision. Not only was the boy turned on by the odor of women, he was turned off and nauseated by the odor of a male, in particular, his own father. Kalogerakis extended my hypothesis. Not only was olfaction operative in the excitatory response to the heterosexual object, but it was also operative in the rivalry response to the same-sex object as demonstrated by the aversive olfactory reaction. Since 1959, I have gathered a great deal of additional supporting data. I have had at least five male patients who recalled a negative reaction to their father's odor. Toby Bieber has reported (1971) one male homosexual who could immediately turn off a homoerotic response by recalling a male's anal odor. Female odors pleased and excited this patient. Freud postulated that there was no instinctual mechanism to determine heterosexual object choice. I think that all humans, excluding those with chromosomal, hormonal, and gonadal anomalies of the type described by Money and the Hampsons (1957), have an inborn mechanism involving olfaction that guarantees heterosexual responsivity. This phase of the oedipus complex is biologically determined. I think, too, that same-sex rivalry is also biologically rooted. It is identifiable in infrahuman vertebrates and, most probably, humans are no exception.

As to anality in connection with olfaction, I have obtained information, mostly from men, which indicates that anal and body odors, their own and their mother's, play a role in oedipal development. A recent clinical experience is illustrative. A patient who was in love with an erratic woman knew that marriage to her was unwise. When he communicated his doubts to her, she broke off their relationship. As a consequence, he became acutely agitated and depressed. During the depth of his reaction, he had a dream that he was a child back in the kitchen of

his parents' home. His mother was cooking chicken soup
and its wonderful aroma pervaded the room. The patient
himself was sitting on the potty, defecating, and emitting
unpleasant odors. From this dream, the following material emerged. There had been four women in his life,
apart from his mother, with whom he had had a profound
emotional relationship: his first wife who died some years
ago, her mother, another woman some years his senior
with whom he had had an affair for many years, and his
recent amour. He clearly remembered that the mother of
his first wife smelled like his own mother; his wife had
smelled like her own mother, and the other two women
had smelled like his wife. In short, although the patient
did not describe it directly, each woman had smelled like
his mother. Olfaction had played an important role in his
choices and emotional reactions to these women. The
dream in which he is defecating suggests that anality is
a determinant of his sexual response to his mother and is
operant on an oedipal level. After the dream was analyzed, the patient's agitation and depression disappeared
with dramatic suddenness, relief that lasted for several
days, to be followed by mild hypomanic excitement as a
reaction to his discovery.

The anal component in the sexuality of men and women
seems to differ. Male patients not infrequently contribute
clear evidence of interest in their mother's anus and of an
unconscious wish to have had anal intercourse with the
mother. Certainly most adult males find female buttocks
sexually arousing, yet a comparable interest in men's buttocks seems not to be present in most women — a difference in sexual behavior well worth further investigation.

As to the use of the anus as a substitute genital: in both
sexes the proximity of the anus to the genitals and the

similarity of innervation make the anus particularly suitable as a paragenital organ. The anterior wall of the rectum is in close approximation to the sexual organ in both sexes. In the female, the anterior wall of the rectum and the posterior wall of the vagina are palpated as one structure and in the male the anterior wall is adjacent to the prostate and seminal vesicles. When genital masturbation is suppressed or extinguished, children may discover anal masturbation as a substitute. Genital masturbation may be interfered with or entirely extinguished by direct prohibition or by a boy's own castration fears about handling his genitals; or, in the case of a girl, fears about vaginal injury. After the oedipal phase has been established, arousal by the cross-sex parent or siblings may stimulate genital masturbation. Generally, there is no consciousness that the stimulus is an incestuous object. If fear of retaliation is great, genital functioning may be suppressed and the anus may then take on the function of the genital. Some male homosexuals are incapable of genital insertion and they use the anus as a receptive genital organ. In these men, their anus may become symbolic of a vagina. Several heterosexuals whom I have treated have masturbated anally. With the restoration of their genital functioning, including the capability of genital masturbation to orgasm without anxiety, anal masturbation disappeared.

A recurring question concerns the relationship between the oedipal constellation and psychopathology. Why is it, many ask, that the oedipus complex, while ubiquitous, is so much more important in some individuals than in others? Freud never directed himself centrally to this question. The only explanation he offered concerns constitutional factors such as exaggeration of partial impulses, oral or anal, or excessive passivity in the male. In researching the problems in homosexuality, my colleagues and I found that the factors determining the outcome of the biosocial maturational phase known as the oedipus complex are directly linked to family influences, particularly the parents (Bieber et al. 1962). Freud concerned himself with the child's sexual responses and rivalries toward parents, not with parental responses to their children. Parents who do not become disturbed by their sexual responses do not disturb their child's emerging sexuality. I have noted that, in the main, fathers have more anxiety about their sexual responses to daughters than mothers to sons. In one case, a father rejected his daughter when she reached adolescence. He brought in a dream in which he and his daughter were climbing up the side of an active volcano. The volcano was erupting and the lava threatened to destroy both. Though the patient was analytically sophisticated, he had not the vaguest notion of the obvious meaning of his dream when he reported it.

Normally, youngsters become rivalrous with a same-sex parent; it is altogether inappropriate for parents to become rivalrous with children. If a parent's rivalry is significantly acted out, or if it precludes an affectionate relationship, serious psychopathology, sexual and nonsexual, develops in the child. The various ongoing studies of the family and family systems should continue to illuminate the highly complex and varied ways in which parents respond to their child's oedipal development and the ways in which a child adapts to parental reactions to his or her gender and sexuality.

Freud's discovery of the oedipus complex is, in my view, among the truly great contributions to the understanding

of human behavior. His theories, however, are badly in
need of revision and change. This chapter represents an
effort in that direction.

Chapter 19

The Libido Theory

The libido theory has been criticized from its inception, yet its major principles continue to influence psycho-analytic thinking and, by and large, constitute accepted doctrine. Comprehensive criticism of the libido theory would require a good-sized volume; this chapter only discusses selected points which are clearly vulnerable.

The term *libido* was first used by Freud (1894a) in refer-ing to psychic sexual desire. Twenty years later, in "On Narcissism" (1914), libido became sexual psychic energy, and a year later, in his 1915 revision of *Three Essays on Sex-uality* (1905a), he wrote that libido was "a force of variable quantity by which the processes and transformation in the spheres of sexual excitement can be measured." Thus, libido was conceptualized as the force or energy that was the mental counterpart of sexual somatic excitations.

In summary the libido theory states that the mind is an apparatus for mastering excitation. Sexual excitation is manifested as an excitatory process in erotogenic organs. The excitations are transformed and related in a way — never made clear — to psychic energy or psychic states of tension. When psychic tension is raised beyond certain levels of tolerance, a state of *Unlust* arises. The state of *Unlust* promotes activity to secure discharge of tension with accompanying states of gratification. Psychic energy can be accumulated and is stored in the reservoir of ego libido. When this reservoir becomes overfull, the libido flows out to objects to cathect them, with resulting relief or impoverishment of ego libido, depending on the amounts of libido cathected.

The libido has not only quantity; depending on its organ of origin, it also has quality. If it arises from oral excitations, it is oral libido; from anal excitations, it is anal libido. The particular quality of cathected libido determines the nature of the object relationship. In turn, once cathected on an object, the object directs the development, expression, and vicissitudes of that particular qualitative level.

The normal stages of libido development proceed from oral to anal to genital levels of organization. Psychopathology is characterized by regression from later stages of libido organization to earlier ones, caused either by vicissitudes at later stages of organization or by the regressive pulls of fixation from earlier levels. If regression even to the earlier, oral stages of libidinal cathexis does not provide sufficient discharge, libido is introverted and taken back into the ego-libido reservoir to seek discharge in narcissistic pleasure channels. Fixation at a narcissistic level, derived from excessive pleasure, can constitute the force determining the detachment from object libido and the return to narcissistic modes of gratification.

In *Beyond the Pleasure Principle* (1920) the concept of a death instinct and its derivative, the aggressive instinct, was added to the libido theory. The biological source of this instinct was not identified. The aggressive instinct had to be projected outward, otherwise it soon would lead to the death of the organism. The aggressive instinct was also directed to objects. To preserve the objects from extinction, aggression had to be fused with the constructive influences of Eros. Aggression generally existed in this fused form. Occasionally, defusion took place, liberating the aggression and resulting in destructive behavior toward objects. If the aggressive instinct was introverted, it led to self-destructiveness—masochism and suicide. The energies of libidinal and aggressive instincts existed in the "id" as unbound, volcanic, free-flowing forces. In its bound form, these energies were at the service of the ego and superego.

The libido theory rests upon the following assumptions:

1. Instincts are forces; they are the ultimate determinants of all activity.

2. Instinctual forces are manifested in somatic processes.

3. The somatic processes create demands upon mental life.

4. The true purpose of an organism's life is to fulfill instinctual needs.

5. A psychical apparatus mediates the needs of the organism and functions according to certain laws and principles.

In *An Outline of Psycho-Analysis* (1940), Freud made his final statement on his major assumptions about instinct. "The forces which we assume to exist behind the tensions caused by the needs of the id are called instincts. They represent the somatic demands upon mental life. They are the ultimate cause of all activity." His definition of instinct is vague and his failure to achieve a well-focused picture of instincts may be attributed to his attempt to link real biologic processes to a fictitious metapsychology. With the continued elaboration of the metapsychology, the concept of instinct becomes more and more abstruse.

FREUD'S INSTINCT THEORY: TWO ERRORS IN LOGIC

Freud's instinctivist concepts were apparently derived from his clinical observations. The wealth of sexual material that his patients brought to him and the salience of their sexual difficulties led him to conclude that sexual factors were etiologically operative in the neuroses. In 1894b, Freud stated, "In all cases I have analyzed, it was in the sexual life that a painful affect — of precisely the same quality as that attaching to the obsession — had originated. On theoretical grounds, it is not impossible that this affect may at times arise in other spheres; I have merely to state that hitherto I have not discovered any other origin." In this paper, Freud still reserved the possibility that there were other etiological sources of the neuroses but he never pursued alternate avenues of inquiry and by 1905, he unequivocally maintained the primacy of sexuality as the cause of neuroses. Moving from the view that sexuality was an important etiological factor in the neuroses to the position that it was the primary and basic cause was a big jump in logic that I believe was unwarranted and erroneous. He held this view throughout his life and all challenges to it were met by ever-widening concepts of what sexuality was until it was ultimately conceptualized as the all-pervasive Eros.

Freud's second major jump in logic was the assumption that, as sexual conflicts were the primary cause of neuroses, the sexual instinct was the primary instinct that caused all human behavior, normal and pathological. He constructed a concept of human sexual development, personality development, and interpersonal relations based on this idea.

Freud was a great simplifier, a reductionist, and a dualistic thinker. His concept of conflict, central to his description of the neurosis, presumed a minimum of two opposing forces. For simplification, he reduced all conflict to this basic minimum. In his earlier work he reduced conflict to that between libidinal and ego instincts; libido was primary and self-preservative instincts were secondary. He thought that the id was present at birth and was the initial psychic agency. The self-preservative instinct was a function of the ego, and the ego developed later out of the "cortical layer of the id" (1940). It was the task of the self-preservative instinct to watch over the libidinal instinct and to guide it to safe expression. After his studies of narcissism, however, Freud concluded that since there is love of self, the ego itself must be libidinized and made part of the libidinal structure; therefore, the ego instincts could no longer be considered the force that conflicted with the sexual instincts. This idea threatened his concept of conflict. In order to preserve his dualistic structure, a new conflicting force had to be found. In 1920, partly out of a need for a new force and partly because he was unable to explain the traumatic neuroses of World War I, Freud reformulated the libido theory. The repetition of the traumatic experience in the dreams of patients suffering from traumatic neurosis was interpreted as the manifestation of an instinct that existed prior to the libido and was more basic. He called it the instinct to repeat. Again he turned to childhood experiences to find corroboration for this instinct and found it in the repetitive tendencies of children at play, as in the repetitive patterns seen in games, their love of repetition in stories, and so on. The traumatic neurosis was explicated as a condition that resulted from having been overwhelmed by the excessive stimuli of fright when unprotected by the defense of anxiety. Dreams supposedly contributed the anxiety that had not existed in the traumatic situation and, thus, a defense was provided in an attempt to master the traumatic experience. Freud's conclusion about the cause of traumatic neurosis is not compatible with clinical experience. In World War II, the service people who succumbed to traumatic neurosis were found to have suffered from anxiety before their military experience.

From his observations of repetitive dreams in traumatic neuroses, Freud derived the concept of the repetition compulsion and the death instinct. The death instinct was viewed as a repetition compulsion driving the organism to the inorganic state preceding life. The opposite of the death instinct was the life instinct, Eros, which was now the force holding all the cells of the organism together. Eros was no longer the force derived only from the sexual excitations. Where originally libido was the psychic representation of sexual desire, as Eros, it became a uniting force, not only in man, but in all living things. Eros was the force in evolution that made unicellular organisms unite and become multicellular; at the same time it was the force that made humans unite to form groups. It was the force behind constructive processes within the organism and in the environment. The new formulations left metaphysics for frank mysticism, and, according to Freud's own statement, were highly speculative. He was not at all sure that he himself believed them. Nevertheless, in *Group Psychology and the Analysis of the Ego* (1921), he stated that "a group is clearly held together by a power of some kind: and to what power could this feat be better ascribed than to Eros, which holds together everything in the world?"

SEXUALITY AND MOTIVATION

Freud's writings reveal his awareness of the many needs of children, the influence of hostile, detached parents, the power of authority, the meaning of rejection, dependency, sibling rivalry, and competitive behavior in general. He did not, however, accord them genetic importance by themselves, but incorporated them in an expanded concept of sexuality. The classical psychoanalytic view of sexuality came to mean something very different from the ideas held by other scientists, biological and social, and has been one important reason for the isolation of psychoanalysis from the other sciences. Warmth, affection, cooperative behavior—whether expressed between members of the same or opposite sex—was considered sexual. In the earlier writings, all human emotion was seen as sexually determined and, later, as sexually or aggressively determined. Since the concept of sexuality became so expanded, there was no longer any clear definition of sexuality per se. There is still a need for a definition of sexuality that would be meaningful to all analysts and other scientists.

As part of the libido theory, Freud constructed a theory of sexual development based upon oral, anal, and genital phases. Many of the variables relative to the child-parent relationship, such as the need for support, dependency, stimulation, affection, and guidance were subsumed under the oral phase. Other phenomena relating to discipline and authority were subsumed under the anal phase. The phenomena closest to a consensual view of sexuality were subsumed under the genital phase. The observations that related to the oedipus complex were integrated into the genital phase. Freud's theoretical reasoning on the oral and anal stages of sexual development do not, on critical analysis, appear valid. On the other hand, I have been able to confirm for myself many of his *observations* relating to the genital phase, and I fully accept the validity of the oedipus complex as he described it.

As a further extension of the libido theory, Freud formulated his structural metapsychology. The id was a simple extension of the libidinal instincts; the ego, of the self-preservative instincts. The superego was added later to include certain aspects of child-parent-authority relationships. Freud's dualistic concept of conflict always pitted one against the other — libido against ego instincts, the id against the ego, the ego against the superego. Even the word *ambivalent* asserts only two forces. A more advanced concept would provide for many elements in a conflict; ambivalence would be more accurately termed *multivalence*. Despite the theoretical failings of the early constructs, they dealt with important areas of human conflict. Whatever operational value those constructs have, the later concepts of Eros and Thanatos have none.

Thanatos, as the aggressive instinct, is an unrelated combination of reasoned self-assertiveness and destructive hostility. The combination of those two characteristics into a single entity confuses rather than elucidates. Interestingly, Freud never completely accepted his later formulations, nor did he renounce his earlier ones.

The libido theory is a motivational theory of human behavior. It comes under the broader category of theories of causality. A motivational theory assumes purposeful causality and that there are organized, goal-directed impulses which, at a cognitive level of organization, constitute wishes. In the libido theory, the instinct is the motivating force. It is translated through somatic processes into psychic energy which propels the organism toward goal-directed behavior. This constellation of events is reflected subjectively in desires that demand satisfaction; instinctual satisfaction is the ultimate purpose of all behavior. The libido theory further assumes that instinctual gratification is the purpose of life itself. The theory is teleological and so contains the potential for error implicit in teleology, that is, once it is assumed that all behavior is purposeful, one has to give purpose to it, appropriate or not.

Clearly, not all human behavior is purposeful. Anatomical and functional pathology of the central nervous system can produce nonpurposeful behavior. The dyskinetic movements of extrapyramidal disease are not purposeful although patients may assign purpose to the movements. I have asked chorea patients why they jerk around and some have answered, "Because I want to." A frightened individual who freezes helplessly in a panic state or faints is not behaving purposefully. The determinants of these phenomena must be differentiated from an assumed purpose. An anxiety reaction with a hyper-mobilizing effect in the face of a perceived danger has adaptational value within limits; however, in most instances, as far as it concerns integrated behavior, anxiety may produce behavior that is neither purposeful or desirable. In psychoses, acute and chronic, much of the behavior is a reflection of disturbed central nervous system physiology, although the disturbances may be caused by adaptational failure arising out of psychological conflict and pathology. Certain of the behaviors observed in the neuroses, particularly in the psychosomatic syndromes, such as the restlessness seen in hyperthyroidism, represent a breakdown in adaptation.

Freud's premise that "everything I do I wish to do at some level of my existence," assumes omnipotence and omnipotent control. Stated in instinctual terms, the premise becomes, "Everything I do, I am driven to do by my instincts." Instincts transfer omnipotence from the individual to his biological drives and thus makes of instinct an omnipotence. The premise is carried to its ultimate conclusion when purpose is assigned to life itself and when "the power of the id is the true purpose of the individual's existence" (1938).

Freud's attempt to reduce all motivation to libido and aggression produced the same results as with his theories of sexuality. The specific motive in its integrated state was atomized and lost in panmotivationalism. Among the classical psychoanalysts, Heinz Hartmann (1951) was the first to break with Freud's dualistic motivational system. Hartmann postulated autonomous, independent ego functions. According to his reformulation, the ego no longer required all its motivational energy from the instinctual id; the ego could energize behavior whose ultimate motivation was no longer assigned to instinctual libido or aggression. Hartmann created the basis for a multi-motivational psychology in Freudian theory and broke with a fundamental assumption of the libido theory, that all behavior is ultimately instinctual and that all pleasure is ultimately sexual.

INSTINCT AND SOMATIC PROCESS

Having assumed a sexual instinct, Freud then investigated where and how it functioned. Of his first explorations (1894a) he states:

> In the sexually mature male organism somatic sexual excitation is produced — probably continuously — and periodically as a stimulus. In order to define the idea more clearly, let us interpolate that this somatic sexual excitation takes the form of pressure on the walls of the vesiculae seminales which are lined with nerve endings; this visceral excitation will then actually develop continuously but only then will it be sufficient to overcome the resistance in the paths of conduction to the cerebral cortex and express itself as a psychical stimulus. Thereupon, the constellation of sexual ideas existing in the mind becomes charged with energy, and a psychical state of libidinous tension comes into existence, bringing with it the impulse to relieve this tension.

This statement reveals the basic postulates of Freud's answer to the "where" and "how" which became further elaborated into the economic aspect of the libido theory. These three postulates are as follows.

1. Instinct is manifested somatically in an excitatory process which is probably continuously operative. Freud neither fundamentally developed nor changed the idea that the sexual or libidinal instincts were manifested in somatic excitation. He probably derived the idea from evidence of excitation in sexual activity but he was unable to find any somatic source for the aggressive instinct. His inability to root the aggressive instinct in the soma very likely contributed to his doubts about the validity of the idea. The probable continuity of the somatic excitation, as expressed in 1894, became definite continuity in 1905. Freud was forced to take this position. Never definitely stated but always implied, the somatic excitation in some way produced psychic energy. If the somatic excitation was not continuous, psychic energy could not be continuous either. A psychic apparatus working without a constant source of energy was an untenable idea. I believe Freud was also somewhat misled by his concepts about hysterical symptoms. He viewed such symptoms as a partial defense against unacceptable libidinal drives and as a partial gratification of these drives. If a symptom could be continuous for days or longer, it meant that a continuous sexual state must also exist. Had he viewed the symptom solely as a defense, he might have recognized that a constant defense does not imply a constant attack by sexual impulses, but merely a constant threat of attack, which is very different.

The idea of continuous excitation has nothing in physiology or biology to support it. It is physiologically untenable, since excitatory states are always followed by refractory periods. A total organism in constant excitation would not survive very long. One might argue that, since Freud thought that all organs were capable of producing libido, if some were in a refractory state, another could take over. I will discuss this line of reasoning later on.

2. The excitatory process takes place in an organ. In 1894, Freud initially chose the testicles as the organ of excitation. The concept was completely mechanical and was concerned with the distention of the seminal vesicles. He rapidly dropped this idea and by 1905 had already oriented himself to the erotogenic zones as the major organs of excitation. In 1922 he stated that "the sources of these component instincts are the organs of the body and, in particular, certain specially marked *erotogenic zones.*" The organ, which at any moment is the seat of the exciting process, is at that moment also the source of the libido. The organ is the site of transformation from the continually flowing inner somatic stimulation to continually flowing libido. The immediate aim of the instinct—that is, the behavioral response directed by the libidinal energies—is to secure the release of the energy generated by the exciting process in the organ, by bringing some external stimulus to the excited organ (Freud 1922, p. 119).

Freud thus localized the "continually flowing inner somatic source of stimulation" that originated in "an exciting process in an organ" throughout the body, but essentially in the erotogenic zones. Since the mouth, anus, and genitals were designated as the three major erotogenic zones, one could assume that an exciting process would have to be present in one or another of the three zones to account for the continuously flowing excitation. One could further assume that upon reaching the genital level of organization, the genital becomes the major organ of continuing excitation.

These ideas about continuous excitation can easily be tested. The presence of excitation can, of course, be determined subjectively through sensations and objectively through observing motor, vasomotor, and secretory activity. The mouth, anus, and genitals are easily inspected. During sexual activity, one is aware of the specific sexual sensations. Objective observation of the genitals during sexual excitement reveals motor, vasomotor, and secretory activity. When one is not involved in sexual activity, there is no evidence of an excitatory process in the genitals. In the normal adult, for most of a twenty-four hour period, there is no evidence of excitatory processes in the genitals or anus. The mouth, in terms of motor activity, is more active throughout the day than either anus or genitals. The mouth is a component part of nonsexual functions such as eating, breathing, and talking. Even if such motor activity were interpreted as responses to libidinal needs of the mouth, it would be the most important erotogenic zone and all people would be "oral characters." But even the mouth is quiescent for significant periods each day. Since the three major erotogenic zones are free from observable evidence of excitation for significant periods, alternative conclusions follow, viz., (a) the somatic basis of the libido theory is based on theoretical constructs, not on observable biological processes; or, (b) the erotogenic organs are not the major source of libido. Orality, anality, and genitality, and the theoretical structures linked to those zones, have no valid somatic basis.

Though many adherents of the libido theory recognize its inconsistencies, they have felt secure in the idea that at least the theory was rooted in biology. Its somatic basis, however, is dependent upon its own constructs, which are couched in biological terms. But nothing in biology, as we know it, corresponds to the somatic constructs of the libido theory.

In his theories of how erotogenic organs participate in sexual and personality organization, Freud assigned characteristics to these organs that are generally assigned to an organism as a whole—the fallacy of treating a part as a whole. For example, the somatic excitatory process in the mouth sets up "a peculiar feeling of tension which in itself is rather of a painful character" (1905a). Psychically, this is represented as an oral desire. The organism is then driven to obtain an external object which is brought to the mouth to satisfy the desire and give pleasure. The mouth is thus conceived of as creating desire and of driving the individual into action to satisfy that local desire.

Freud stated that the organism is at the service of the demands of the organs, while in fact, the total organism is thought of as having a desire and that behavior is organized to satisfy it. The organs serve together with all other organs to fulfill the needs of the organism as a whole. Freud's organ orientation is reflected in such terms and concepts as oral drives, oral desires, oral gratifications.

A. V. Wolf (1956) has demonstrated how the apparent organ needs derive from total body needs. Thirst is a powerful drive, like hunger and sex. The physiologist, Walter B. Cannon, evolved a theory that thirst results from a drying of the mouth and throat—a theory based on the idea of organ deprivation. It is known as the "dry mouth" theory, which is now disproven. Wolf established that the sensation of thirst was determined by the osmotic pressure of body fluids. When the osmotic pressure of body fluids is raised one or two percent by intravenous injection of a hypertonic saline solution, thirst is felt; it is mediated through osmoreceptors in the hypothalmus, which are the real sensory organs of the thirst reflex. Wolf's work is an excellent example of a systemic need that can be misinterpreted as an oral or local need.

3. *The excitatory processes have an important relationship to psychical states of tension and psychic energy.* In 1894 Freud had already formulated a concept of a mental or psychic energy. What this energy is or where it comes from was not explained. Presumably, it was set off by a psychical stimulus which itself was set off by somatic excitation. The analogy to induction-coil dynamics is implied though not stated. The origin and nature of this energy nevertheless remain unclear, as does the psychical state of libidinous tension which somehow came into existence. After Freud made his unsuccessful attempt to express his psychopathological findings in terms of neuroanatomy, neurophysiology, and physics, he gave up all attempts to deal with the brain as the organ of mental processes (1895). Instead, he constructed a fictitious model, the psychic apparatus, with its own anatomy—the id, ego, and superego—and with its own physiology centered on the idea of psychic energy. With characteristic dualism, Freud elaborated a somatopsychic apparatus, dichotomizing the organism into a body and mind. The linkage between the two, unclear in 1894, remained unclear throughout Freud's work. He never clarified how the somatic excitation became psychic energy. He came closest to an explication by the statement that the erotogenic zones were the organs of transformation. He attempted to use psychic energy itself as an explanation of the linkage. The somatopsychic apparatus was half-real and half-fictitious. The somatic half, so far as it referred to the body, was real. The psychic half, with its anatomy and

physiology, was an imaginary, fictitious model. In the *Outline of Psycho-Analysis* (1940), Freud states, "We assume that mental life is the function of an apparatus to which we ascribe the characteristics of being extended in space and of being made up of several portions—which we imagine, that is, as being like a telescope or microscope, or something of the sort. The consistent carrying through of a conception of this kind is a scientific novelty even though some attempts in that direction have been made previously."

Fictitious concepts can be important tools for ordering and explaining known phenomena and for predicting new ones. They are so used in many sciences today. In discussing the fictitious concepts of Freud's metapsychology, Else Frankel-Brunswick (1954) defends the need for fictitious theoretical constructs in psychoanalysis. My criticism of Freud is not that he used fictitious concepts, but that he so interlaced the fictitious with the phenomena he was explaining that the two became indistinguishable.

Freud used the concept of psychic energy as a device to explain the linkage between biophysiological sexual phenomena and sexual behavior and psychological phenomena, but it became not only the explanation of the linkage—it was the link itself. Psychic energy supposedly originated in the erotogenic zones, real anatomic structures. The excitatory processes said to occur in the mouth, anus, and genitals were so ingeniously linked with fictitious psychic tensions and psychic energy, that the fusion of reality and fiction came to be regarded as totally real. The interpenetration of fictitious concepts with reality occurs extensively in Freud's metapsychology. This interpenetration and Freud's tendency to state a hypothesis, then treat it as proven, have influenced the widely held view that psychic energy is a realistic physiological process.

In "The Psychodynamic Action of Chlorpromazine and Reserpine," Ostow and Kline state (1956), "Since paralysis agitans may be produced by large doses of either drug, the speculation is offered that psychic energy is generated in the globus palladus." Not only have the authors accepted psychic energy as reality, they are attempting to locate the part of the brain in which it is produced.

Norbert Wiener (1950) had this to say:

> One of the most abused terms in biology and psychology is that of energy. In its Aristotelian connotation, it signifies the potential of action, and is not really physical, but rather a metaphysical term. Under these conditions there is perhaps some justification for using it for the tendency of an animal to follow a certain tropism, or for the mind to seek a certain goal. However, it is impossible in this day and age to use the term without a strong suggestion of its physical use, and this suggestion seems to be actually intended by many of those who employ it in the science of life. In physics, energy is a quantity which represents one of the constants of integration of a certain system of ordinary differential equations, etc. . . . In the employment of the word by Freud and by certain schools of physiologists, neither justification (for the use of the term energy) is present; or at the very most, no one has proved it so. There was a plethora of materialistic biological writing at the end of the last century in which the language of physics was bandied around in a very unphysical way. The same sort of quantity was now termed an energy and now a force regardless of the fact that the laws of transformation of force are widely different from those of energy. Chief among these books was *The Riddle of the Universe* by Ernst Haeckel. It is in the line of this scientific

journalese that one finds the words "force" and "energy" interchangeably applied to whatever it is that drives the moth into the light and the flatworm away from it. However, the moth is not pulled by the light nor is the flatworm pushed away from it. They are steered—the one toward the light and the other away. In this steering process, all the energy which the animal possesses in any true physical sense is ultimately converted into heat. . . . Whatever energy it (i.e. the organism) possesses bears no simply stateable relation to its motion. Thus the proper language for end-seeking processes is not that of energy, but of steering and directing. Energy is a thirty-two dollar word of the pseudoscientific psychologist.

Fictitious concepts lean heavily on analogy and metaphor but its use in scientific matters can be dangerous. The flexibility that analogy and metaphor provide permits an easy construction of systems that are cohesive, logical, and internally consistent—a plausibility that readily lends itself to confusion with reality. As to psychic energy, the central question is, does it have any special value in clarifying behavior, normal or pathological? Wiener stated that when used in psychology, the term "energy" is misleading; it implies a relationship to physical science that, in fact, it does not have. We know nothing about the energy dynamics of mental processes. We do not know whether mental processes require energy or are themselves reflections of cerebral energy systems. Considerations about quantity when we do not know the quality of a process are surely far-fetched.

The concept of psychic energy has no special advantage. Does it enhance one's comprehension of human relationships and behavior to say that an individual is cathecting another with libido, instead of saying that one is *relating* to another, and then to detail the nature of this relationship? Can all human complexities be described in oral, anal, or genital terms? What is the advantage of saying that libido is withdrawn over saying that the person has withdrawn? The assumption underlying the narcissistic neuroses is that libido has been withdrawn from objects and is being discharged through narcissistic channels of gratification. From birth on, the individual is related to the environment; the relatedness may be disturbed, even disorganized, but a relationship exists. Examination of patients with a so-called narcissistic neurosis (i.e., psychosis) does not reveal signal evidences of gratification.

Libido theory formulations often follow the laws of physics more closely than those of psychology. In "On Narcissism," Freud (1914) states, "We were struck only by the emanation of this libido — the object cathexis which can be put forth and drawn back. We perceive also, broadly speaking, a certain reciprocity between ego-libido and object-libido. The more that is absorbed by one, the more impoverished does the other become." In other words, the more one loves another, the more impoverished the ego-libido becomes. What are the signs of impoverished ego-libido? If Freud meant that a person in love loves himself or herself less, then observations of reasonable people in love do not confirm this idea. If he is referring to a "love-sick" person who cannot eat or sleep and has to cling to the love object, Freud is describing the anxiety manifestations accompanying the loving of people with neurotic problems. If impoverishment of ego-libido implies a diminished capacity for narcissistic pleasure, then again, anxiety-free people in love, including so-called narcissistic types, retain a capacity to enjoy sensuality. If Freud's statement refers only to the mechanical idea that there is a limited quantum of libido and if it flows to one site it leaves another, then a concept of physics is being applied that has no relevance in psychology.

The pleasure principle is another example of Freud's attempt to express psychological processes in terms of mechanics. Stated in psychological terms, the pleasure principle has observable validity in that it asserts that individuals are motivated to perform acts that give pleasure and will tend to avoid any that produce pain. In 1892, however, Freud and Breuer translated the pleasure principle into physical terms, using Fechner's constancy principle, which was itself derived from Helmholtz's principle of constancy governing the laws in fixed systems. In 1920, Freud described it in these terms:

> For if the work of the mental apparatus is directed to keeping the quantity of excitation low, then anything that is calculated to increase that quantity is bound to be felt as adverse to the functioning of the apparatus, that is, as unpleasurable. The pleasure principle follows from the constancy principle—actually the constancy principle is inferred from the facts which forced us to adopt the pleasure principle. Moreover, a more detailed discussion will show the tendency which we thus attribute to the mental apparatus is subsumed under a special case under Fechner's principle of the tendency towards stability to which he has brought the feelings of pleasure and unpleasure into relation.

Freud ran into difficulties with his physicalist formulations. He viewed foreplay in sexual activity as raising psychic tension and increasing *Unlust*. Since the constancy principle asserts that the psychic apparatus would try to keep excitation low, Freud could not explain why one would attempt to extend foreplay since it would create *Unlust*. Nor could the constancy principle explain why individuals seek out stimulating experiences which also disturb the supposedly desirable homeostatic psychic balance. The physical constancy principle is inconsistent with the findings (after Freud's time) that stimulation is necessary for cerebral integration; that without it the organism fails to develop properly and once developed, does not remain integrated without it.

Is the concept of psychic energy or, for that matter, the entire libido theory, useful? Most psychoanalysts, traditional and others, do not refer to energy concepts in their daily practice, since there is no operational value in doing so. After he had already reformulated the libido theory, Freud himself, in 1922, stated that the cornerstones of psychoanalysis were: the recognition of unconscious mental processes; the theory of resistance; the importance of sexuality and of the oedipus complex. He made no direct mention of the libido theory. The entire theory can be discarded without sacrificing any of the stated cornerstones of Freudian psychoanalytic theory.

Chapter 20

The Superego

Freud's view of morality and of man's relation to society is most clearly reflected in his concept of superego. The superego was conceived of as an agency of the mind that became a repository for internalized social structures in the absence of parents and social authority. Their authoritarian codes were represented in the superego as a kind of police agent whose function was to guard against the expression of pleasurable but antisocial id impulses. In the *Outline of Psycho-Analysis* (1940) Freud wrote: "The superego may bring fresh needs to the fore but its main function remains the limitation of satisfactions" (p. 148). Freud's view of man's nature was strikingly similar to theological fundamentalist precepts. Man was selfish and sought pleasure. Indeed, one of Freud's central ideas was that man's pleasures were in basic conflict with the needs of society at large. Drives toward gratification, the egoistic urges, were located in and energized by an instinctual id, itself completely under the control of a hedonistic pleasure principle. Its aim was to achieve gratification at any cost, heedless of the needs of reality and society. "It almost seems as if the creation of a great community would be most successful if no attention had to be paid to the happiness of the individual" (p. 140).

The instinctual id was depicted, not only as a seething cauldron brimming over with surging Dionysian pleasures, it was also represented as a repository for sociopathy. Antisocial acts resulted from a breakthrough of elements in the instinctual id from the controlling forces of the superego, while socially constructive acts were the evidence of a well-functioning superego powerful enough to screen out immoral instinctual impulses. In superego theory, structure was emphasized over content and moral behavior was, by and large, handled in generalities; it was posed in simplistic opposition to immoral behavior. They are not, however, simple opposites along a conceptual continuum of good-bad. Socially constructive (moral) and antisocial (immoral) acts belong to entirely different sources and categories of behavior and personality, as shall be discussed later on.

The aggressive instincts, like the sexual, were also seen as pressing for expression and gratification and, unless controlled, presented an even greater threat to society than the sexual instincts. Unchecked, aggressive instincts would lead to the extinction of humankind. All men would be murderers. According to Freud's anthropological-fictional schema, they, in fact, once were. Did not the early brothers, like the later conspirators against Caesar, band together and murder the primal father? Murder, not sex, seemed to be man's original sin. Clearly, there had to be a powerful psychic agency such as the superego to protect society against the individual's unbridled aggression and his polymorphous perverse sexuality. Freud (1930) stated:

> aggressiveness is introjected, internalized; it is, in point of fact, sent back from where it came from—that is, it is directed towards . . . [one's] own ego. There it is taken over by a portion of the ego which sets itself over against the rest of the ego as superego which now in the form of conscience is ready to put into action against the ego the same harsh aggression that the ego would have liked to satisfy upon other extraneous individuals. The tension between the harsh superego and the ego that is subjected to it is called by us the sense of guilt; it expresses itself as a need for punishment. Civilization therefore obtains mastery over the individual's dangerous desire for aggression by weakening it and disarming it and by setting up an agency within him to watch over it like a garrison in a conquered city. (p. 123)

Yet, Freud recognized man's need to be part of a group. He termed this need the altruistic urge but, again, it was seen to be in opposition to egoistic urges. "In the process of individual development, as we have said, the main accent falls mostly on the egoistic urge (or the urge to happiness), while the other urge (altruistic) which may be described as a cultural one, is usually content with the role of imposing restrictions" (p. 140).

The egoistic and altruistic urges find good fit within Freud's structural theory; the former appear to be

synonymous with instinctual id impulses and the latter
with superego. In many different ways Freud (1938) re-
stated the same premise: society's function is to restrict
man's hedonism while man tries to achieve gratifications.
The superego, as an agency of the mind, internalized the
interests of society and "its main function remains the
limitation of satisfactions" (p. 148).

MORAL BEHAVIOR

I have observed in young children who were in the pre-
oedipal era (and, according to Freudian theory, still
uninfluenced by the superego which would not yet have
developed) evidence of generosity, kindness, and consideration. I believe such behaviors to be the product of
innate, programmed, affectional potentials evoked by the
appropriate stimuli. Between the ages of six and twelve
weeks the normal infant will respond with smiles and coos
to the stimulus of adult smiling and head nodding. Affectional affects become part of a reciprocally interacting
stimulus-response system between child and parent. The
appropriate parental stimulus (head nodding and smiling)
stimulates pleasure and smiling in the infant, which in
turn stimulates pleasure and smiling in the parent, reinforcing the smiling and pleasurable stimulation in the
infant. Biological maturational phases are species-specific
and do not vary significantly from one normal child to
another. Differences, then, depend upon how the parent
initiates and manages this reverberating, reciprocal system of interaction. Where the parent-child affectional
system develops satisfactorily, children develop the affectional behavior of humans; they become "humanized"
as Robbins (1956) has emphasized (p. 289). Serious

distortions in the developing affectional parent-child system produce disturbed children to whom we may refer as defectively humanized. They become the so-called affectionless characters whose moral behavior will be grossly impaired. Harlow's (1965) experiments demonstrated that monkeys brought up in isolation were incapable of object-related sexuality or of participating in social interaction with other monkeys. In humans as well, membership in a peer group, particularly in preschool and preadolescent eras, seems to be a prerequisite for the development of normal adult social behavior. Morality defined as humane and socially constructive attitudes and behavior can logically be associated with a system of affectional affects. A morality based on humanization articulates naturally with cooperative, socially constructive behavior. A morality based on sublimated behavior derived from the inhibition of instinctual urges and mediated through the conscience-stricken superego suggests a continuity between morality and original sin. Further, a morality which depends upon strength of inhibition proposes a kind of motivational brinksmanship which maintains the personality at the uneasy edge of temptation. Morality powered by the superego can be compared to the use of ever greater repressive police action in civil disorders. If the police perform well and there are enough of them, there will be law and order; if not, chaos reigns. It is as if the civil disorders in large cities today are the consequences of judicial leniency and inadequate police protection—a notion maintained by many citizens who do not accord causal primacy to the social, economic, and political processes determining the disturbances. Similarly, if the variegated dynamic processes operant in determining sociopathy are not accorded primacy (and these processes involve anxiety, inhibition, perceptual and cognitive distortions among other variables) attention is directed instead to the primacy of the inadequate police functioning of the superego.

A society where man's biological and human needs can be satisfied through equitable, democratic social arrangements has the material base for moral behavior. Where there is scarcity because of inequitable distribution of wealth, where there is social stratification, where there are haves and have-nots, the social base for moral behavior is constricted and irregular. Such anxieties are characterized, at least in part, by the immorality of scarcity where one man's gain is another man's loss and where conflicts exist between the social need for cooperative behavior on the one hand, and competitive struggles for personal gratification, if not survival, on the other.

In Freud's conception of man's relationship to society, the gratification of instinctual needs comes into conflict with society, whose needs are in turn seen as running counter to that of individual, hedonistic urges which have to be repressed. This construct implies that the only kind of society reconcilable with the expression of egoistic urges is a totally immoral society, Nazi Germany for instance, in which the leadership can gratify every instinctual wish; they can murder, rob, indulge any sexual fantasy, yet remain as the power elite within their society. Throughout history the prerogatives of the power elite permitted them to have gratifications not accorded the common man. The conflict between egoistic and altruistic urges has theoretical relevance for the powerless and underprivileged. Social revolutions are struggles to reconstruct society in such a way that egoistic needs would not be antagonistic to altruism and would be concordant with a moral society.

IMMORAL BEHAVIOR

The terms *immorality* and *morality* are more at home in philosophy than in psychiatry. Immoral behavior stripped of value judgments by the psychoanalyst appears as neurotic, psychopathologic, or sociopathic syndromes.

Psychoanalysts have been in the vanguard among those who would free sexuality and relegate the puritanical code to the past. Yet such terms as *perverse* and *perversion* continue in use though they have moralistic connotations. By and large the psychopathies and sociopathies are used to designate grossly antisocial behavior. The terms in themselves have no moralistic meaning but they carry a pejorative nuance, and, in this sense, have a moralistic overtone. In attempting to explicate these syndromes, classical psychoanalysis has directed its attention centrally to superego theory. Explanations for sociopathy remain oriented around the notion of superego defects; yet antisocial (immoral) behavior almost always turns out to be the aftermath of anxiety and inhibition rather than of untethered impulses that have escaped from the watchdogs of the superego. Psychoanalytic studies reveal that stealing, rape, prostitution, drug addiction, and so forth, occur in individuals who are profoundly inhibited in sexual and work functions. A rapist is one whose sexual organization is so defective that he cannot fulfill romantic and sexual desires with women who would accept his advances. To consider rape an act motivated by a rush of sadistic sexual impulses that have overcome a defective superego like a prison breakout past a sleepy guard, is to locate psychopathology in a weakened, metapsychological abstraction rather then in the defective cognitive and psychosocial systems involved.

The idea that prostitutes are sexually inhibited usually evokes amusement, if not amazement, among psychoanalytic students; the prostitute is supposedly the personification of Erotica. Clinical examination reveals prostitutes to be sexually frigid; they are incapable of a monogamous love relationship for any length of time; many are homosexual (Greenwald 1958). The psychodynamic underpinnings of their sexual inhibitions include profound early disturbances in their relationship with their mother, fears of a dominating, hostile, rejecting mother on whom there is often a pathologic dependency, and absent or inadequate paternal affection, protection, and support. Disturbances in affectional affects are invariably present among the schizophrenic fraction of the prostitute population, and it is a sizeable fraction. Successful treatment of prostitutes is rare, yet when it is achieved I believe it is through resolving the fears that determine and maintain sexual and other inhibitions, not by creating new ones.

Don Juanism, or male heterosexual promiscuity, is also usually viewed as an expression of great sexual freedom; it is less likely to be regarded as sociopathic when men seek numerous sexual partners than when women do. But as in prostitution, Don Juanism is associated with sexual inhibition. Should the Don Juan begin to love any one woman, he develops profound anxiety, frequently verging on panic. His anxiety requires flight which he may rationalize by claiming a loss of interest and by extolling the qualities of the new favorite. Within a socioethical frame of reference, sexual promiscuity is a time-honored symptom of immorality, a symptom that articulates with the dynamics of structural theory where a weakened, defective superego permits uncontrolled expression of sexual impulses. In operational terms, however, promiscuity and apparent immorality are the consequence of psychopathological syndromes of fear and inhibition. Sexual deviations such as homosexuality are also the consequences of fears, not of defective moral values.

The notion that sociopaths do not experience anxiety or guilt does not accord with my clinical observations. The absence of anxiety and guilt would not be inconsistent with the "sick superego" theory, though this does not appear to be the explanation. The sociopaths I have examined experience anxiety, guilt, and depression which they may deny, repress or attempt to anesthetize through the use of drugs. The suicide rates among them, particularly narcotics addicts, are significantly higher than among nonsociopaths in comparable age groups.

THE SUPEREGO AND EXPERIENTIAL INFLUENCES

Freud's statements about the effects of individual experiences with parents and other authority figures on the evolution and structure of the superego are often contradictory. They vary from descriptions of the superego as a repository of highly specific parental introjects (i.e., parental tastes, class values, etc.) to statements suggesting that experience has essentially little influence on the superego:

A portion of the external world has, at least partially, been abandoned as an object and has instead, by identification, been taken into the ego and thus become an integral part of the internal world. This new psychical energy continues to carry on the functions which have hitherto been performed by the people (the abandoned object) in the external world: it observes the ego, gives it orders, judges it, threatens it with punishment exactly like the parents whose place it has taken. We call this agency the *superego* and are aware of it in its judicial functions as our *conscience*. . . .

The superego is in fact the heir to the oedipus complex and is only established after that complex has been disposed of. For that reason its excessive severity does not follow a real model but corresponds to the strength of the defence used against the temptation of the oedipus complex. Some suspicion of this state of things lies, no doubt, at the bottom of the assertion made by philosophers and believers that the moral sense is not instilled into men by education or acquired by them in their social life but is implanted in them from a higher source. (1940, pp. 205-206)

Yet, a few sentences later Freud states:

the superego continues to play the part of an external world for the ego although it has become a portion of the internal world. Throughout later life it represents the influence of a person's childhood, or the care and education given him by his parents and of his dependence on them—a childhood which is prolonged so greatly in human beings by a family life in common. And in all this it is not only the personal qualities of these parents that is making itself felt, but also everything that had a determining effect on them themselves, the tastes and standards of the social class in which they lived and the innate dispositions and traditions of the race from which they sprang. (p. 206)

Experience shows, however, that the severity of the superego which a child develops in no way corresponds to the severity of the treatment which he has himself met with. The severity of the former seems to be independent of that of the latter. A child who has been very leniently brought up can acquire a very strict conscience. But it would be wrong to exaggerate this independence; it is not difficult to convince oneself that the severity of upbringing does also exert a strong influence on the formation of the child's superego. What it amounts to is that in the formation of the superego and the emergence of a conscience innate constitutional factors and influences from the real environment act in combination. (1930, p. 130)

Although Freud wrote extensively on the theory of parental introjection into the superego, one finds little in his writings which distinguishes one superego from another except for a single parameter, the quantitative polarity of severity and leniency. Throughout, the superego is referred to as though it were an organ like the liver; one is pretty much like another. The superego model is severe and puritanical; in fact, the introjections often resemble not a parent so much as an angry, punitive deity whose main function remains "its limitation of satisfactions." Indeed, Freud (1930) depicted the superego to be quite an angry god—and a paranoid one, as the following quotations reveal: "For the more virtuous a man is, the more severe and distrustful is its behavior so that ultimately it is precisely those people who have carried saintliness furthest who reproach themselves with the worst sins" (p. 125). He stated that once the superego is constructed, "Instinctual renunciation now no longer has a completely liberating effect; virtuous continence is no longer rewarded with the assurances of love. A threatened external unhappiness—loss of love and punishment on the part of external authority—has been exchanged for a permanent internal unhappiness, for the tension of the sense of guilt" (1930, p. 127). And, "If civilization is a necessary course of development from the family to humanity as to a whole—then . . . there is inextricably bound up with it an increase of the sense of guilt, which will perhaps reach heights that the individual finds hard to tolerate" (1930, p. 133). With this dismal view of morality, it would have been appropriate for Freud to have added, "where superego was, there shall ego be."

Of the many complex and varied developmental influences, if any parameter of personality is experientially determined, it is one's moral and ethical values. Even those values that may have biological roots in the affectional system ultimately depend for its outcome on the attitudes and behavior of significant others, parents, peer group, reference group, and so forth. Moral values differ from culture to culture and in a complex heterogeneous society as our own, from group to group. The oedipus complex does not account for this diversity. In all societies with a nuclear family structure the oedipus complex is essentially similar yet moral and ethical values may differ radically.

METAPSYCHOLOGICAL VERSUS
ADAPTATIONAL APPROACH

"As long as things go well with a man his conscience is lenient and lets the ego do all sorts of things; but when misfortune befalls him he searches his soul, acknowledges his sinfulness, heightens the demands of his conscience and imposes abstinences on himself and punishes himself with penances" (1930, p. 126).

Some people respond to misfortune as Freud described but many do not. What determines the different ways which people cope with adversity? Does superego theory explain the differences most usefully? In the late 1950s a psychiatric research team at Memorial Hospital in New York City, of which I was a member, was studying, among other things, psychological reactions to the diagnosis of malignancy (see chapter 14). Upon learning the diagnosis, each patient understandably experienced a reactive depression. In one group, however, there was an overlay of psychopathological depression with self-accusatory content. These patients held themselves accountable for becoming ill. Some had maintained the belief that if one ate the proper food, slept well, exercised regularly, and did not carouse but led a sober life, illness, surely serious illness, would be avoided. Their security operations relative to maintaining good health had been based on vaguely formed, nonverbal beliefs about omnipotent control. When they became ill, it followed that they must have done something wrong; why else would their security system break down? Other patients whose security operations also involved omnipotent control assigned the omnipotence to a deity. These individuals felt that they had sinned. Attempts were then made to seek out their past instances of wrongdoing which would justify their present punishment. Some patients who had been religious nevertheless did not regard themselves as sinners. "I have led a good life. If this could happen to me when there are so many people who are evil, maybe there is no God." These patients were prepared to give up their magical security system rather than distort reality for themselves. The patients who did not distort reality and did not rely upon magic, adapted to their misfortune most effectively; they expressed no self-accusations nor needs to do penance. The notion of a punishing conscience in the face of adversity applied to but one segment of the group studied, but even in these cases, there is no explanatory gain in the idea that the superego becomes severe when things go badly for the ego.

THE SUPEREGO AND THE OEDIPUS COMPLEX

The oedipus complex is not so much a theory as it is a constellation of observable data; it can be repeatedly observed — and not only psychoanalytically — in children and adults. Where Freud's inferences derived directly from observations of the family romance they were psychological, not metapsychological.

The oedipus complex confronts the individual with at least three major moral issues: incest, stealing, and murder. The oedipus complex is predicated on the biological fact that heterosexual responsiveness begins at about the third year of life and that the nuclear family provides the setting in which this interpersonal conflict unfolds. Though a child's sexual responses are not confined to family members, the intimacy of family relations guarantees the inclusion of his cross-sex parent and siblings as objects stimulating sexual responses. The sexually determined competitive attitudes which accompany this new phase bring the child into conflict with a parent of the same sex around whom were organized affectional attitudes and security operations, begun in the recent pre-oedipal past. The child must now attempt to extinguish both incestuous impulses and his sexual rivalry since he needs to preserve affectional and security ties. The precedence of family integrity required the invention of an incest tabu, and the value to children of family integrity promotes the repression of incestuous and rivalrous impulses. The need to control, repress, or extinguish hostile feelings toward the same-sex parent does not derive entirely from external prohibitions and fears of retaliation, but also from a biosocial need to preserve positive affectional ties. The ways in which parental attitudes and behavior influence the resolution of the oedipus complex (and other social aspects of childhood) help shape the ultimate course of moral and ethical values.

The oedipus complex concerns a special type of murder—murder for gain. The law and ethical codes distinguish among various types of killing: self-defense, revenge, and murder for gain or expediency, the last type being represented in the oedipus complex. A son's patricidal wish is not inconsistent with love for his father in the ambivalent relationship with which we are familiar. The paid killer and the military mercenary do not necessarily hate the victims whom they kill only for gain. Impulses to murder for gain are also present among rivalrous siblings. In these situations, however, murderous impulses are associated with rage and hatred, at least initially. In the adult the impulse to murder for gain has a tap root in the oedipus complex.

Freud believed that the murderous impulses associated with the oedipus complex determined the origin of the need for a superego. Although the oedipus complex is a central determinant in personality development, it does not seem to be the prototype for all situations which evoke murderous impulses and defenses against it. Various species-specific behavioral patterns among social animals preclude intraspecies killing. These patterns have been well described by ethologists who have furnished convincing evidence that at least in some species such behaviors are likely to be innate. Similar species-protective mechanisms are probably operant in humans and may account for the revulsion experienced when, for example, one sees another human severely mangled. The hypothesis that revulsion under such circumstances is a reaction formation against an impulse to kill does not take into account species-specific, preservative, biological, defensive integrations. Built-in mechanisms, such as revulsion among humans under the threat described, are clearly not as effective in us as in other members of the animal kingdom, since only man with his vaunted conscience has exterminated countless millions of his own kind.

The development of normal affectional response systems probably constitutes the most important guarantees against intragroup murder. Socially based cooperative ties and mutual concerns strengthen affectional affects, giving meaning and substance to moral codes against murder. The fear of murderous retaliation (legal as well as interpersonal) is also a potent deterrent.

Morality that derives from the oedipus complex is essentially a family morality. Thou shalt not kill thy father or brother, thy sister or mother. How far this precept extends to community, state, nation and beyond, depends upon economic, political, and social factors. The power elite may sometimes circumvent family morality. The history of royal families is replete with murder of close kin for the sake of power; later, the killers were accepted as rightful and lawful monarchs by the populace. In some primitive societies, intertribe murder is limited to token gestures; in others, a successful warrior is measured by the number of heads taken. Civilized societies score their successes in accordance with their technology, for example, the number of planes shot down, and which side has the higher enemy body count at the end of a day's battle. The social killer experiences pride, not guilt, for he is fulfilling a societal ideal and his own ego-ideal. The warrior's superego rewards him with a feeling of pride for his predations, yet the main function of the superego is to prohibit murder for gain. During the Nazi occupation of western Europe, betrayers not infrequently exposed Jews to the Gestapo as a simple way of appropriating Jewish property; they were neither punished nor excommunicated by their own group for participating in programmed murder. And later, when justice, retribution, and reparations were being considered by an international court of law, the concerns for minorities were uneven; the Nazi mass murder of gypsies, for instance, received comparatively little attention. In sum, the superego has been conceived of as an immutable structure which, if intact, remains as an established guardian of morality whereas, in fact, group and individual standards of morality and ethics change with time and circumstance in ways not provided for by the static concepts of superego function.

Stealing can be understood only in the social context in which it takes place. Where there is poverty in the midst of plenty, stealing from the rich to give to the poor may not be at all immoral. Robin Hood is a legendary hero, not a common thief. A parent who steals food from a rich man's kitchen to keep his family from starving need not believe his act is immoral and therefore should have no guilt about it; parental guilt would reflect neurosis, not realistic, adaptive behavior. On the other hand, a starving prisoner, say, in a concentration camp, who steals from another starving prisoner would be likely to feel guilt. Superego theory does not leave room for the behavioral dynamics which form part and parcel of complex, changing social realities. In general, stealing is a manifestation of psychopathology when it occurs among children or adults of means. The child of a middle-class family who steals almost always has psychiatric difficulties rooted in a disturbed and defective parent-child relationship. The complexity of the stealing syndrome cannot be accounted for simply by the failure of parents to instill adequate values of honesty. Whatever part the oedipus complex plays in engendering impulses to steal, the ultimate fate of such impulses is determined by the totality of social experience.

GUILT AND THE SUPEREGO

Freud distinguished between two stages in the evolution of guilt. The first involved fear of loss of love for violating the wishes and directives of power figures upon whom the helpless child was dependent. The second essential stage involved the internalization of authority with the development of the superego. Freud said (1930, p. 135): "A great change takes place when the authority is internalized through the establishment of a superego. The phenomenon of conscience then reached a higher stage. Actually, it is not until now that we should speak of conscience or a sense of guilt." The indiscriminate fear of violating directives of power figures may, of course, be differentiated from a cognitive, discriminating conviction that one is performing an antisocial act. In my view, however, the distinction does not rest upon the internalization of a fictitious superego as Freud postulated; rather, it depends upon conviction, that is, strong confidence in one's belief. Although convictions may evolve as the consequence of an automatic, submissive, uncritical acceptance of parental values, and may be compatible with the concept of internalization, they may also represent independent thought arrived at through the selection of alternatives. Choice is particularly relevant as a child grows into adolescence and adulthood and as he continues to form and revise ideas and convictions about questions of morality. The concept of automatic internalization of parental values does not account for human cognitive faculties in determining individual judgments nor does it leave room for changing moral convictions as social maturation proceeds.

Freud's concept of guilt as the punishment of the ego by the harsh superego for attempts at gaining unacceptable gratifications has several limitations. For one, it excludes guilt induced by guilt-provoking parents. Their children tend to manifest guilt reactions very easily even in situations where they are innocent of any wrong doing and where guilt is entirely inappropriate. Parents who inculcate guilt feelings as a technique of domination are usually egocentric, exploitative, perfectionistic, and intolerant of shortcomings in their child, whom they regard as personal property. A child's resistance against acting in accordance with his parents' neurotic demands may elicit from them guilt provocations such as, "You're killing me" or "You're making me sick." He learns to respond in ways which will circumvent such parental behavior. In such families, the child experiences guilt for *not* doing what his parents wish, not just for *doing* some unacceptable

instinctual act. Guilt associated with the lack of fulfillment of parental wishes may be unrelated to introjection.
An adult may feel guilty if he does not phone his mother
daily if this is what she expects, but his guilt reaction may
disappear when she dies and he may not experience the
same reaction with anyone else. Some such individuals
may avoid relationships with guilt provocateurs. But
those who remain vulnerable to guilt provocation by
valued objects have developed the potential to react
with guilt to cues or expressions of dissatisfaction,
contempt, or pain by others. One might say that under
the circumstances discussed, a potential to react with
guilt has been internalized, if one wishes to use a
gastrointestinal metaphor.

Superego theory does not account for a type of commonly experienced guilt that accompanies self-destructive
acts, as in masochistic self-sabotage where success or the
fruits of success are destroyed. When a businessman
destroys an established, successful enterprise, or when an
athlete sabotages a well-deserved victory, guilt is experienced for having destroyed something of value. In 1916
Freud described problems about achievement among
"those wrecked by success" in his paper on character
types. He cited the case of a young woman who was finally
in a position to marry the man she loved but could not
accept her good fortune and soon broke down in a hopeless psychosis. In this instance, one might speculate theoretically that superego guilt stopped her from fulfilling her
oedipal strivings in marrying a valued love object identified with father. Superego theory does not provide for
guilt experienced in destroying a valued relationship nor
for the guilt about causing suffering to a rejected fiancé.
This type of guilt might usefully be termed masochistic

guilt. I have discussed the problem of masochism else-where and will not pursue it here (see chapters 9 and 10). Others have referred to this type of guilt as existential guilt. The renunciation of fulfillment and pleasure may elicit masochistic guilt. This is the converse of superego guilt which explains but one category of guilt, that is, the guilt experienced when one fails to renounce forbidden pleasures.

In the range of affects associated with goodness and morality is the emotion we term compassion. According to Schopenhauer it represents the essential ingredient of the moral man. Where is compassion located in structural theory? Certainly not in the superego which is said to have no compassion for the ego. On the contrary, it uses the energies of the aggressive drives against the ego. Surely, compassion does not reside in the id. All that is left is the ego; compassion must be an ego function. If this is so, morality is only partially accounted for by the superego.

In conclusion, the concept of the superego, like the con-cepts id and ego, presents the limitations and theoretical fallacies that characterize the structural and libido theories. Id, ego, and superego are but metaphorical, fic-titious constructs that have been reified by articulating them with reality structures in a way that creates an aura of realism. The energies of the id (a fictitious concept) are supposedly derived from somatic organs and processes (real structures), and the ego (a fictitious concept) has at its disposal all the resources of the organism—perceptual, motor, intellectual, and so forth (all real organs and pro-cesses). The superego contains the introjects (a fictitious concept) of parents (real objects). Reification of metaphor is a serious logical fallacy and has no place in science. Not only does reification abound in metapsychology, but many constructs are anthropomorphized, a poetic device that tends to obscure a clear presentation of human motivation and behavior; for example, "the superego treats the ego harshly." Whatever heuristic value it once may have had, this type of thinking is no longer acceptable. With the enormous development of psychoanalysis in the last twenty-five years, personality theory not only can be more consistently related to observational data but can also articulate more validly with biological and other social sciences. Metapsychology as a scientific methodology is today an anachronism that is hardly consonant with the sophistication of ideas in the present world.

Chapter 21

Cognitive Psychoanalysis and Moral Values

Moral values constitute an order of beliefs associated with the ethical aspects of behavior as expressed in interpersonal transactions and, more broadly, social acts that society may deem to be right or wrong, good or bad, virtuous or evil. In every culture, at any given time, prevailing mores affect and are affected by societal values and standards of morality. At first, moral values are learned through the family, where behavior and affective experiences are initially patterned and directed. Later, through a continuity of the reinforcing influences of social institutions, one comes to accept the moral values of one's time as the givens of social reality. One's own moral values are then thought to be right, socially constructive, inviolate, and inexorable. Personal motives and behaviors that threaten to violate established moral standards precipitate feelings of guilt, diminish self-esteem, and evoke expectations of rejection.

Philosophers, of course, and in more recent decades, sociologists, have lavished much thought and ink on the nature and role of moral values. Three aspects seem most germane to our discipline:

1. *The psychoanalyst and moral values.* People move into their work orbit with a developed system of moral values. The psychoanalyst enters the profession no differently. In general, the beliefs of psychoanalysts conform to popularly held ethical values; however, as a group they tend to be philosophical and, since they are likely to have given much thought to more abstract subjects, at least in certain particulars, their moral values will have been modified. They will have thought a great deal about themselves in relation to others and contemplated upon their clinical experience and personal psychoanalysis. Inevitably, psychoanalysts become more deeply involved with questions about value systems than colleagues in the more purely medical specialties. As a behavioral scientist, the analyst delineates motivations and evaluates behavior itself, using for the most part a medical model. Gross dichotomies, such as normal and healthy versus sick and pathological, are refined to become nonneurotic and normal versus neurotic or psychotic, assertiveness versus submission, and so forth. The medical model has been sharply criticized, notably by Thomas Szasz and others who agree with him. They assert that, in essence, psychoanalysts use a medical model as a cover-up for translating culture-bound value systems of good and bad into scientific-sounding language. I do not believe that the

central issue is the misuse of the medical model or that it conceals naive, moralistic notions. Psychoanalysts must direct themselves to two basic questions. Do one's moral values influence diagnostic judgment? If so, does it then follow that the judgments are necessarily based upon biased criteria derived from a submissive conformity to cultural mores?

An example of psychoanalytic bias is a statement by Freud (1917) that appears in the *Introductory Lectures*: "We actually describe a sexual activity as perverse if it has given up the aim of reproduction and pursued the attainment of pleasure as an aim independent of it" (p. 316). This would be consonant with the ethical tenets of some religions but as a statement of science it is insupportable, judgmental, and moralistic. Actually, the terms *perverse* or *perversions* have been replaced by the more neutral *sexual deviation*. In our era of sexual liberation, pleasure-motivated sexuality has psychoanalytic and societal moral support. Masturbation is another example. In the past, psychoanalytic attitudes toward masturbation articulated with the prevailing mores. Professional bias against masturbation has now virtually disappeared, a change in clinical attitudes that reflects the shift in moral values.

2. *The psychoanalyst and moral judgment.* Psychoanalysis began as a therapeutic innovation and treatment remains its major orientation. Moral values are an implicit part of all professions concerned with therapeutics. The healing professions have traditionally been directed toward the welfare and betterment of people's lives and have fostered development and improvement in the physical, mental, and, in more recent years, economic and social spheres. The analyst's goal, that of resolving the psychopathology

of his or her patients, is therefore a positive moral value. One of the directives of the Hippocratic oath enjoins the physician to suspend all moral judgment in the treatment of patients, whether sinners or saints. Moral judgment, however, must be differentiated from moral evaluation. If I were confronted by a thief, my defensive, aggressive response would evoke a moral judgment that might lead to the thief's arrest. However, in a therapeutic context, say, as prison psychiatrist, I would evaluate the predatory act as antisocial but I would have to free myself from hostility, aggression, and antipathy toward the prisoner. My therapeutic orientation toward him would also involve determining the motivation and meaning of his socially destructive behavior.

Within the framework of therapeutics and to the extent that one cannot dissociate oneself from moral judgment, countertransference becomes a determining and contaminating variable. In the presence of a kleptomaniac, one might lock away the family silver. This is not countertransference; it is, rather, the legitimate right to protect oneself from an acting-out patient. Self-protection need not stimulate countertransferences. The enjoinder to suspend moral judgment and to adhere to the role of healer can sometimes present difficult challenges and, perhaps, insurmountable problems. An analyst might find that treating a Nazi evokes irrepressible counterreactions of hatred and moral judgment which would interfere with the legitimate course of treatment. But, as in other instances, psychoanalytic principles governing the resolution of countertransference must prevail. If moral judgment cannot be successfully suspended, if countertransference cannot be resolved, then the analysis must be terminated.

3. *Psychoanalysis and ethical and moral systems.* In my view, the goal of moral and ethical systems should be to provide standards for developing and maintaining optimal development and cooperation in human relationships. Based upon this aim, psychoanalysis can be a reference source for evolving new, more sophisticated ethical systems and for testing old ones. Psychoanalysis has the know-how to evaluate the human condition in all its stages—from early life to old age, and to determine the nature and extent of familial and extrafamilial influences and pressures. By studying patients who have decompensated psychiatrically and tabulating their condition on a continuum of mild to severe, the commonality and range of stress points for a given population can be determined. In this sense, the psychoanalyst is a social microscopist who is in a position to make broad contributions to sociology and political science and contribute to sociopolitical arrangements most suitable to human groups. Certainly, if data were pooled, it would be no insurmountable task to demonstrate which aspects of social structure and processes promote feelings of rejection, anxiety, and low self-esteem and which influence the ability to pursue happiness. It is now a commonplace that differential social acceptance and status stratification are not commensurate with the moral values espoused by a democratic society; and further, that a highly disparate distribution of wealth induces competitiveness discordant with the tenets of brotherly love. To demonstrate its psychiatric effects on populations and its effects on the moral fabric of society is perhaps the moral responsibility and challenge of psychoanalysis today.

Psychoanalysis has evolved during an era in which a sexual revolution has radically altered sexual moral values. The revolution is not yet over. New guidelines remain to be established so that a rationally based sexual ethic can evolve. There are many questions that need to be answered. What are the psychoanalytic views regarding premarital and extramarital sexual relations? and how are these views to be arrived at? We must look to systematic methods for gathering reliable data on which to base moral precepts. For example, one could compare a population who have had premarital sexual relations with a matched population who have not, then compare the two groups for sexual effectiveness, capability of forming a stable, heterosexual love relationship, work effectiveness, level of social relatedness, and so forth. I have found that young married people, under the age of thirty-five, who have not had premarital intercourse tend much more often to suffer from neurotic difficulties than those who have had premarital intercourse. I have also found that individuals of either sex who have had the advantage of higher education and are still virgins at the age of twenty-two or twenty-three are also more likely to have neurotic problems than educated young people who at that age had started to have intercourse. Those who are unable to avail themselves of the advantages of a more liberal sexual ethic, for whatever reason, are more likely to have psychiatric problems. One could say, then, that it is moral for men and women of about the age of twenty-two to have sexual intercourse whether or not they are married.

But how about the ages eighteen or sixteen or fourteen? At the present time, one must individualize with each patient and evaluate a concatenation of data. Standards of sexual behavior for the very young await studies which must be done if we are to formulate knowledgeable guidelines.

The question of extramarital relations puts us in the middle of a lake, surrounded by the shores of stern morality and virtue. Yet, psychoanalytic experience articulates in certain ways with traditional views. The psychoanalytic contribution to a new morality in marriage may rest, at least in part, upon the repeated observation that if a spouse is physically and psychologically capable of good sexual and affective relatedness, then the partner's extramarital activity is almost always neurotically determined.

If we grant the proposition that a psychoanalyst's viewpoint is shaped by personal beliefs and value systems, that moral values are part of his or her "mind set" and hence play a determining role in what is observed about patients and how the data are ordered, then clearly the analyst's beliefs and moral values must be based upon the best available information and not upon traditional mores, mythology, and folkways. As analysts, we are trained to be cognitively aware of the psychodynamic processes operant in our patients and of our countertransferences. So must we be consciously aware of the assumptions on which our moral values are based, and how they have been derived.

References

Abraham, R., and Finesinger, J. (1950). Guilt reactions in patients with cancer. *Cancer* 6:474–482.

Adorno, T. W., Frankel-Brunswick, E., Levinson, D. J., and Sanford, R. N. (1950). *The Authoritarian Personality*. New York: Harper & Row.

Arieti, S. (1950). New views in the psychology and psychopathology of wit and of the comic. *Psychiatry* 13:43–62.

Attardo, N. (1966). Symbiotic factors in adolescent addiction. *Journal of the Long Island Consultation Center* 4:30–46.

Bard, M. (1955). Use of dependence for predicting psychogenic invalidism following radical mastectomy. *Journal of Nervous and Mental Disease* 22:152–160.

Bard, M., and Dyk, R. B. (1955). Psychodynamic significance of beliefs regarding the cause of serious illness. *Psychoanalytic Review* 43:146–162.

Bard, M., and Sutherland, A. M. (1955). Psychological impact of cancer and its treatment: adaptation to radical mastectomy. *Cancer* 8:656–672.

Bateson, G., and Mead, M. (1942). *Balanese Character: A Photographic Analysis.* New York: New York Academy of Sciences.

Beck, A. T. (1976). *Cognitive Therapy and Emotional Disorders.* New York: International Universities Press.

Bergler, E. (1949). *The Basic Neurosis.* New York: Grune & Stratton.

Bieber, I. (1937). Grasping and sucking. *Archives of Neurology and Psychiatry* 37:704–707.

———(1940). Grasping and sucking. *Journal of Nervous and Mental Disease* 91:31.

———(1959). Olfaction in sexual development and adult sexual organization. *American Journal of Psychotherapy* 13:851–859.

———(1967). Sex in psychoanalysis. In *The Biology of Sex,* ed. A. Allison, pp. 240–254. London: Penguin Science Survey.

———(1972). Sex and power. In *Science and Psychoanalysis* 20.

———(1974a). The concept of irrational belief systems as primary elements of psychopathology. *Journal of The American Academy of Psychoanalysis* 2:91–100.

———(1974b). Masked depression in relation to work, pleasure and sexuality. In *Masked Depression,* ed. S. Lesse. New York: Jason Aronson.

Bieber, I., Dain, H., Dince P., Drellich, M., Grand, H., Gundlach, R., Kremer, M., Rifkin, A., Wilbur, C., and Bieber, T. (1962). *Homosexuality: A Psychoanalytic Study.* New York: Basic Books.

Bieber, I., and Drellich, M. G. (1959). The female castration complex. *Journal of Nervous and Mental Disease* 129: 235–242.

Bieber, I., and Fulton, J. F. (1938). Relation of cerebral cortex to grasp reflex and to postural and righting reflexes. *Archives of Neurology and Psychiatry* 39:433-454.

Bieber, I., and Herkimer, J. K. (1948). Art in psychotherapy. *American Journal of Psychiatry* 104:10 627-631.

Bieber, T. B. (1971). Group therapy with homosexuals. In *Comprehensive Group Psychotherapy*, ed. H. I. Kaplan and B. Sadock, pp. 518-533. Baltimore: Williams and Wilkins.

Breuer, J., and Freud, S. (1893-1895). Studies in hysteria. *Standard Edition* 2.

Bridger, W., and Birns, B. (1968). An analysis of the role of sucking in early infancy. *Science and Psychoanalysis* 12:156.

Cantril, H., et al. (1952). Psychology and scientific research in human behavior. In *The Transactional Point of View*, ed. F. P. Kilpatrick, pp. 195-212. Hanover, New Hampshire: Institute for Associated Research.

Chein, I., Gerard, D. L., Lee, R. S., and Rosenfeld, E. (1964). *The Road to H.* New York: Basic Books.

Chessick, R. R. (1960). The pharmacogenic organism in the drug addict. *Archives of General Psychiatry* 3:545-556.

Drellich, M. G., and Bieber, I. (1968). The psychological importance of the uterus and its functions. *Journal of Nervous and Mental Disease* 126:322-336.

Drellich, M. G., Bieber, I., and Sutherland, A. M. (1956). Psychological impact of cancer and cancer surgery: adaptation to hysterectomy. *Cancer* 9:1120-1126.

Dyk, R. B., and Sutherland, A. M. (1956). Adaptation of the spouse and other family members to the colostomy patient. *Cancer* 9:123-138.

Ellis, A. (1962). *Reason and Emotion in Psychotherapy.* New York: Lyle Stuart.

Erikson, E. H. (1959). Identity and the life cycle. *Psychological Issues* Monograph 1. New York: International Universities Press.

———(1963). *Childhood and Society,* 2nd ed. New York: Norton.

Frankel-Brunswick, E. (1954). The meaning of psychoanalytic concepts and confirmation of psychoanalytic theories. *Scientific Monthly* 79:293–300.

Freud, S. (1894a). On the grounds for detaching a particular syndrome from neurasthenia under the description "anxiety neurosis." *Standard Edition* 3:90–120.

———(1894b). The neuropsychoses of defence. *Standard Edition* 3:43–61.

———(1895). Project for a scientific psychology. *Standard Edition* 1:295–397.

———(1900). The interpretation of dreams. *Standard Edition* 4 and 5.

———(1905a). Three contributions to the theory of sex. In *The Basic Writings of Sigmund Freud,* ed. A. A. Brill. New York: Random House, 1938.

———(1905b). Three essays on the theory of sexuality. *Standard Edition* 7:130–243.

———(1908). Character and anal erotism. *Standard Edition* 9:167–176.

———(1913). On beginning the treatment. *Standard Edition* 12:121–144.

———(1914). On narcissism. *Standard Edition* 14:73–102.

———(1915a). Instincts and their vicissitudes. *Standard Edition* 14:109–140.

———(1915b). Observations on transference love. *Standard Edition* 12:157–171.

———(1916). Some character types met with in psychoanalytic work. *Standard Edition* 14:309–333.

———(1917). Introductory lectures in psychoanalysis. *Standard Edition* 16.

——(1919). A child is being beaten. *Standard Edition* 17: 172–201.

——(1920). Beyond the pleasure principle. *Standard Edition* 18:7–64.

——(1921). Group psychology and the analysis of the ego. *Standard Edition* 18:67–143.

——(1922). Two encyclopedia articles. *Collected Papers,* vol. 5, pp. 107–135.

——(1923). The ego and the id. *Standard Edition* 19:3–68.

——(1924a). The economic problem of masochism. *Standard Edition* 19:157–162.

——(1924b). The economic problem in masochism. *Collected Papers,* vol. 2, pp. 255–268.

——(1930). Civilization and its discontents. *Standard Edition* 21:59–145.

——(1940). An outline of psycho-analysis. *Standard Edition* 23:141–207.

Galenson, E. (1977). Paper presented at symposium of Society of Medical Psychoanalysts, New York City.

Ganger, R., and Shugart, G. (1966). The heroin addict's pseudoassertive behavior and family dynamics. *Social Casework* 47:643–649.

Glover, E. (1956). *On the Early Development of the Mind.* New York: International Universities Press.

Goldfried, M. R., and Goldfine, A. P. (1975). Cognitive change methods. In *Helping People Change,* ed. F. H. Kanfa and A. T. Goldstein. New York: Pergamon.

Goldfried, M. R., and Sabicinski, D. (1975). The effects of irrational beliefs and emotional arousal. *Journal of Consulting and Clinical Psychology* 43:504–510.

Goodman, R. S., and Gilman, A. (1965). *The Pharmacological Basis of Therapeutics.* New York: Macmillan.

Greenwald, H. (1958). *The Call Girl.* New York: Ballantine.

Harlow, H., and Harlow, M. K. (1965). *Behavior of Non-human Primates,* ed. A. M. Schien, H. Harlow, and F. Stollvitz. New York: Academy Press.

Hartmann, H. (1951). Ego psychology and the problem of adaptation. In *Organization and Pathology of Thought.* New York: Columbia University Press.

Horney, K. (1937). *The Neurotic Personality of Our Time.* New York: Norton.

————(1950). *Neurosis and Human Growth.* New York: Norton.

Kalogerakis, M. (1963). The role of olfaction in sexual development. *Psychosomatic Medicine* 25:420–432.

Kardiner, A. (1939). *The Individual and His Society.* New York: Columbia University Press.

————(1978). *My Analysis with Freud.* New York: Norton.

Kinsey, A. C., Pomeroy, W. B., and Martin, C. E. (1948). *Sexual Behavior in the Human Male.* Philadelphia: W. B. Saunders.

Kinsey, A. C., Pomeroy, W. B., Martin, C. E., and Gebhard, P. (1953). *Sexual Behavior in the Human Female.* Philadelphia: W. B. Saunders.

Krafft-Ebing, R. von (1892a). *Psychopathia Sexualis,* 12th ed. New York: Physicians and Surgeons Book Co., 1937.

————(1892b). Sadism and masochism. In *The Sexual Revolution,* ed. M. Krich. New York: Dell, 1963.

————(1892c). *Psychopathia Sexualis,* translated from the 12th Edition by F. S. Klaf. New York: Stein and Day, 1963.

Lantos, B. (1943). Work and the instincts. *International Journal of Psycho-Analysis* 24:114–119.

Lindner, S. (1878). Das Saugenanden Fingern, Lippen, etc. bei den kindern (Ludeln). *Jahrbuch für Kinderheilk* 14:68–91.

Masters, W. H., and Johnson, V. E. (1966). *Human Sexual Response.* Boston: Little, Brown.

Menninger, K. A. (1942). Work as sublimation. *Bulletin of the Menninger Clinic* 6:170–182.

Money, J., Hampson, J. S., and Hampson, S. L. (1957). Imprinting in the establishment of gender role. *Archives of Neurology and Psychiatry* 77:333–336.

Neff, W. S. (1965). Psychoanalytic conception of the meaning of work. *Psychiatry* 28:324–333.

Nyswander, M. (1956). *The Drug Addict as a Patient.* New York: Grune & Stratton.

Opler, M. K. (1956). Cultural anthropology and social psychiatry. *American Journal of Psychiatry* 113:302–311.

Ostow, M., and Kline, N. (1956). The psychodynamic action of chlorpromazone and reserpine. Abstracts from the Official Program of the 1956 Mid-winter meetings of the American Psychiatric Association.

Perry, S. C., and Klerman, G. L. (1980). Clinical features of the borderline personality disorder. *American Journal of Psychiatry* 137:165–173.

Rado, S. (1926). The psychic effects of intoxicants. *International Journal of Psycho-Analysis* 7:396–413.

———(1933). The psychoanalysis of pharmacothymia. *Psychiatric Quarterly* 2:211–223.

———(1956). An adaptational view of sexual behavior. In *Psychoanalysis of Behavior,* pp. 201–202. New York: Grune & Stratton.

———(1959). Panel discussion on individual and family dynamics. *Science and Psychoanalysis* 2:53–56. Grune & Stratton.

———(1969). Overreactive disorders: emergency dyscontrol and descending dyscontrol. In *Adaptational Psychodynamics: Motivation and Control,* ed. J. Jameson and H. Klein. New York: Jason Aronson.

Reich, W. (1945). *Character Analysis.* New York: Orgone Press.

Reik, T. (1941). *Masochism in Modern Man.* New York: Farrar and Straus.

Robbins, B. S. (1956). Sigmund Freud. *Psychotherapy* 1: 289-295.

Savitt, R. A. (1963). Psychoanalytic studies in addiction: ego structure in narcotic addiction. *Psychoanalytic Quarterly* 32: 43-47.

Schmideberg, M. (1956). Multiple origins and functions of guilt. *Psychiatric Quarterly* 30:471-477.

Selye, H. (1947). The general adaptation syndrome and the disease of adaptation. *The Pharos of Alpha Omega Alpha* 2: 16-26.

Spitz, R. (1945). Hospitalism. *Psychoanalytic Study of the Child* 1:53-74.

————(1965). *The First Year of Life.* New York: International Universities Press.

Strachey, J. (1955). Editor's introduction. *Standard Edition* 2.

Sullivan, H. S. (1956). *Clinical Studies in Psychiatry.* New York: Norton.

Sutherland, A. M., Orbach, C. E., Dyk, R. B., and Bard, M. (1952). Psychological impact of cancer and cancer surgery: adaptation to dry colostomy. *Cancer* 5:857-872.

Thompson, C. (1959). The interpersonal approach to the problem of masochism. *Science and Psychoanalysis* 2:31-37.

Thorpe, W. H., and Zangwill, O. L. (1961). *Current Problems in Animal Behavior.* London: Cambridge University Press.

Waxenberg, S. E., Drellich, M. G., and Sutherland, A. M. (1959). The role of hormones in human behavior. *Journal of Clinical Endocrinology and Metabolism* 19:193.

Wickler, D., and Rasor, R. (1953). Psychiatric aspects of drug addiction. *American Journal of Medicine* 14:566-570.

Wiener, N. (1950). Some maxims for biologists and psychologists. *Dialectica* 4:3.

Wolf, A. V. (1956). Thirst. *Scientific American* 194:70–76.

Zimmering, P., Toolan, J., Safrin, R., et al. (1952). Drug addiction in relation to problems of adolescence. *American Journal of Psychiatry* 109:276–278.

Source Notes

Chapter 4. Biosocial Determinants of Neurosis. In *Etiology of Neurosis,* edited by J. Merin and S. Nagler, pp. 16-27. Palo Alto: Science & Behavior Books, 1966.

Chapter 5. Psychoanalysis 1938-1978—A View from the Chair. In *Changing Concepts in Psychoanalysis,* edited by S. Klebanow. New York: Gardner Press, in press.

Chapter 6. Transference and the Sex of the Analyst. Previously unpublished.

Chapter 7. Disorders of the Work Function. *Science and Psycho-analysis* 16:92-98. New York: Grune & Stratton, 1972.

Chapter 8. Pathological Boredom and Inertia. *American Journal of Psychotherapy* 5:215-222, 1951. Presented as a lecture at Cooper Union, New York, N.Y., 1949.

Chapter 9. The Meaning of Masochism. *American Journal of Psychotherapy* 7:433-449, 1953.

Chapter 10. Sadism and Masochism. In *Handbook of Psychiatry, Volume III,* edited by S. Arieti, pp. 256-272. New York: Basic Books, 1966.

Chapter 11. Sadism and Masochism: Phenomenology and Psychodynamics. In *Handbook of Psychiatry, Volume III,* 2nd ed., edited by S. Arieti, pp. 316-332. New York: Basic Books, 1974.

Chapter 13. Pathogenicity of Parental Preference. *Journal of the American Academy of Psychoanalysis* 5:291-298. Copyright © 1977, American Academy of Psychoanalysis. Reprinted by permission of John Wiley & Sons, Inc.

Chapter 14. Depressive and Paranoid Reaction. *A.M.A. Archives of Neurology and Psychiatry* 78:301–311, September 1957. Copyright © 1957, American Medical Association.

Chapter 15. Psychological Adaptation to Serious Illness and Organ Ablation. In *The Psychological Basis of Medical Practice,* edited by H. Lief, V. Lief, and N. Lief, pp. 318–322. New York: Harper & Row, 1963.

Chapter 16. Dreams of Hospitalized Male Heroin Addicts: A Psychodynamic Appraisal. *Interaction,* Fall 1978, pp. 3–14.

Chapter 17. Treatment of the Ambulatory Schizophrenic. In *Treatment of Schizophrenia in Office Practice,* edited by A. Rifkin. New York: Grune & Stratton, 1957.

Chapter 18. Biosocial Roots of Childhood Sexuality. In *Sexuality and Psychoanalysis,* edited by E. Adelson, pp. 161–174. New York: Brunner/Mazel, 1975.

Chapter 19. A Critique of the Libido Theory. *American Journal of Psychoanalysis* 18(1): 52–68, 1958.

Chapter 20. Morality and Freud's Concept of the Superego. In *Moral Values and the Superego Concept in Psychoanalysis,* edited by S. Post, pp. 126–143. New York: International Universities Press, 1972.

Chapter 21. Psychoanalysis and Moral Values. In *Moral Values and the Superego Concept in Psychoanalysis,* edited by S. Post, pp. 244–252. New York: International Universities Press, 1972.

Index